PERSPECTIVES ON COUNSELING THEORIES

Louis E. Shilling

Texas Woman's University

Prentice-Hall, Inc., Englewood Cliffs, New Jersey 07632

Library of Congress Cataloging in Publication Data

Shilling, Louis E.
  Perspectives on counseling theories.

  Includes bibliographies and index.
    1. Psychotherapy. 2. Counseling. I. Title.
  [DNLM: 1. Counseling. 2. Psychotherapy. 3. Psycho-
  analytic therapy. WM 420 S5557p]
  RC480.S368 1984   616.89'14   83-13849
  ISBN 0-13-660365-3

Editorial/production supervision and
  interior design: Helen J. Maertens
Cover design: Wanda Lubelska Design
Manufacturing buyer: Ron Chapman

**To Catherine, the *sine qua non* of all my perspectives
and to Andy, the light of our love.**

Printed in the United States of America

10 9 8 7 6 5 4 3 2 1

ISBN 0-13-660365-3

Prentice-Hall International, Inc., *London*
Prentice-Hall of Australia Pty. Limited, *Sydney*
Editora Prentice-Hall do Brasil, Ltda., *Rio de Janeiro*
Prentice-Hall Canada Inc., *Toronto*
Prentice-Hall of India Private Limited, *New Delhi*
Prentice-Hall of Japan, Inc., *Tokyo*
Prentice-Hall of Southeast Asia Pte. Ltd., *Singapore*
Whitehall Books Limited, *Wellington, New Zealand*

CONTENTS

FOREWORD

It is a rare privilege to read a book on counseling theories that is theoretical and at the same time practical. Dr. Shilling departs from the usual sterile presentation and includes personal observations and experiences.

This book presents excellent chapters on the Adlerian and Carkhuff approaches to counseling. These perspectives are seldom included in most other counseling theory textbooks.

Dr. Shilling includes a section on training of the counselor in each chapter and illustrates each approach with a case study. In the introduction a clear position is stated which outlines some basic differences between counseling and psychotherapy. Multicultural counseling is seldom included in traditional textbooks. The greatest asset the counselor brings into the helping relationship is the personhood of the counselor. Dr. Shilling is to be commended for his sections on the counselor as a person and characteristics of the present and future counselors who depart from routine helping and facilitate the growth of the populations they seek to serve.

As a counselor educator, I highly recommend this fresh, thorough, yet concise approach to counseling theories. The reader will enjoy and appreciate the unique presentation of both traditional and emerging concepts of helping.

Clifton T. Sparks, Ph.D.
Professor, Counselor Education
Dean of College of Education
Texas Woman's University

PREFACE

This book is intended as a first text in a graduate-level course typically called "Theories of Counseling." It presupposes little or no prior knowledge of counseling and is intended to provide a general survey of what I believe to be the more important movements, approaches, or perspectives in the field today. It is by no means exhaustive, either in the number of perspectives treated or in the depth in which each has been covered. It is not, and was not intended to be, completely original. The comments at the beginning and end of each chapter and the organization of the chapters are mine. Almost all of the rest are my words expressing the thoughts of others. The net result is—I hope—a clear picture of nine major perspectives on counseling: a picture "taken" with my mind but "developed" with yours.

As have many authors in recent years, I, too, have struggled with the problem of sexist and/or racist language. I am totally and unalterably opposed to sexism or racism in any sense; but I also owe it to you, my reader, to be clear. Whenever possible, I have avoided the generic pronoun except in those cases when clarity of meaning demanded it.

A few notes about the text itself are in order. In general, the perspective chapters follow this outline:

```
I   Historical Development
    A Personal Background
    B Theoretical Background
II  Theory of Personality
    A Definition of Terms
```

There are five departures from this outline. The psychoanalysis, client-centered, and HRD chapters all have an additional section entitled "Current Status." I have added this because I believe these perspectives, in their current use, are sufficiently different from their original formulation and need updating. This is not to say that the other perspectives have not continued to develop. The other departures involve the behavior therapy chapter in which there is no "Personal Background" section because there is no one person sumarily responsible for the perspective and the psychoanalysis chapter in which the headings use the term "therapist" rather than "counselor" because few, if any, psychoanalysts see themselves as counselors. A case study is included with each perspective, but not all of them are typescripts because suitable ones were not available. Finally, the order of presentation of the perspectives roughly follows an insight/action dimension culminating in what I believe to be the most effective union of insight and action.

I could not in good conscience conclude the writing of this text without acknowledging those who made and/or allowed me to do it. My deepest appreciation goes first to those seminal thinkers upon whose perspectives I have chosen to comment; my students, whose probing questions have made me think deep thoughts; my clients, who need to know that I have and can deliver something they need; my teachers, who opened my mind to new perspectives; all my friends and colleagues, whose encouragement helped to keep me going; and Jerome B. Katz, MD of the Topeka Institute for Psychoanalysis, who went out of his way to help with some hard-to-get information.

LES

CHAPTER ONE
INTRODUCTION

COUNSELING OR PSYCHOTHERAPY

Efforts to distinguish counseling from psychotherapy have been less than totally successful. Some think that no distinction is necessary; others think it is essential. It is unlikely that a master's degree school counselor would think of herself as a psychotherapist—and even less likely that she would be allowed to function in that capacity. Most psychologists and psychiatrists don't like to be called counselors; but, when the function of counseling is described, they acknowledge that they share some of its procedures. Adding to the confusion is the recent proliferation of "used-car counselors," "bereavement counselors," and "investment counselors," to name just a few.

Eysenck—tongue in cheek—defined psychotherapy as "an unidentified technique applied to unspecified problems with unpredictable outcomes. For this technique we recommend rigorous training" (1961, p. 698). Wolberg, somewhat more seriously, defined psychotherapy as "the treatment by psychological means of problems of an emotional nature in which a trained person deliberately establishes a professional relationship with the patient with the object of (a) removing, modifying, or retarding existing symptoms; (b) mediating disturbed patterns of behavior; and (c) promoting positive personality growth and development" (1967, p. 3).

Counseling, as Tyler pointed out, is a word that everyone understands; but no two people understand it in quite the same way. Even within the profession, there is agreement, but not unanimity. The American School Counselor Association (ASCA), a division of the American Personnel and Guidance Association (APGA), defined counseling as "a confidential, accepting, non-evaluative, permissive, face-to-face relationship, in which the counselor uses his knowledge and competencies to assist the pupil to resolve better those problems and issues which he would normally resolve less satisfactorily without counseling assistance" (Loughary, Stripling, & Fitzgerald, 1965, p. 99). The 1980 APGA Licensure Commission's model licensing bill, developed to persuade state legislators to license counselors for private practice, stated, "The practice of counseling within the meaning of this act is defined as . . . the application of counseling procedures and other related areas of the behavioral sciences to help in learning how to solve problems or make decisions related to careers, personal growth, marriage, family, or other interpersonal concerns" (p. 23). The American Mental Health Counselor's Association (AMHCA) Certification Committee defined professional counseling as "the process of assisting individuals or groups, through a helping relationship, to achieve optimal mental health through personal and social development and adjustment to prevent the debilitating effects of certain somatic, emotional, and intra- and/or interpersonal disorders" (1979, p. 24). The American Psychological Association's (APA) Division of Counseling Psychology (1968) defined counseling as work with individuals or groups with personal, social, educational, and vocational concerns. In sum, then, definitions of counseling by both APGA and APA are quite similar: both specify a trained counselor working with concerns, conflicts, or anxieties related to personal, social, educational, or career decisions.

Areas of Possible Difference

Is there, then, a difference between counseling and psychotherapy? Efforts to answer this question with any finality have met with little success. Brammer and Shostrom (1977) suggested that counseling and psychotherapy lie on a continuum—but at opposite ends. On this continuum, counseling and psychotherapy can be differentiated on the basis of goals, clients, practitioners, and methods.

Goals.   Hahn and Maclean (1955) proposed that counseling is concerned with preventative mental health, while psychotherapy concerns itself with remediation. Counseling may be more involved with situational distress, while psychotherapy deals with personality reorganization. Of course, a client who needs personality reorganization probably also needs assistance with situational distress.

Clients.   Some attempts have been made to distinguish between counseling and psychotherapy on the basis of client functioning: counselors work with "normals," while psychotherapists deal with neurotics and/or psychotics. Although such distinctions were once rather commonly made, they are no longer; partly because the labels "normal," "neurotic," and "psychotic" have lost much of their meaning and usefulness as discriminators.

Practitioners.   It can be said that a well-trained counselor is indistinguishable from a well-trained psychotherapist. Both have basic training in personality theory, psychopathology, and research methods, as well as in interviewing and testing techniques. Both have had a formal internship of one or two years in addition to several practicum experiences; both hold the doctor's degree. The relatively untrained therapist is likely to hold a master's degree in social work or psychology (clinical or educational), while the relatively untrained counselor usually holds a master's degree in counseling and guidance. (Note that in each case, the individual is *relatively* untrained; i.e., relative to the doctoral-level practitioner.) The master's-level practitioners typically endure thirty to forty semester-hours of course work, which typically includes no more than one or two on-campus practicum courses. Thus the differences among practitioners may be great or little.

Settings.   At one time, therapists were more likely to be found in mental health settings or private practice, while counselors were almost exclusively found in educational settings. Recently, these distinctions have all but vanished. Counselors are now employed in Veterans Administration hospitals, mental health agencies, rehabilitation centers, correctional institutions, substance abuse centers, probate courts, juvenile homes, family counseling agencies, and family crisis centers. As more and more states pass counselor licensure laws (e.g., Virginia, Arkansas, and Texas), more and more counselors will be going into private practice. Competency requirements for license are more stringent than for the typical master's degree program. More and more colleges and public school systems are hiring psychologists and psychotherapists.

Methods.   Here, too, there is so much commonality that almost all distinctions are blurred, if not eradicated. However, it is generally true that counseling is characterized by briefer treatment, more use of psychological examination, more concern with clients' day-to-day problems, greater emphasis on conscious activities such as decision-making and problem-solving, and more emphasis on inter- rather than intrapersonal dynamics.

Summary

Counseling and psychotherapy *may* be distinguished on the basis of *goals* (counseling: situational distress; psychotherapy: personality reorganization); *practitioners* (most counselors are trained at a master's level, while most psychotherapists are trained at a doctoral level); and *methodology* (counseling usually deals with problem-solving and decision-making, while psychotherapy confronts intrapsychic dynamics). Even in these areas, however, there is so much overlap that broad generalizations about differences are of little value. It would seem that the most practical discriminations would involve a knowledge of individual practitioners and their usual *modus operandi*. This indistinct identity of professionals can cause some severe problems for the naïve consumer. Therefore, practitioners should inform clients, in some way, of their training and general treatment methodology, fees, as well as any other consumer-related information.

EFFECTIVENESS

Based on cumulative knowledge garnered from research going back over two decades, Carkhuff and his associates have concluded that the ingredients of effectiveness in any context may be summarized in an equation (Carkhuff & Berenson, 1976, p. 176):

$$\text{Effectiveness} = \frac{\text{Effective}}{\text{People}} + \frac{\text{Effective}}{\text{Programs}} + \frac{\text{Effective}}{\text{Organization}}$$

Explaining the elements of this effectiveness equation, Carkhuff and Berenson point out that personal effectiveness is a function of the individual's interpersonal skills and specialty area skills. The former involve the person's ability to relate to others, while the latter include those skills peculiar to a specific function or area of performance. Thus, an effective counselor has the skills to relate to his or her clients and to guide them in the resolution of their problems. An effective high school English teacher has the skills to relate to her students and to teach them the intricacies of the plot development in Arthur Miller's *The Crucible*. An effective bank teller has the skills to relate to his customers as well as to keep his accounts balanced. Another way to state this is that personal effectiveness is a function of the quantity and quality of responses in your skills repertoire.

The mark of an effective program is systematization. Effective programs achieve their goals through systematic planning, development, implementation, and use of feedback to adjust the system (Carkhuff, 1981):

1. All effective systems receive input. The system must be open to, and facilitative of, all stimuli impinging upon it. This means that those planning

and developing the program must function at a high level of energy in order to be attentive to incoming stimuli.

2. All effective systems process data. The effective system analyzes the input, diagnoses its needs in relation to the analysis, personalizes its goals, and individualizes its action programs to achieve the goals.

3. All effective systems are shaped by feedback. An effective system learns the degree to which its product is effective and uses this feedback as new input to stimulate the learning process once more.

Effective organization is simply a systematic way of relating effective people to effective programs. One type of effective organization is a functional hierarchy of effective people operating effective programs. In this case, the more effective people oversee the activities of the less effective; and the most effective individual directs the whole operation. Another way to look at effective organization is as a functional explanation of how and why effective people and effective programs work; i.e., as a theory. It is in this latter sense that the concept of "effective organization" is used in this chapter.

The effectiveness equation, then, suggests a paradigm for examining the effectiveness of counseling:

$$\frac{\text{Effective}}{\text{Counseling}} = \frac{\text{Effective}}{\text{Counselor}} + \frac{\text{Effective}}{\text{Programs}} + \frac{\text{Effective}}{\text{Theory}}$$

THE COUNSELOR AS AN EFFECTIVE PERSON

As long as there have been counselors, they and others have sought to determine the personality characteristics that enable an individual to be an effective counselor. Despite years of research, the exact qualities that distinguish effective from ineffective counselors are still elusive. Part of the problem is semantic. We use words like *empathic, warm, genuine,* and *flexible;* but we are not able to operationalize these terms with any real measure of accuracy. Another big hurdle is the outcome problem. We just don't know what "cured" means, although we are pretty sure it means something different for each client. There is no sure way to quantify healing. Nevertheless, we do know something about the personal characteristics of counselors who seem to be effective.

Many researchers have looked at the qualities of the effective counselor *as counselor.* Rogers (1957) posited his "necessary and sufficient conditions," at the core of which were the therapist's qualities of empathy, unconditional positive regard, and congruence. Combs and Soper (1963) found that effective counselors saw their clients as capable, dependable, friendly, and worthy, and perceived themselves as altruistic and nondominating. Carkhuff and his associates redefined Rogers' conditions as accurate empathy, respect, and genuineness, and added concreteness, confrontation, and immediacy (Carkhuff & Berenson, 1967, 1976, 1977; Truax & Carkhuff, 1967). Others have found that these very conditions may work in the context of Rogerian counseling, but not in other therapies (Frank, Hoen-Saric, Imber, Liberman, Nash, & Stone, 1978).

At about the same time, others were investigating the idea that effective counselors were, first, effective people (Allen, 1967; Carkhuff, 1966). Schoben (1957) identified four characteristics of healthy development: (a) willingness to accept personal responsibility for behavior, (b) capacity for interpersonal relationships, (c) obligation to society, and (d) commitment to standards and ideals. Rogers (1962) posited three characteristics of the fully functioning person: (a) an increasing openness to experience, (b) continued growth toward becoming a process, and (c) increasing trust in your own organism. Dreikurs (Dinkmeyer & Dreikurs, 1963) described the healthy personality in terms of courage. The courageous person can look at a situation, task, or event in terms of possible solutions and actions, rather than potential threats or dangers.

Maslow (1968, 1970) studied self-actualizing people and found that, as a group, they manifested the following characteristics: (a) the capacity to tolerate and even welcome uncertainty in their lives, (b) acceptance of self and others, (c) spontaneity and creativity, (d) a need for privacy and solitude, (e) autonomy, (f) the capacity for deep and intense interpersonal relationships, (g) a genuine caring for others, (h) a sense of humor, (i) innerdirectedness, and (j) the absence of artificial dichotomies within themselves (e.g., weak/strong).

Carkhuff has elaborated several schemata of the effective helper or the whole person (Carkhuff & Berenson, 1976, 1977). His most recent formulation reworked Maslow's theme (Carkhuff, 1981). In it, Carkhuff illuminated the following dimensions as indicative of self-actualizing people: (a) physical fitness and the physical energy that flows from it, (b) emotional commitments to a mission outside oneself, (c) interpersonal relations that lead to incorporating the missions of others, (d) substantive specialty skills leading to skilled expertise, (e) learning skills leading to the processing of data, and (f) teaching skills leading to the communication of content. In short, actualizers are skilled, while nonactualizers are unskilled.

Summary

What kind of person must I be to be an effective counselor? Given the scope of the question—what is presented here is only the tip of the iceberg—any attempt to summarize an answer is probably futile, if not foolhardy. However, in order to stimulate your thinking on the matter, here's how I see it (this afternoon).

Effective counselors are first effective people. You can't help me if you don't have your act together. And even if you have it together, you still can't help me if you run out of steam before you get to me. So I think the first mark of effective people is that they have the physical energy to do what they need or want to do. Not Ms. or Mr. Americas, not NFL linebackers, but high-energy folks.

A second characteristic of effective people is that they know who they are and are comfortable with who they are while working systematically—but not frantically—to become more than they are. I am frightened by people, especially counselors, who have "arrived": they know all there is to know (if they don't know it, it isn't worth knowing); they have had all the valuable experiences (if they haven't done it, it is probably sinful); and they are above any strong emotion except righteous indignation, which they can whip out at the drop of a hat. I believe that effective people, because they are comfortable with who they are, have no need to be defensive about who or what they are not. Because they know where they are going, they are not afraid of people who are on a different path. Because they are courageous (Dreikurs' term) they don't have to have all the answers, just the confidence that there are answers, and the energy to look for them.

A third quality of effective people is that they possess a sense of community, which Adler called "social interest" (Ansbacher, 1977). They are relatively optimistic about life and altruistic in their dealings with others, yet maintain a critical problem-solving attitude toward behavior. They believe deeply in the creative potential of all humans to become more than they are, and they are ready to participate in facilitating that growth.

Finally, effective people "put their money where their mouths are": they are committed to action, not just talk. Effective people don't curse the darkness, they light candles; if they have a problem, they work on it; they don't tell you how good they are, they demonstrate it over and over.

COUNSELING AS AN EFFECTIVE PROGRAM

Many psychotherapeutic approaches have developed over the past century—especially during the last three decades. A curious fact is that each of them tries to explain its success, its rationale for change, in terms of some single factor that distinguishes it from the rest. Thus, psychoanalysts make the unconscious conscious; behavioral therapists put all their eggs in the learning basket; Rogerians seek to unleash the creative potential of the self-actualizing tendency; transactional analysts analyze interpersonal transactions; others seek peace through blood-curdling screams.

Curative Factors

Research from a variety of sources (Carkhuff, 1969; Carkhuff & Berenson, 1976; Frank et al., 1978; Liebermann, Yalom, & Miles, 1973; Marmoor, 1976; Truax & Carkhuff, 1967; Yalom, 1975) has made it quite clear that in no instance can success in counseling or psychotherapy be attributed to such single factors. Rather, a substantial number of variables enters into the process, including the personalities of both counselor and client, the nature of the client's problem, the degree of the client's motivation, the function and skills of the counselor, the hope and expectation that the counselor's qualities generate in the client, the client's own assets and deficits, the potential contributions or deficits inherent in the client's environment, and—perhaps most important of all—the quality of the relationship that develops between counselor and client (Marmoor, 1976).

Corsini and Rosenberg (1955) and Yalom (1975) developed lists of "curative factors" in group therapy, but Marmoor's list is more general and encompasses the other two. According to Marmoor, there are at least eight major factors present in all effective psychotherapies (1976, pp. 6–7):

1. A good *counselor-client relationship* based on the counselor's genuine interest in, and empathy for, the client, and the client's motivation to be helped.
2. *Release of tension* through the client's discussion of problems with a helping person in the context of hope and expectation of help.
3. *Cognitive learning* based on the counselor's effort to help the client better understand the reasons for the problem.
4. Either direct or indirect *operant conditioning* through the counselor's reinforcement of the client's healthy functioning and extinction of the client's unhealthy functioning.
5. Effective *suggestion and persuasion* by the counselor.
6. Identification with the counselor; at least in patterns of problem-solving behavior.
7. *Repeated reality testing* through rehearsal of new adaptive techniques.
8. If the client is to persist in reality testing despite setbacks, and if behavior change is to be internalized, then the continuing *emotional support* of the counselor is essential.

After twenty-five years of psychotherapy research, the Johns Hopkins Group came to the following conclusions: "The effectiveness of all forms of psychotherapy largely depends upon their ability to restore morale, primarily through achieving two interrelated goals. The first is to combat destructive emotions and attitudes such as fear or despair and foster health promoting ones such as hope and self-confidence. Contributing to these is the second goal: to enhance the patient's sense of mastery or control over himself and thereby over his environment" (Frank et al., 1978, pp. 172–173).

Burton (1976) generally agreed with the above analysis, but added a wistful (if not pessimistic) note: "It becomes more and more apparent that we are awaiting, if not a new Freud, then one who will give us a new conception of man: his psyche, his purpose, and his spirit" (p. 326).

This concern with a view of human nature is really the heart of the matter. The individual counselor's view of human nature will affect his or her approach to, and work with, clients. But the view that the developer of a theory or model of counseling takes toward human nature affects the entire theory as well as generations of practitioners who use it. Of course, at the heart of this problem—"heart of hearts" if you wish—is the philosophical/theological problem of free will versus determinism. Although the range of opinions about this issue is almost unlimited, there are no definitive or universally accepted answers from a scientific viewpoint. Actually, the practicing counselor can function quite well without a final resolution to the philosophical problem, provided he or she has a working hypothesis to fall back on.

Ford and Urban (1963) suggested that people are either "pilots" or "robots." Pilots are capable of determining their own course and assuming responsibility for their voyage. Robots appear to be self-directing, while their behavior is actually determined either biologically or environmentally. Of course, in real life, there is not quite so neat a dichotomy. People do make choices, yet at other times act as if they did not or could not make a choice. Perhaps there is some pilot and some robot in each of us. The problem for the counselor is to decide whether he or she views human nature as mostly pilot or mostly robot. The decision will affect both theory and practice.

Everyone's experience demonstrates that periodically problems arise that must be solved, decisions that must be made, courses of action that must be chosen or abandoned. Rare is the individual who solves all problems, makes only right decisions, always chooses the best course of action. Yet people do solve problems. Therefore, they possess the ability to think and rethink, to decide and redecide, to behave and change their behavior. Surely, then, a mark of an effective counseling system is that it helps people to rethink, redecide, and change behavior.

Goals

Carkhuff's (1981) definition of an effective program embraced the idea that such programs reach operationalized goals through systematic planning, development, implementation, and use of feedback. An operationalized goal is simply one that is defined in terms of observable, measureable behaviors. Thus, a change in attitude is not an observable, measureable behavior and is not an operationalized goal; losing four pounds in two weeks is. Systematic planning, developing, and implementing involve developing an action plan consisting of a series of steps, each one of which is an operationalized goal. Using feedback means that the efficiency and efficacy with which each step is mastered is monitored, in order that the program can be adjusted on the basis of the feedback thus obtained.

Now that the adjectives are out of the way, we can look at the noun: *goal*. What are the appropriate goals of counseling? Are there inappropriate goals of counseling? Do the goals of counseling, the counselor, and the client differ? Unfortunately, all of these questions are easier to ask than to answer.

The goals of counseling, counselor, and client are—or may be— different. The goals of the client typically involve some developmental task. Frequently, clients express their goals in somewhat unrealistic terms: "Help me to get over my alcoholism—but not give up drinking," or, "Help me to pass this course—but not waste my time studying," or, as Augustine prayed, "Lord, make me continent—but not yet!"

The counselor's goal might be to teach the alcoholic that it is not possible to go on drinking without remaining an alcoholic. It might also be to enhance his or her professional stature or augment a sagging bank account: less noble, perhaps but not ignoble (unless they are the counselor's only goals). More typically, the counselor's goal is to help clients attain the goals they (the clients) have identified. It would be inappropriate for a counselor to determine a goal for a client or to direct a client toward goals dictated by the counselor's values or needs.

Just as there are inappropriate goals for the client, so also there are inappropriate goals for counseling (the system) and for the counselor. Counseling is a psychological, not a theological, discipline; therefore, "to inculcate Christian (or Jewish, or Islamic) principles" is not an appropriate goal or function of psychological counseling. This is not to say that a Christian, Jewish, or Islamic counselor should not *live* by his or her religious principles. It is to say that a system of psychological counseling is neither Christian nor anti-Christian; Jewish nor anti-Jewish; Islamic nor anti-Islamic. The goals of counseling are the goals of the counseling process. These goals have been variously described, and, indeed, are uniquely defined in each of the several approaches described in subsequent chapters.

Summary

As I see it, counseling is a system or program; therefore, effective counseling has the qualities of an effective program; it proceeds systematically through mastery steps to the attainment of an operationalized goal. The mastery steps of counseling involve certain curative factors present in all effective counseling approaches, such as the personal qualities and functional skills of the counselor, the motivation of the client, and the quality of the relationship that develops between counselor and client. The "map" that guides the counselor in his or her use of these curative factors for the client's benefit is the counselor's view of human nature.

THEORY AS EFFECTIVE ORGANIZATION

The third ingredient of effectiveness is an effective organization, which is defined as a systematic way of relating effective people to effective programs. Since a theory tries to answer the question "why" by organizing and integrating knowledge, it would seem that the best way to put effective programs into the hands of effective people is through an effective theory (Carkhuff & Berenson, 1976).

Theory in General

A theory does more than answer the question "why"; it also answers "who," "what," "when," "where," and "how." An explanatory theory gives direction to practice. It allows the practitioner to corral many seemingly different events under one rubric, thus facilitating predictions about future events.

In addition to predicting new facts or relations, a working theory also organizes and integrates what is already known into a meaningful whole, a gestalt. A formal theory has certain characteristics. First, it is based on stated postulates or assumptions— "givens"—which are accepted without proof. Second, the terms or concepts by which the theory is formulated and communicated must be operationally defined. Third, the terms or concepts should bear a cause-and-effect or other logical relationship to each other. Finally, hypotheses must be constructed from the assumptions, terms, and relationships. The hypotheses should serve as testable predictions of what should be true if the assumptions, definitions, and deductions are verified. If the hypotheses are not supported by experiment or observation, then the theory must be revised and new hypotheses generated (Patterson, 1980).

Theories are really neither good nor bad, true nor false. A more accurate dichotomy would be working or not working. A theory may be working; i.e., validated, without being totally accurate. It may provide an adequate explanation for most (but not all) areas it covers. No theories are totally correct in all aspects. There have been several formulations of the criteria for evaluating a theory. All support the idea that a workable theory should not be trivial; it should be internally consistent and free of ambiguities; it should be comprehensive; it should be capable of being tested; and, finally, it should have a direct bearing on practice. Let it be said at the outset that no theory of counseling or psychotherapy meets all these requirements.

In an attempt to find a theory of abnormal behavior, Price (1972) argues that we really don't have a theory as such, but, rather, a set of conflicting perspectives or points of view. A similar revision seems to be in order in regard to theories of counseling: they are more like points of view than theories in the formal sense. This would explain the diversity among the various "theories" of counseling: each of the formulators of the "theories" is looking at the same thing—human nature—but seeing it from a different perspective. Just as different observers of an automobile accident will give differing accounts of the same event, so the various theorists give their own perspectives of the same human nature they are all observing. Some have elected to call their formulation a "theory"; others, a "model"; and still others, an "approach". Because of the confusion and lack of precision, it seems to me that *perspective* is the most accurate and least confusing term to apply to the ideas presented in the following chapters.

For the practicing counselor, the important issue is not which perspective to choose, but that he or she has a perspective that, in fact, explains the client's behavior and guides counselor intervention. A counselor who attempts to function without a consistent perspective to explain human nature and behavior, without a model for action based on the perspective, is not only unscientific, but is likely to be (at best) not helpful and (at worst) seriously harmful even to the least needy of clients.

Substantive elements of a perspective of counseling ought to include the following (Burks & Stefflre, 1979):

1. *Assumptions about human nature.* Does the perspective deal with the innate goodness or evil of human nature? determinism or voluntarism?
2. *Beliefs about behavior change and learning.*
3. *A commitment to stated goals of counseling.*
4. *A definition of the role and function of the counselor.* What is the general stance taken by the counselor—interpreter, teacher, supporter, friend, etc.— and by what techniques is this stance implemented?
5. *Evidence supporting the perspective.* What evidence is there that the proponents of the perspective empirically test their hypotheses and revise the perspective on the basis of obtained results?

Personal Perspective

As you develop your own point of view, you should look at each of the perspectives relevant to your practice in the light of the foregoing discussion, particularly the "substantive elements," and compare their perspectives with your own. For example, what is your view of human nature? Are humans innately good or evil—or neither? Free or determined? Which perspectives best express your own view? How is behavior acquired? Is human behavior determined by some configuration of genes, or do we learn to behave in certain ways? In either case, what are the implications for your practice? What are the appropriate and inappropriate goals of counseling? How will you determine which is which? What kind of person do you believe the counselor should be? Are you that kind of person? If not, what can you do to become so? Are you doing it? What kinds of counselor behaviors (techniques) do you think are most likely to facilitate the process of counseling? How familiar are you with those techniques, and how skilled are you in using them? What are you doing to become more skilled? When examining a perspective or considering a practice, do you look for supporting evidence? What "hardnosed" research do you have to support your own perspective? At this point in your career, you probably lack answers to most, if not all, of these questions. Not to worry. Be looking for the answers as you study this text and begin your practice.

Summary

A theory is a working explanation of what works, who makes it work, and when, where, why, and how it works. In counseling I prefer to talk about perspective or point of view rather than theory; but, in any case, it is imperative that a practicing counselor have a perspective to guide his or her practice. Since all working theories or perspectives are imperfect and need constant updating, it is unwise to adhere slavishly to one point of view. On the other hand, if a perspective is going to work for you, it must reflect your point of view.

Years ago, I read about an old country preacher in the mountains of North Carolina, renowned throughout the entire Piedmont for his fiery sermons—and full services. One day the Charlotte *Observer* sent a reporter to interview the minister and determine the secret of his success. After the services, the reporter went up to him, introduced himself, and "popped the question." The old man thought a while, smiled, and drawled, "Wal, fust Ah studies m'self full, then Ah thinks m'self clear, then Ah prays m'self hot, then Ah just lets go!" I have tried to follow that advice with one addition: before I "lets go" I "works m'self into shape." You might consider a similar program.

CROSS-CULTURAL COUNSELING EFFECTIVENESS

Cross-cultural counseling implies major differences between counselor and client. As a result of these differences, the counselor will be tested frequently by the client for competence, trustworthiness, and lack of similarity (between counselor and client). Counselors who are able to meet these challenges successfully are culturally skilled counselors (Sue, 1981, pp. 105–110):

1. The culturally skilled counselor is one who has moved from ethnocentrism to valuing and respecting differences. Other cultures are seen as being as valuable as the counselor's own.
2. A culturally skilled counselor is aware of his or her own values and biases and how these may affect minority clients. As a result, such a counselor strives to avoid prejudice and stereotypical labeling.
3. The culturally skilled counselor will have a good understanding of the sociopolitical system's operation in the United States with respect to its treatment of minorities.
4. A culturally skilled counselor is one who is comfortable with differences that exist between the counselor and client in terms of race and beliefs.
5. A culturally skilled counselor is aware of his or her limitations in cross-cultural counseling and is not threatened by the prospect of referring a client.
6. The culturally skilled counselor possesses specific knowledge and information about the particular groups he or she is working with and continues to update that information.

7. The culturally skilled counselor must clearly understand the value assumptions inherent in the major schools of counseling and how they may interact with the values of the culturally different client.

8. The culturally skilled counselor must be able to generate a wide variety of verbal and nonverbal messages.

9. The culturally skilled counselor must be able to send and receive messages accurately and appropriately.

Thus, the culturally skilled counselor will be aware that (a) economically and educationally disadvantaged clients may not be amenable to "talk therapy"; (b) self-disclosure may be incompatible with the oppressive experiences of Blacks and Native Americans; and (c) many minority clients prefer an active/directive approach to an inactive/nondirective stance.

Summary

Effective counselors, developing effective programs for their clients through an effective organization (perspective), will be culturally skilled counselors. Such practitioners will take the time and make the effort to understand and become comfortable with the client's perspective, to enter the client's environment in order to see the client's world through the client's eyes. On the other hand, effective counselors also see the client and the client's frame of reference from the broader perspective of the world as it is: a world in which the culturally different client is different. In the United States, this means that the nonwhite client has to make it in a predominantly white world. Therefore, culturally skilled counselors do not limit their client's horizons to the ghetto, the barrio, or the reservation.

How comfortable are you with a culturally different client? A client of differing religious or political views? What do you know about other cultures and their views and practices? What do you really know of your own culture? How comfortable are you with you?

REFERENCES

ALLEN, T.   Effectiveness of counselor trainees as a function of psychological openness. *Journal of Counseling Psychology,* 1967, *14,* 35–40.

AMERICAN MENTAL HEALTH COUNSELOR'S ASSOCIATION.   The Board of Certified Professional Counselors procedures. *American Mental Health Counselor's Association Journal,* 1979, *1,* 23–38.

AMERICAN PERSONNEL AND GUIDANCE ASSOCIATION,   *Licensure Committee action packet.* Washington, D.C.: 1980.

ANSBACHER, H. L.   Individual psychology. In R. Corsini (Ed.), *Current personality theories.* Itasca, IL: F. E. Peacock, 1977.

BRAMMER, L. M., & SHOSTROM, E. L.   *Therapeutic psychology: Fundamentals of counseling and psychotherapy* (3rd ed.). Englewood Cliffs, NJ: Prentice-Hall, 1977.

BURKS, H. M., & STEFFLRE, B.   *Theories of counseling.* New York: McGraw-Hill, 1979.

BURTON, A.   The integration of behavior change. In A. Burton (Ed.), *What makes behavior change possible?* New York: Brunner/Mazel, 1976.

CARKHUFF, R. R.   *The counselor's contribution to facilitative processes.* Urbana, IL: R. W. Parkinson, 1966.

CARKHUFF, R. R.   *Helping and human relations: A primer for lay and professional helpers,* vol. I. New York: Holt, Rinehart, & Winston, 1969.

CARKHUFF, R. R.   *Toward actualizing human potential.* Amherst, MA.: Human Resource Development Press, 1981.

CARKHUFF, R. R., & BERENSON, B. G.   *Beyond counseling and therapy.* New York: Holt, Rinehart, & Winston, 1967.

CARKHUFF, R. R., & BERENSON, B. G.   *Teaching as treatment: An introduction to counseling and psychotherapy.* Amherst, MA.: Human Resource Development Press, 1976.

CARKHUFF, R. R., & BERENSON, B. G.   *Beyond counseling and therapy* (2nd ed.). New York: Holt, Rinehart, & Winston, 1977.

COMBS, A. W., & SOPER, D. L.   Helping relationships as described by good and bad teachers. *Journal of Teacher Education,* 1963, *14,* 64–67.

CORSINI, R., & ROSENBERG, B.   Mechanisms of group psychotherapy: Processes and dynamics. *Journal of Abnormal and Social Psychology, 51, 1955,* 406–411.

DINKMEYER, D., & DREIKURS, R.   *Encouraging children to learn.* New York: Hawthorn Books, 1963.

EYSENCK, H. J.   The effects of psychotherapy. In H. J. Eysenck (Ed.), *Handbook of abnormal psychology.* New York: Basic Books, 1961.

FORD, D. H., & URBAN, H. B.   *Systems of psychotherapy: A comparative study.* New York: Wiley, 1963.

FRANK, J. D., HOEN-SARIC, R., IMBER, S. D., LIBERMAN, B. L., & STONE, A. R.   *Effective ingredients of successful psychotherapy.* New York: Brunner/Mazel, 1978.

HALL, C. S., & LINDZEY, G.   *Theories of personality* (2nd ed.). New York: Wiley, 1970.

HAHN, M. E., & MACLEAN, M. S.   *Counseling psychology* (2nd ed.). New York: McGraw-Hill, 1955.

LIEBERMANN, M. A., YALOM, I. D., & MILES, M. B.   *Encounter groups: First facts.* New York: Basic Books, 1973.

LOUGHARY, J. W., STRIPLING, R. O., & FITZGERALD, P. W. (Eds.).   *Counseling: A growing profession.* Washington, DC: American Personnel and Guidance Association, 1965.

MADDI, S. R.   *Personality theories: A comparative analysis.* Homewood, Ill.: Dorsey, 1968.

MARMOOR, J.   Common operational factors in diverse approaches to behavior change. In A. Burton (ed.), *What makes behavior change possible?* New York: Brunner/Mazel, 1976.

MASLOW, A. H.   *Toward a psychology of being.* New York: Van Nostrand Reinhold, 1968.

MASLOW, A. H.   *Motivation and personality.* New York: Harper & Row, 1970.

PATTERSON, C. H.   *Theories of counseling and psychotherapy* (3rd ed.). New York: Harper & Row, 1980.

PRICE, R. H.   *Abnormal behavior: Perspectives in conflict.* New York: Holt, Rinehart, & Winston, 1972.

ROGERS, C. R.   The necessary and sufficient conditions of therapeutic personality change. *Journal of Consulting Psychology,* 1957, *22,* 95–103.

ROGERS, C. R.   Toward becoming a fully-functioning person. In A. Combs (Ed.), *Perceiving, behaving, becoming.* Washington, DC: Association for Supervision and Curriculum Development, 1962.

SCHOBEN, C.   Toward a concept of the normal personality. *American Psychologist,* 1957, *12,* 183–190.
STEFFLRE, B., & METHANEY, K.   *The function of counseling theory.* Boston: Houghton Mifflin, 1968.
SUE, D. W.,   *Counseling the culturally different: Theory and practice.* New York: Wiley, 1981.
TRUAX, C. B., & CARKHUFF, R. R.   *Toward effective counseling and psychotherapy.* Chicago: Aldine, 1967.
TYLER, L.   *The work of the counselor* (3rd ed.). New York: Appleton-Century-Crofts, 1969.
WOLBERG, L. R.   *The technique of psychotherapy* (2nd ed.). New York: Grune & Stratton, 1967.
YALOM, I. D.   *The theory and practice of group psychotherapy.* New York: Basic Books, 1975.

CHAPTER TWO
PSYCHOANALYSIS

Since few, if any, counselors use psychoanalysis in their professional practice, you may wonder why this chapter is included in a text for beginning counselor trainees. I have included it for at least two reasons. First, it was the first: Sigmund Freud is grandfather to all of us associated with the behavioral sciences, and especially to those of us who are psychologists and/or counselors. We ought to know our roots. Second, all of us who are Freud's heirs have either adopted, adapted, or (we think) improved upon his system. Therefore, in order to understand the changes, we must first understand what was changed. Beyond that, there are, no doubt, some sinister, primordial urges repressed into the farther reaches of my unconscious which could illuminate the real reason for my including this chapter.

HISTORICAL DEVELOPMENT

Personal Background

Sigmund Freud was born on May 6, 1856, in Freiberg, Moravia (now a part of Czechoslovakia) of devout Jewish parents. When he was about three, the family moved to Leipzig, and a year later, to Vienna, where

Freud remained until the Nazi invasion of 1938. Freud was certainly aware of and probably experienced the antisemitism prevalent in Vienna even then.

In the fall of 1873, Freud entered the University of Vienna as a medical student, despite the fact that he really didn't want to be a physician, but was more interested in studying the historical and cultural development of the human race. His frequent references to mythology attest to that interest as well as to the extent of his reading in that area. Interest in theoretical issues notwithstanding, Freud did not see himself as a social activist or reformer. Apparently he decided that making a living was more important than being a theorist! At any rate he took three years longer than necessary and was finally awarded the M.D. degree in 1881. He had been working in Brücke's physiology laboratory since 1876; but, because his Jewish background slowed his advancement in the university system, he was compelled by economic necessity to enter the practice of medicine. In 1884, he began service as a physician in the department of nervous diseases at the Vienna General Hospital. Often, there were no patients with nervous disorders admitted to the hospital, because the superintendent had no interest in such cases; however, the doctors in charge of admissions circumvented the superintendent and thus provided Freud with patients during his fourteen-month stay at the hospital. His clinical publications finally won him a lectureship in neuropathology in 1885, and that same year he was awarded a travel grant that enabled him to study the problem of hysteria with Charcot in Paris.

In 1886, he married and opened a private practice in Vienna—with little success. In July 1897, while he was troubled by sharp mood swings, a fear of dying, and the inability to continue writing, Freud began his self-analysis. As a part of his self-analysis, he used his dreams as a window on his own consciousness. In 1902, he was promoted to associate professor, and he remained at this level for 18 years. Freud finally achieved full professorship in 1920 and retained that rank until he fled Vienna in 1938 after the Nazi book burnings (which included his works). He died in London in 1939 of cancer of the jaw (Abeles, 1979; Mack & Semrad, 1967).

Theoretical Background

Freud began his private practice at a time when the medical community was largely unaware of what is now considered psychological—as opposed to somatic or physiological—phenomena. Essentially, all disorders were seen as physiological, and treatment was universally physical. While working at Brücke's physiology institute, Freud became associated with Josef Breuer and was impressed by Breuer's successful treatment of "Anna

O." While in Paris, he also observed Charcot's use of hypnosis in the treatment of hysteria. In 1887, Freud began using hypnosis in his own practice but by 1892 had given it up in favor of the concentration method. In this technique, the patient (with eyes closed) was asked to lie on a couch and concentrate on a particular symptom, trying to recall the memories associated with it. Both Freud and his patients came to believe that the urging, probing, questioning of the concentration method interfered with the free flow of thought. As a result, he gradually (1892-1895) developed the free-association technique. This procedure worked particularly well with patients who had developed hysterical disorders. Freud found that these patients initially were unable to think of a sufficient cause for their symptoms; but, as they continued to free associate, they would remember an event immediately preceding the onset of the symptoms that caused considerable disturbance. This emotionally disturbing event seemed invariably to be connected with some aspect of the patient's childhood.

This discovery led, in turn, to the conclusion that very often these memories had been inhibited because they involved sexual experiences or other painful events. When his patients seemed reluctant to talk about these memories, Freud attributed it to an unwillingness to cooperate—resistance. The more he investigated this phenomenon, the more he became convinced that it was due, not to an active, conscious resistance, but rather to an unconscious force in the patient's mind. He described this force as repression. Freud considered repression to be at the core of symptom formation.

At first, Freud was unaware of a salient unitary factor in the disturbances of his patients; but when he reexamined the first eighteen cases he had analyzed, he found a sexual component in each. Further examination of nonhysterical symptoms, such as obsessions, compulsions, and phobias, revealed that these patients were also bothered by the residual effects of early sexual experiences. These adult ideas or wishes were unacceptable to the patient because of moral or ethical values. They had initially neutralized the disturbing thoughts by banishing them from awareness. Unfortunately, they didn't stay banished: later experiences unleashed them, usually in disguised form. Thus the symptoms manifested both the original wish and the self-reproach generated by the wish. Freud also discovered that many of his patients' "memories" of childhood sexual activities were, in fact, only fantasies. Consequently, he focused on unconscious wishes and desires as the prime determinants of psychopathology (Rader, 1976). In fact, Freud (1962) offered what may be taken as an operational definition of psychoanalysis. In it he combines the notions of repression, unconscious mental activity, and transference: repression, which is the foundation of psychoanalytic theory, requires a process of unconscious mental activity, which, in turn, is revealed through transference.

THEORY OF PERSONALITY

Definition of Terms

Abreaction.   The emotional release or discharge resulting from recalling to awareness a painful experience that has been repressed because it was consciously intolerable is called *abreaction*.

Anxiety.   Anxiety is apprehension, tension, or uneasiness that stems from the anticipation of danger, the source of which is largely unknown or unrecognized.

Castration complex.   This is a group of emotionally charged ideas that are unconscious and that refer to the fear of losing the genital organs, usually as punishment for forbidden sexual desires. It includes the childhood fantasy that female genitals result from the loss of a penis.

Catharsis.   In one sense, catharsis refers to the therapeutic release of ideas through a "talking out" of conscious material accompanied by the appropriate emotional reaction. At a deeper level, catharsis refers to the release into awareness of repressed material from the unconscious.

Concentration method.   The forerunner of free association, this early technique required that the patient concentrate upon a particular symptom and then try to recall memories associated with it.

Conscious.   That part of the mental life the individual is aware of at any given time is known as the *conscious*.

Countertransference.   Countertransference is the analyst's conscious or unconscious reaction to the patient.

Defense mechanism.   Defense mechanisms or ego defenses are specific intrapsychic processes that operate unconsciously and are employed to give relief from emotional conflict and freedom from anxiety.

Drive.   A drive is a genetically determined, psychic constituent that, when operative, produces a state of psychic excitation. This excitation or tension impels the individual to activity.

Ego.   That part of the personality structure that is the mediator between the person and reality is called the *ego*. Its prime function is the perception of reality and adaptation to it. It also serves to mediate between the demands of the id and the superego.

Fixation.   When psychosexual maturation is arrested at one level, this delay is called *fixation*.

Free association.   Free association is the spontaneous, uncensored verbalization by the patient of whatever comes to mind. It is the primary technique for releasing repressed material.

Homeostasis.   The tendency of an organism to maintain a constancy and stability in its internal environment is known as *homeostasis*.

Id.   The id is the part of the personality structure that harbors the unconscious, instinctive desires and strivings of the individual.

Instinct.   An instinct, according to Freud, is a primal trend or urge that cannot be further resolved.

Libido.   Libido is a psychic drive or energy usually associated with the sexual instinct.

Narcissism.   Narcissus was a figure in Greek mythology who fell in love with his own reflected image. Narcissism is self-love as opposed to love of another.

Oedipus complex.   Oedipus was a figure in Greek mythology who murdered his father and married his mother. Here, it refers to the attachment of the child to the parent of the opposite sex. This attachment is accompanied by envious and aggressive feelings toward the parent of the same sex.

Penis envy.   In the literal sense, this refers to the female's envy of the male's penis. More generally, it is used in reference to a female's wish for male attributes, position, or advantage.

Pleasure principle.   This refers to the basic psychoanalytic concept that humans instinctively seek to avoid pain and discomfort and strive for gratification and pleasure.

Preconscious.   *Preconscious* refers to thoughts that are not in immediate awareness but can be recalled to awareness by conscious effort.

Primary process.   Psychoanalysts use this term for the generally unorganized mental activity characteristic of unconscious mental life. It is marked by the free discharge of psychic energy and excitation without regard to the demands of the environment, reality, or logic.

Reality principle.   This is the concept that the pleasure principle is normally modified by the inescapable demands and requirements of the external world.

Resistance.   Resistance is the individual's conscious or unconscious psychological defense against bringing repressed material to light.

Secondary process.   Mental activity and thinking, characteristic of the ego and influenced by the demands of the environment, is known as *secondary process*.

Superego.   The superego is that part of the personality structure associated with ethics, standards, and self-criticism. It is formed by the infant's identification with important and esteemed people in early life, particularly parents.

Training analysis.   This is a character analysis of a prospective analyst carried out for the purposes of training the individual in the concepts and problems of psychoanalysis.

Transference.   This term refers to the unconscious "transfer" to others (usually to the analyst) of feelings and attitudes that were originally associated with important figures (usually parents) in early life.

Transference neurosis.   Transference neurosis is an artificial neurosis occurring only during psychoanalytic treatment. The analyst represents one or both parents as if he or she were the original parent(s) in the patient's original infantile setting.

Unconscious.   The unconscious is that part of the mind or of mental functioning whose content is unavailable to direct access by the individual. It is the repository of repressed material.

View of Human Nature

Although psychoanalytic theory is very complex, and at points difficult to fathom, there seem to be seven basic assumptions about human nature (Allen, 1977, p. 60):

1. Personality is a closed energy system fueled by instinctive biological urges.

2. These urges are directed toward reduction of biological tension and come into conflict with environmental constraints and moral prohibitions.

3. Psychic growth results from successfully meeting the changing and conflicting demands of the instincts, the environment, and society.

4. Growth proceeds through fixed developmental stages; the needs of each stage must be fulfilled before a person can progress to subsequent stages.

5. Human activities are overdetermined—i.e., all behavior is the result of both conscious and unconscious determinants. Human action is never free in the sense of being random or spontaneous.

6. The unconscious determinants of behavior are rule-governed and operate according to a dynamic model. They exert much more important influences on thoughts and actions than do conscious determinants.

7. Since equilibrium among the complex forces that compete with one another is difficult to maintain, growth is easily thwarted; thus, the state of healthy normality is difficult to achieve.

In the psychoanalytic literature, there are many references to instinctual drives, or simply to instincts. "Drive" is a more accurate translation of Freud's term *Triebe*. He revised his motivational theory several times, finally arriving at the concept of sex and aggression as the two drives most associated with psychopathology. They are characterized by three fundamental features not shared by other drives. Sex and aggression are (a) *interpersonal*—they are directed at other people; (b) *plastic*—they can be satisfied in a number of ways; and (c) *postponable*—they need not be satisfied immediately.

Freud found that his patients experienced intense conflicts that were largely unconscious, often seriously affecting their behavior or feelings. These conflicts, unlike those that are conscious, are generally inappropriate, impervious to reason, are not easily resolved, and are rooted in childhood experiences. The basis for such conflicts is laid between certain drives, wishes, or feelings and the demands of reality or the "shoulds" and "oughts" of conscience. If such wishes and drives were acknowledged in consciousness, they would arouse severe anxiety and guilt. Defense mechanisms are unconscious avoidance responses that prevent both the recognition and the execution of such wishes, and, thus, enable one to avoid unpleasant feelings and anticipations of punishment. Freud assumed that drives differ in intensity, because his patients manifested considerable variation in the intensity of their suffering and their concern with themselves and their world. This led him to the conclusion that normal and abnormal are only quantitatively different; i.e., they differ in degree, not in kind (Price, 1972; Rader, 1976).

Structure of Personality

In *The Interpretation of Dreams*, Freud attempted to set forth a topographical theory of the mind. He divided the mind into three regions—unconscious, preconscious, and conscious—based on their relationship to consciousness. He derived this theory from dream interpretation, analysis of neurosis, and the study of the psychopathology of everyday life—humor, jokes, slips of the tongue, and so forth.

The unconscious. The unconscious is the repository for repressed thoughts and feelings. Ordinarily, the material in the unconscious is unavailable to awareness and can become conscious only through the preconscious, which acts as a censor or gatekeeper. The repressed ideas can become conscious only when the preconscious is overpowered (neurotic symptom or psychotherapy), relaxes (hypnosis or dream states), or is fooled (jokes).

The unconscious is associated with what Freud called "primary process thinking," which is directed toward wish-fulfillment and the discharge of instinctual energy: operations of the pleasure principle. Thus, the unconscious typically disregards logic, revels in contradictions, refuses to say "no," has no conception of time, and presents wishes as already fulfilled acts. The content of the unconscious is limited to wishes seeking fulfillment, which provide the material for dreams and neurotic symptom formation. Finally, the unconscious contains the mental representatives and derivatives of the instincts, especially the sexual instincts (Mack & Semrad, 1967).

The preconscious. This region of the mind is not present at birth but develops as the child interacts with the environment. Elements in the unconscious can become conscious only by being linked to words and then reaching the preconscious. On the other hand, one of the functions of the preconscious is to act as censor, repressing wishes and desires, thus keeping them in the unconscious. The type of mental activity associated with the preconscious is called *secondary process thinking*; and it is aimed at avoiding unpleasure (not just pain), delaying instinctual discharges, and marshalling mental energy in the service of external reality and logic (Mack & Semrad, 1967).

The conscious. Freud saw the conscious as a kind of sense organ of awareness working closely with the preconscious. While an individual may become conscious of perceptual stimuli from within the organism, only those elements in the preconscious could enter the conscious; the rest of the mind is unavailable to awareness. If you visualize the mind as an iceberg, the one-tenth tip visible above water is the conscious mind, the water line itself is the preconscious, and the nine-tenths below water is the unconscious (Mack & Semrad, 1967).

With the publication of *The Ego and the Id* in 1923, Freud added a new point of view to the topographical model. To explain more thoroughly the intrapsychic conflicts an individual is beset by, Freud divided the mind into id, ego, and superego while still retaining the earlier unconscious, preconscious, and conscious. He distinguished between primary process and secondary process. The former is the more primitive mode, disorganized, illogical, and not subject to the constraints of reality or time. The major purpose of primary process thinking is the speedy discharge of mental energy. The *pleasure principle* is the term used to describe the undifferentiated tension-avoidance effort intrinsic to primary process. Secondary process, on the other hand, is more organized and restrained. It is characterized by reflection and submission to the exigencies of reality, time, and logic. Freud formulated the reality principle as the regulatory mechanism for secondary process thinking. It is based on the capacity to delay immediate gratification for future satisfaction (Abeles, 1979).

The id.   Freud saw the id as the original system of personality. A newborn infant is all id. It does not develop over time, but remains unchanged. It is an unorganized chaos, "a cauldron of seething excitement" (Freud, S., 1933, p. 103). It contains the instincts and is the source of psychic energy. Its function is to discharge energy released in the organism and to keep the level of tension as low as possible. To do this, the id seeks to gratify instinctual drives immediately. The id may seek gratification and discharge of tension directly through a motor reflex or indirectly through wish-fulfillment (primary process). Since the id does not distinguish between subjective reality and objective reality, the primary process may produce hallucinations or dreams in order to gratify the instinctual drives of the id. The operations of the id are unconscious, but it is not synonymous with the unconscious, because some superego functions are also unconscious (Price, 1972).

The ego.   As the infant interacts more and more with the external world, a part of the id becomes differentiated as the ego. The ego develops out of the id because of the organism's need to cope with the real world. Like the id, the ego pursues gratification; but unlike the id, it does so while taking into account the demands of the external world. For example, the ego is able to delay a short-term gratification in order to ensure a long-term gratification in the future. Thus, the ego is ruled by the reality principle and operates by way of secondary-process thinking. The ego relies on past experience to make judgments about the most effective way to obtain gratification. The ego, then, is the organized part of the id and is referred to as the executor of the personality. Among the functions of the ego are (a) to develop and maintain a sense of reality, (b) to test reality through objective evaluation and judgment of the external world, (c) to adapt to reality by using one's own resources to arrive at satisfactory solutions, (d) to control and regulate instinctual drives, (e) to develop mutually satisfying object relations, and (f) to defend itself (the ego) against threat (Mack & Semrad, 1967).

The superego. During the third—genital (see below)—stage of development, children undergo the Oedipal conflict: boys wish to possess their mothers and girls their fathers. These wishes are frustrated by the same-sexed parent, and the resulting hostility—unacceptable to parents—is met with punishment. Thus, through a series of developmental situations, the values (positive as well as negative) of the parents are internalized by the child. The portion of the ego that introjects or internalizes these parental (and/or societal) values is called the *superego,* which is made up of two subsystems: the conscience and the ego-ideal. The conscience—values introjected from others—represents things the individual believes should not be done. The ego-ideal—values learned by the child—represents things the individual would like to do. Either or both are in frequent conflict with the id, but these conflicts operate largely at an unconscious level.

In his original writings, Freud presented these three regions of the mind as organized principles; but the tone of later works by both Freud and his followers made them appear to be reified, to be given a life and reality of their own (Mack & Semrad, 1967).

Development of Personality

Freud maintained that personality is pretty well formed in the first five years of life. He postulated a series of psychosexual stages of development that, while allowing for some variation among individuals, remain basically the same for all. To understand Freud's theory fully, you must remember that he used the term "sexual" in a much broader sense than is usually used today. For Freud, the erogenous zones included the mouth and anus, as well as the genital organs. Sexuality involves a stimulation of all the erogenous zones (not necessarily simultaneously); thus, it may be more closely associated with the concept of "pleasure" than genital sexuality. Nevertheless, Freud believed that the erogenous zones are important in the development of personality because they provide the first source of excitement for the infant. Furthermore, the child's stimulation of these zones frequently leads to parental censure, which, in turn, leads to frustration and anxiety. Freud posited three pregenital stages: oral, anal, and phallic. Following these is the latency stage—a period of five or six years of quiescence. The latency stage then blossoms into the final, enduring, genital stage (Price, 1972).

Oral stage. During the infant's first year, the primary source of pleasure/tension-reduction is the mouth. Initially the mouth is used for incorporation—taking in food. After teeth have erupted, the infant draws pleasure from biting as well as sucking and swallowing—incorporation.

These two kinds of activity—incorporation and biting—may be manifested later in distinctive character traits. For example, the child who was fixated on incorporation may become the gullible adult who "swallows" all he or she is told. The biting child may become a verbally aggressive adult, a "backbiter."

Since the infant is almost totally dependent upon the mother for both protection and nourishment at this stage, the relationship between mother and child poses two possible threats to future stability. If the relationship is too close and too comfortable, the child may be overly dependent. On the other hand, if the relationship is too distant and anxiety-producing, the child may develop insurmountable feelings of insecurity. If the relationship is characterized by appropriate warmth and closeness without being overwhelming, the child should develop affectionate and trusting ties to others in later life (Abeles, 1979; Price, 1972).

Anal stage.   During the second year, the child begins to be aware of pressure on the anal sphincter as a source of discomfort. Just as the child discovers how to relieve this discomfort, the parent begins to impose toilet-training demands. This is the first major conflict between parent and child. Once again, the quality of the relationship between parent and child is crucial. If the parents are excessively harsh, the child may rebel by retaining the feces, and, over time, develop an "anal retentive" personality—stingy and obstinate. If the relationship is relaxed and the child is praised for his efforts, the basis is laid for a creative, productive adulthood (Abeles, 1979; Price, 1972).

Phallic stage.   Between the ages of three and five years, the psycho-sexual development of boys and girls becomes differentiated on the basis of whether or not they have a phallus. During this period, the boy identifies with his penis and manifests intense interest in his genitals. Sexual fantasies and curiosity about sex increase, and masturbation is more frequent. The threat of castration becomes frightfully real when boys discover that girls do not have penises, and girls feel deprived and envious when they become aware that they do not have penises. Freud was adamant in his conviction that both boys and girls value the phallus highly and have fears about castration.

A prominent feature of the phallic stage for both sexes is the Oedipus complex, which presupposes that a child is drawn erotically to the parent of the opposite sex. At the same time, the child experiences angry impulses and wishes toward the parent of the same sex. The boy sees his father as a rival for the affection of his mother. He can either fantasize about taking his father's place (becoming his mother's lover) or supplanting his mother (becoming his father's lover). The former is referred to as the positive Oedipus complex, while the latter—relatively infrequent—is known as the negative Oedipus complex. In the positive Oedipus complex, the child fears that his father will punish his rival by removing the offending organ—castration anxiety. In the negative complex, the boy fears that he will come to resemble his mother: without a penis. In either case, he loses his identity.

Girls may relate to the father as a rival for their mother's affections; but, as a rule, they do not feel as intensely about the rivalry as boys do. Frustrated by weaning and toilet training, the little girl begins to draw away from her mother and toward her father. The resentment is deepened when she blames her mother for not having provided her with a penis. As the feelings toward the father intensify, the little girl fantasizes about having her father's penis and about removing her mother as a rival. Soon the desire to have a penis gives way to the desire to have a child by the father (Abeles, 1979).

Latency stage. By the time the child has reached the age of five or six, the storms of the Oedipal phase have diminished and their memories are repressed. Overtly sexual feelings are replaced by feelings of affection, and the strength of the hostility wanes. During this stage, the ego is fortified. The child increases cognitive activities, spends more time with children of the same sex, and adheres more consistently to the reality principle. All of these changes are indicative of secondary-process functioning. More and more parental values are introjected, forming the nucleus of the superego. The latency period lasts until puberty, which typically occurs at about age eleven, but may come anywhere between nine and fourteen (Abeles, 1979).

Genital stage. While the first three stages of development can be characterized as narcissistic, during the genital stage, this self-love begins to change into a love of others. With the beginning of puberty, the child enters a stage of development that hopefully will culminate in mature heterosexual behavior. In this ultimate stage of development, the normal individual does not get pleasure from oral, anal, or autoerotic activities; and he or she is not bothered by castration anxiety or an unresolved Oedipus complex. Rather, the greatest pleasure is received from a relationship with a member of the opposite sex. The effects of the pregenital stages do not entirely disappear, but become fused with the effects of the genital stage. Thus, the final personality organization of the individual is a function of all developmental stages as they persist in the adult character (Abeles, 1979; Price, 1972).

Development of Maladaptive Behavior

According to Mack and Semrad (1967), the theory of neuroses (hysteria, obsessional neuroses, and the phobias) is the core of the pyschoanalytic concept of psychopathology. Neuroses develop when there is an intrapsychic conflict between drives—usually sexual—and fears which conflict prevents the drives from being gratified in reality. When the libidinal energy of the drive is not discharged, the drive itself must be repressed. However, the process of repression only renders the drive unconscious; it does not dissipate its power or energy. As a result, the pent-up energy of the repressed drive erupts as a neurotic symptom.

Throughout the development of the personality, many vicissitudes may contribute to the development of maladaptive behavior or psychopathology. Deprivation of maternal warmth and caring in the first few months of life may impair ego development. Failure to make the appropriate identification weakens the ego for its role as executor of personality. Parental inconsistency, excessive harshness, or overpermissiveness may result in inappropriate functioning of the superego. Conflicts among instinctual drives may diminish the ego's ability to sublimate one or another of the conflicting drives, thus inhibiting the autonomous functions.

In summary, neuroses arise because of an imbalance between impulses seeking "release" and the dynamic forces whose function it is to control them. When the impulses cannot be tolerated in consciousness and cannot be effectively defended against, the ego has no other recourse but to form symptoms, which are then identified as neurotic. Thus the primary purpose of neurotic behavior is the reduction of tension or conflict (Mack & Semrad, 1967).

In the course of his clinical practice, Freud found that his patients, with the help of his new technique of free association, could recall childhood experiences that, without the vehicle of free association, remained buried in the unconscious. Moreover, these experiences were traumatic—fearsome—because they threatened the relationship between parent and child. Frequently the experiences were sexual activities or fantasies. In order to protect the ego in the relationship, the child denied the experience and repressed its memory. Thus the ego defense of repression is directed against impulses, drives, and, especially, direct expression of sexual instinct, in order to enable the individual to conform to the demands of the external world. When the traumatic childhood experience was repressed, the excitement associated with it was also repressed. Since excitement is psychic energy and energy is never lost, the repressed energy remained in the id in the form of libidinous drives. In adult life, some current event may release the energy through a new outlet, but the memory of the original experience remains repressed. The new outlet may be a manifest symptom.

Anxiety. The release of the libidinous energy constitutes a threat to the ego, and anxiety signals the presence of danger to the ego. Freud described anxiety as an unpleasant feeling that is associated with the excitement of the autonomic nervous system. He differentiated three types of anxiety: (a) reality anxiety, (b) neurotic anxiety, and (c) moral anxiety. In all three types, the ego is threatened with being overwhelmed by internal or external forces. They differ only in the source of the anxiety: the real world of the ego, the unconscious world of the id, or the parental injunctions of the superego.

Reality or objective anxiety is an unpleasant emotional experience resulting from the individual's perception of danger from the real world. The jogger's fear of being struck by a car while running along the road has an objective basis in reality. It is the ego that experiences the threat of reality anxiety, and it is the ego that learns to cope with reality anxiety by avoiding the threatening situation. In the case of neurotic anxiety, the ego fears being overwhelmed by the instinctual demands of the id. Neurotic anxiety may be expressed in three ways: free-floating anxiety, phobia, and panic reaction. The person experiencing free-floating anxiety has a chronic apprehensiveness of impending danger. The phobic experience is an intense, irrational fear of some specific object or event. The panic reaction is characterized by the sudden appearance of an intense debilitating fear with no apparent cause. Moral anxiety is the result of a conflict between the impulses of the id and the regulatory functions of the superego. It is usually accompanied by intense feelings of guilt or shame.

Whatever the source of the anxiety, neuroses result from that quantitative distribution of energies, not merely from the presence of conflict. Behavior, then, is pathological when it becomes unmanageable and interferes with the day-do-day life of the individual (Price, 1972).

Defense Mechanisms

If anxiety signals the presence of danger to the ego, how does the ego handle this danger? According to Freud, there are two ways. Either the ego makes use of realistic problem-solving or it resorts to irrational and unconscious methods to distort or deny reality. Freud called these irrational methods defense mechanisms or ego defenses. Defenses arise early in the individual's development as a result of the ego's efforts to mediate between the pressures of the id and the requirements of external reality. These several ego defenses have two characteristics in common: (a) they are unconscious, and (b) they function to deny or distort reality. While abnormalities in the development and/or functioning of the defenses are associated with pathology, the defenses themselves are not pathological. In fact, they serve an essential function in maintaining "normal," balanced well-being.

Although there is no unanimity among psychoanalysts regarding either the number of ego defenses or their relative importance, the following have received the most general support and are presented in order of removal from reality. For example, rationalization distorts reality only minimally; while denial, at the bottom of the list, totally rejects reality (Abeles, 1979; Freud, A., 1966; Price, 1972):

Rationalization.   A person who explains his behavior in socially acceptable ways is using rationalization to maintain his self-esteem. A student who flunks an exam distorts the reality by explaining that all his study time was spent sitting up with a sick friend (it's rationalization even if he *was* sitting up with a sick friend!). The angry father who, paddle in hand, tells his son, "this will hurt me more than you" is also using rationalization.

Repression.   This is the mechanism by which threatening instinctual impulses from the id, which are in conflict with the ego or superego, are removed from consciousness. Repression may function in any of several ways: it may distort auditory or visual perceptions, or it many obliterate memories associated with traumatic or painful events. The adolescent boy who is unable to remember fondling his younger sister has repressed the painful memory.

Displacement.   Displacement refers to replacing the object of impulses with a substitute object. For example, the man who enjoys pornographic movies instead of actual sexual activity, and a woman who expresses her anger at her husband by being cross with her children are both using displacement.

Identification.   When a person takes the character traits of another and makes them his own, he is using identification. One may identify with a loved one to minimize the pain of loss (a widow who runs for her deceased husband's political office), with a sense of guilt feelings in order to punish oneself (the reformed addict who becomes a drug abuse counselor), or with an aggressor in order to master—or mask—terror (the hostage who joins with his or her captors).

Conversion.   Conversion refers to the transformation of the psychic impulses into a somatic disturbance. For example, hysterical paralysis of the arm could be a symbolic compromise between a wish to masturbate and the superego's prohibition against that wish.

Isolation.   This refers to the splitting of an idea that is remembered (conscious) from the affect that accompanied it and is repressed (unconscious). This can be a common aspect of normal thinking; but it may also explain an obsessional client's ability to handle violent or disturbing thoughts in a calm, detached way.

Reaction formation. This defense enables an individual to express an unacceptable impulse by transforming it into its opposite. One of the primary characteristics of reaction formation is its exaggeration: the individual "doth protest too much." Sometimes both the original impulse and its opposite (reaction formation) exist side-by-side: the love-hate relationship.

Undoing. Undoing is an attempt to cancel out or nullify an act previously committed (in reality or in fantasy) by certain counteractions. The ritual or obsessive-compulsive behavior of some neurotics (e.g., hand-washing or incantations) are typical.

Projection. In this defense, something unacceptable in the self is attributed to (projected onto) another. Thus, the individual who experiences sexual feelings toward another, but cannot accept these feelings, may defend against them by accusing the other of making "improper advances." "He loves me" really means "I love him."

Denial. Denial is a relatively primitive mechanism and is often found in children. When circumstances of reality frustrate an id impulse, denial intervenes to protect the ego from the frustration of the real situation. Examples of denial in action are the abused child's clinging to the abusing parent or a mother's continuing to rock her dead child.

THEORY OF THERAPY

Rationale for Change

Change occurs in psychoanalysis when the unconscious becomes conscious. This means that the ego is strengthened, the superego is reduced or eliminated, and the client is more aware of the id. In the process of being cured, the patient deals with the facts of his or her life, as well as the fantasies that can be recalled. In other words, cure, in psychoanalysis, involves the undoing of repression, so that both the repressive forces and the repressed strivings are safely and effectively accounted for. One of the primary objectives of psychoanalytic therapy is to facilitate the patient's production of material (Fine, 1973).

Process of Therapy

Psychoanalysis usually proceeds through three major phases: orientation, transference neurosis, and termination. Freud compared these three phases to the opening, middle, and end games of chess (Stewart & Levine, 1967).

Orientation. During the opening phase of treatment, the analyst tries to get a sense of the story of the patient's life: a picture of the major conflicts that confront the patient, together with attempted solutions. The second concern of the initial phase is the establishment of a good working relationship with the patient. This involves, among other things, training the patient to be a patient.

At the beginning of analysis, the patient is informed about the "fundamental rule": free association. During the initial phase, the analyst keeps close watch over any departures from the fundamental rule, which are usually interpreted as resistances. Even the "resistances" are explored through free association (Abeles, 1979; Stewart & Levine, 1967).

Transference Neurosis. Transference neurosis develops as the patient becomes more preoccupied with the present than with the past and particularly with the process of analysis itself. It is characterized by a somewhat variable but sustained network of transferences, in which the patient reproduces much of the essential material from the past. This new information is a kind of refocused set of patterns that is directed toward the analyst and appears as a response to the whole analytic environment. Originally, the transference neurosis was considered a serious obstacle to therapy; but, when analysts realized that through it they could observe first-hand many of the patient's childhood conflicts and attempted solutions, the transference neurosis became the central concern of analysis.

By the time analysis is well into this second phase, the relationship between analyst and patient is so firmly established that it can bear the stresses of the transference neurosis. The primary concern at this point is whether or not the patient is beginning to develop the power of self-observation—the ability to objectively evaluate his or her own emotional experience (Freud, A., 1966; Stewart & Levine, 1967).

Termination. This phase begins when the patient has finally relived much of the infantile situation and has begun to resolve infantile conflicts in effective ways. The goal of analysis has been reached if the patient becomes free enough to develop in his or her own way. Perhaps the most important task of this phase is the dissolution of the positive and negative transference, which, up to this point, has served to move the analysis forward (Stewart & Levine, 1967).

Goals of Therapy

The major goal of psychoanalysis is to alleviate pathological symptoms by bringing repressed thoughts and feelings into consciousness. Psychoanalysis is designed to make the unconscious conscious and to reintegrate previously repressed material into the total personality structure. To the extent that this is achieved, the patient regains control of his or her life, is better able to make decisions and to experience self and others directly, consciously, and accurately. This may involve a large-scale reorganization of the personality structure of the individual. However, since it is not possible to eliminate all personality defects, analysts seek to return the patient to a state of homeostasis—equilibrium.

Among the generally accepted criteria for the effectiveness of treatment are the following: (a) reduction of the conscious need to suffer; (b) fewer neurotic inhibitions; (c) decreased infantile dependency needs; (d) increased capacity for responsibility; (e) success in marriage, social relationships, and work; and (f) ability to experience pleasure (Abeles, 1979).

Training of the Therapist

The first psychoanalytic training institute was established in Berlin in 1920. Its staff was invited by the director in consultation with members of the Berlin Psychoanalytic Society, and its purpose was to supply members to the Society. Training was divided into three major phases: first, the training analysis of the candidate—a period of one to three years of personal analysis; second, theoretical instruction; and third, practical clinical training consisting of supervised analysis and case seminars (Alexander, 1956).

The current *Standards for Training in Psychoanalysis* (American Psychoanalytic Association, 1980) indicates that, to be eligible for training, an individual must have graduated from a Class A medical school and have served a one-year's internship in psychiatry in an approved hospital. The training itself consists of (a) preparatory analysis of at least 300 hours; (b) assigned reading (principally Freud); (c) courses dealing with theory, clinical applications, and techniques of analysis extending over at least three years; (d) continuous case seminars and clinical conferences; (e) supervised clinical work; and (f) advanced training in child analysis. (A list of approved training institutions in the United States is appended at the end of this chapter.)

Function of the Therapist

The work of psychoanalysis is concerned with preparing the patient to deal with the material that has been uncovered and to provide a kind of desensitization of psychonoxious material. At times, the intervention takes the form of instruction, focusing on teaching the patient to be introspective, to be aware of his or her own inner promptings. At other times, the process involves uncovering hidden resistances to the analytic process; at still others, it involves dealing directly with the noxious material.

The analyst's role is to listen, observe, and comment (interpret). It is a highly didactic stance, in which the analyst is both teacher of concepts and guide through a frightening and strange world. Psychoanalysis adopts a problem-solving approach in which a problem is formulated, various solutions are tried, and then, finally, a way out is found. Therapy emphasizes primarily the affective factor. The analyst deals with feelings all the time. Cognition and behavior are understood primarily in terms of the feelings they embody or convey. Interpersonal factors are primary and are conceptualized through the underlying transference.

The therapist should be warm, accepting, and nonjudgmental. An analyst is primarily concerned with the goals of therapy, rather than a precise routine. The therapist must understand the patient's transference maneuvers, resistances, and the specific structure of his or her neurosis. Crucial errors in technique do not arise to any significant degree from premature, partially incorrect, incomplete, or even false interpretations; rather, they are to be seen as a failure to reach the patient at a level where therapy becomes an experience that makes a difference in the patient's life. Perhaps such errors may come under the heading of lack of empathy or faulty technique. Yet, ultimately, it is not the technique that is at fault; rather, it is the therapist's failure to communicate in terms that are emotionally significant and personally meaningful to the patient (Fine, 1973; Rader, 1977; Strupp, 1973).

PRACTICE OF THERAPY

Major Techniques

Free association. The "fundamental rule" of analysis is that the patient agrees with the analyst to be completely candid, revealing everything that comes into his mind, even if it is unpleasant, derogatory, or seems unimportant or inane. This rule is in force throughout therapy, but most particularly during the free-association phase. In a sense, the associations really are not "free," but are governed by certain unconscious forces: (a) the pathogenic conflicts of the neuroses, (b) the wish to get well, and (c) the wish to please the analyst. The interplay among these forces can become very complex and may even threaten the analysis itself.

During free association, the patient lies on a couch in a semidarkened room; the analyst sits at the head of the couch out of the patient's range of vision. The patient is not to choose what to say; nor is he or she to omit anything no matter how trivial, irrelevant, embarrassing, or painful it may seem. The analyst's job is to listen carefully, trying to understand, and then to choose the right moment to interpret what the patient reveals. Among those elements interpreted are resistances, transference, early childhood memories, dreams, and symbolic language (i.e. the symbolic meaning of words used by the patient). Free association continues throughout treatment, except for periodic discussions of the interpretations (Stewart & Levine, 1967).

Analysis of transference. By his acceptance of all material recovered through free association, the analyst provides an atmosphere in which the patient can plumb the depths of his or her soul. Instead of seeing the revelations as weird, sick, or frightening, the analyst accepts the fact of their occurrence. The patient gradually assumes the analyst's attitude toward the material and, thus, is able to become deeply involved in it rather than overwhelmed by it. The patient, in other words, is allowed—even encouraged—to regress safely. Part of this therapeutic regression includes the patient's attributing to the analyst the long-repressed feelings formerly held in relation to significant others in the patient's early life. Thus the patient may want the analyst's love, forgiveness, or guidance; he or she may fear that the analyst will abandon, blame, or ridicule; he or she may become very angry with, or dependent upon, or possessive of, the analyst. The analyst, meanwhile, provides support, understanding, and stability— principally in the form of interpretations. This enables the patient to recognize that these feelings are disrupting life outside therapy as well as within. He or she can then apply the new, more mature understanding to developing more adaptive behavior patterns (Rader, 1977).

Analysis of resistance. Neither resistance nor transference are themselves techniques. It is the analyst's skill in recognizing, facilitating, and interpreting them that constitutes the techniques. With regard to resistance, the analyst first confronts the patient with the resistance (e.g., tardiness, or refusal to accept the analyst's interpretation), then explores and interprets its meaning and significance (Mack & Semrad, 1967).

Dream analysis. Freud first became aware of the importance of dreams when he discovered that in free association his patients frequently described dreams. He concluded that the dream is a conscious expression of an unconscious fantasy. A dream is a commentary on the events of the previous day that arises out of the unconscious part of the mind. Since the unconscious also includes memories of past events, the mechanisms and symbols of the dream may reveal significant information about those past events. The analysis of dreams uncovers material that has been repressed. The dream, which the patient may or may not remember, is called the "manifest dream," and its elements are "manifest dream content." The unconscious thoughts and wishes that occasion the dream and are disguised by it are called "latent dream content." The analyst's job is to discover and interpret the latent dream content, which is the real meaning of the dream (Mack & Semrad, 1967; Stewart & Levine, 1967).

The interpretive process. In classical psychoanalysis, therapeutic intervention is almost limited to interpretation. Thus, the term "psychoanalysis" means to identify and explain (interpret) unconscious conflicts. The analyst focuses the patient's attention on the patient's intrapsychic "events" and on intrapersonal "events" within the analytic setting. Thus, the analysis is focused on the *patient in analysis.* The interpretation of dreams is made within this context: one of the major stimuli for dream formation is the analytic relationship, while the dream provides a fruitful source of information about the transference relationship with the analyst. Finally, interpretation of current conflicts is also offered in order to uncover the defensive maneuvers employed by the patient (Stewart & Levine, 1967).

Treatment Parameters

Freud insisted that his patients commit themselves to hour-long sessions, usually for six days each week. He estimated that psychoanalysis would involve a minimum of six months and might extend well beyond a year. This is far less than most modern analyses.

After the preliminary assessment interviews are over and the patient is accepted as a suitable candidate for psychoanalysis, he or she is instructed to lie on a couch with the analyst out of sight at the head of the couch. The patient is to say everything that comes to mind, omitting nothing, no matter how trivial, off the point, nonsensical, embarrassing, or offensive to the analyst. All that is demanded of the patient is to come regularly, three to six times a week, for a forty-five- to fifty-minute session and to follow this basic rule of free association. On the average, most analyses require between two and five years; some last more than ten. The American Psychoanalytic Association recommends at least four analytic sessions each week (Abeles, 1979; Rader, 1977; Stewart & Levine, 1967).

CASE STUDY   *The following case study is cited from Dewald (1972, pp. 26–30).*

SESSION 2:

Patient: I don't know whether to talk about my present problems or whether I should be talking about my emotional problems.
Analyst: Let's look at your wish to separate them.
P: I just feel unsure about everything. I do have some new problems.
A: What's the detail?
P: We've decided that we're not going to borrow any money for this and instead we are going to get it on our own. *(Elaborates plans)* We're going to have to cut our budget and Tom is going to take some extra jobs and I'll try to get a part-time job. I feel as if there are so many things to do and I'm not even sure that we're going to get them done. I know that I'm going to have a baby in October.
A: What's your feeling about it?
P: I feel happy, but it also makes me mad. Somehow being pregnant makes me somebody. I'm thinking about the money and how I

resent the children about this right now. We wouldn't have any worries about paying for the analysis without them. But I must have things worked out. I somehow expected everyone to give me what I asked for and no one is going to. There are only two people in the world who love me. I think of my mother's call and all she said was that they would investigate the idea of analysis. I have no one to turn to. I have one friend and she offered to loan us $4,000.

A: What's the detail?

P: She went to Mr. Harris and she got divorced. She's through with her treatment now. I'm thinking of how much I feel my resentment. *(Elaborates)* I feel it toward my parents and toward my sister. I feel so jealous of her. I feel as if I'm tied to them with strings, and it has been that way all my life. I hate them. I know that I want to be independent of them and yet emotionally I'm just like a child. It's almost as if I need my parents to feed me and to change my diaper.

A: What's the detail of your feeling about your sister?

P: She's a junior in college and right now she's in Europe with my older sister. . . . I've been through this feeling so many times I just want to be rid of it.

A: What are you referring to?

P: I feel so frustrated. There's nothing that I can do to elicit love from anyone. It makes me mad but there is nothing there. It's like dealing with a statue. I can't hurt it no matter how hard I kick. . . .

A: And what comes to your mind?

P: . . . I can't do anything so I might as well not try. I hate them! What's the good of that? It's just not fair! I want to scream and yell but it wouldn't do anything!

A: You feel as if it's been this way all your life. What are your associations?

P: It's always been this way. I was just born into a family and I just happened to come along. My mother resented me and my father didn't care about anything. If only I had some device!

A: You seem to be holding back some of your feelings and thoughts.

P: I get very anxious when I think about this. I'm thinking of my mother now and how much I hate her! There's no love for me in my mother, and yet I feel that maybe I'm wrong. I want someone to say to me, "Yes, your mother was a . . . "

A: What did you stop at?

P: A bitch.

A: What comes to your mind that you didn't want to use the word?

P: One time my father called her that. If I ever let go I'll explode.

A: What's the detail of the feeling that you might explode?

P: I feel like killing her sometimes. I'd like to take a knife and stab her but I know that I can't, and I don't really want to. Really I'd like to hurt her more some other way. Maybe I could do that by killing myself. That's what she wanted in the beginning anyhow. So I'm not going to give her that satisfaction, but I do blame all of my problems on to my mother. I wonder why? I think it has something to do with my father because she caused him to do what he did and so it all hurt me.

A: Let's not jump to conclusions about why you feel this way. What are your associations to the thought of her causing him to do the things he did?

P: Somehow I feel as if my father's fate was inevitable. She digs at him and she drove him out. *(Elaborates)* She kept him a child. I don't blame my father for his affairs. He couldn't help it. But I do blame my mother for her problems. She's been thirty years trying to get my father under her thumb.

A: What's the detail?

P: If she says jump, he does. He's not having any more affairs now. She mammas him in order to control him. *(Elaborates)* He's not even a man anymore. . . . It would be much better for me now just to run away from them now and have no communication with them. Why do I hate my mother?

A: Let's go back to your fear of exploding if you ever let go of your feelings. What comes to your mind?

P: My hands feel paralyzed right now. I wonder if I want to kill her? I know that I do want to get back at her. I'd like to stand and scream. I did once, but she just sat there and looked at me! Something is holding me back.

A: What comes to mind?

P: . . . (Sobs) . . . I see her lying on the floor and then she is crawling around and I am standing over her, and I'm big and I'm in control and she's completely helpless. . . . I can't stand this.

A: What is it that you can't stand?

P: I can't stand my thoughts.

A: I wonder if you aren't reversing the positions in this image, and if it is you who feels helpless at the moment.

P: I feel as if I'm incapable of handling myself. It's an old feeling that I have all the time. I feel as if something terrible will happen. Maybe I'll black out or something that I don't know. So it is much easier to be controlled and to be told what to do. . . . I am thinking of my children. If this emotion ever gets out I'm afraid I'll go wild and uncontrollable.

A: I think that here you are not distinguishing between the thought or feeling on the one hand, and an action on the other.

P: Yes, yes. *(Sigh)* I feel afraid to go home now. I'm afraid that I'll hurt my children or do something else. I wish I could put my aggression onto the person that I feel it for, but somehow I can't.

A: What comes to your mind?

P: I took it all out on my little sister as I grew up and I do it now with my children. . . . When I stopped seeing Mr. Harris I used to beat the baby and sometimes I felt as if I'd kill her. *(Elaborates)* This is just what my mother did to me.

A: What is the detail?

P: Her hostility towards my father was directed to me. I was bad and I had a temper and sometimes I was uncontrollable and she used to say, "You're so much like your father." . . . Sometimes I'm afraid to leave my children with my parents because I'm afraid that they may physically hurt them. My mother sometimes used to look at me as though she wanted to kill me. *(Elaborates)* . . . I feel helpless now and I couldn't fight back and I feel sorry for this little girl who is so helpless.

A: There seem to be some gaps in your associations. It is as if you're afraid to talk without editing here.

P: Sometime I'll get back at her. I'm just waiting for the chance. . . . this frightens me. . . . I feel as if it's crazy. I can't . . . when I get mad like this, I get a sexual feeling. I've got one now. It happens whenever I get anxious like this. It's as if I'm masturbating.

A: What comes to your mind about the fear of mentioning it directly?

P: I'm afraid of my feelings anyway. I'm afraid that you will think I'm terrible if I tell you these things.

A: If I suggest to you that for the purposes of analysis you let down your usual barriers and say everything that comes to your mind, then what right do I have to have a reaction if you do just that? We'll stop here for today.

In this session, the analyst's main goal is to help the patient learn how to work in analysis. This is what prompted his comments about separating "present problems" from "emotional problems," as well as the various requests for details of information and of feeling.

Applications

Freud was quite explicit about the kind of persons and disorders amenable to psychoanalysis. Patients should be less than fifty years old, endowed with reasonable intelligence, capable of periods of normal functioning, and should not have deep-seated character defects or severe organic disabilities. Furthermore, he advised that patients suffering from massive depression, confusion, or psychosis are not good candidates for psychoanalysis. He acknowledged that psychoanalysis is costly, demanding, and time-consuming. Patients unwilling or unable to withstand these rigors were advised to seek help elsewhere. On the other hand, he reported that many of his patients came to him after failing to find help through other modalities (Abeles, 1979).

In view of the training required, it is highly unlikely that a counselor would use psychoanalysis *per se,* or even psychoanalytic techniques in his or her practice. However knowledge of psychoanalytic theory and practice can facilitate an understanding of (a) the role of early relationships in clients' present lives, (b) the possibility of transference and countertransference in the relationship, (c) the use and misuse of ego defenses.

Current Status

Beginning with the departure of Adler and Jung from the psychoanalytic fold, there have been a number of neo-Freudian approaches to psychotherapy. One of these (Adler's individual psychology) will be discussed in detail in the next chapter. All of the rest are worthy of study—in some other text. The remainder of this section will present a very brief overview of psychoanalytic therapy as an outgrowth of classical psychoanalysis and a representative of the other neo-Freudian therapies. This presentation is adapted principally from Rader (1976).

Since the death of Freud in 1939, *ego psychology* has arisen to correct some of the overemphasis on unconscious phenomena of the *id psychologists*. More attention and importance is now given to the conscious adaptive and controlling functions of the ego. The ego psychology framework has encouraged and suggested modifications in standard psychoanalytic therapy that open that approach to populations previously considered unsuitable for psychoanalysis, such as patients with psychoses or character disorders.

Psychoanalytic therapy sessions are usually held once or twice a week, with the patient and therapist in face-to-face positions throughout. It is the patient's responsibility to produce material, but the fundamental rule of free association may or may not be invoked. As a result, the patient's talk is much more reality-oriented. The focus is on the patient's present life and principally on relationships outside of therapy. The goals of psychoanalytic therapy are more limited than those of psychoanalysis and more focused on the presenting problems. The therapist interacts more frequently with the patient than does the analyst, sharing his or her own attitudes and feelings far more than an analyst would. Although transference reactions do arise, a full-blown transference neurosis is not encouraged as a vehicle for therapy.

The principal aims of psychoanalytic therapy are to help the patients come to know themselves fully, to understand their conflicts and their influence on their behavior, and to become aware of the possibility of responding differently in the future. Treatment involves pointing out derivatives of unconscious conflicts—repressed material. As they become aware of these thoughts, wishes, or feelings, they are better able to reintegrate them into their conscious lives. The therapist's job is to create an atmosphere in which the patients feel free to delve into areas fraught with anxiety, guilt, and shame.

CRITIQUE

Research Support

In an extensive review of the literature pertaining to quantitative research on psychoanalytic therapy, Luborsky and Spence (1978) drew the following conclusions:

Qualities of most suitable patients.   Four initial qualities were identified: (a) better general personality functioning (or absence of severe pathology), (b) younger age, (c) stronger anxiety, and (d) higher educational level. Strong anxiety is an especially positive predictor in patients with good general personality functioning.

Desirable qualities for psychoanalytic therapists.   The little research of this type that exists concerns supervisor's opinions of analytic candidates and indicates that "healthier" analysts will be of more help to their patients than analysts who lack objectivity and self-confidence or are otherwise "unhealthy."

Outcome.   Simple, unspecified outcome studies have not been useful in showing the efficacy of treatment. Better-specified studies had more to say about the nature of treatment and what changes occur during psychoanalysis. Some evidence was found that patients tend to increase their level of experiencing and self-observation and show global improvement, resolution of transference, and increase in ego strength. Controlled comparisons of psychoanalysis and other forms of treatment are almost nonexistent, and those which are extant are inconclusive.

Process of psychoanalysis.   Quantitative studies have been made of four main concepts that encapsulate the patient's adequacy of production during psychoanalytic treatment: meaningfulness, productivity, experiencing, and associative freedom.

Techniques.   There is likely to be much variation in technique from analyst to analyst, and this variation increases with experience. The therapist's accuracy of interpretation is similar to his or her empathy. Both accurate interpretations and empathy are shown best by the therapists who are healthiest.

Evaluation

Psychoanalytic theory and practice have had a tremendous impact on modern life. Freudian concepts abound, not only in psychology and psychiatry, but also in literature, the arts, political science, marketing, education, and even humor. Thus, it is alarming to discover that despite its wide acceptance, it is not yet adequately supported by objective empirical evidence. It has neither been proved nor disproved. In fact, it remains virtually untested.

Contributions. Psychoanalytic theory has provided a basis for understanding personality and mental life in imaginative and symbolic terms—the only terms that can be used to describe nonmaterial processes. It has provided an explanation of the lasting effects of early childhood experiences. It has led the way toward understanding the importance of emotions in human life and of catharsis in therapy (Carkhuff & Berenson, 1977).

Cautions. In response to an American psychologist who had sent him reports of his efforts at the experimental investigation of repression, Freud wrote: "I have reviewed with interest your experimental investigations for verifying psychoanalytic propositions. I cannot value these confirmations very highly since the abundance of reliable observations upon which these propositions rest make them independent of experimental verification" (Rosenzweig, 1977, p. 146). Ever since, much of the research support for psychoanalysis rests on clinical observation. Unfortunately, while clinical observation is empirical, it is not objective: one person (the therapist) observes, records, reports, and interprets the data while, at the same time, interacting with the patient to effect change in the very behavior being observed.

Another major limitation to psychoanalysis is the amorphous, allegorical nature of the theory. There is, in fact, no one body of writings. A corollary of this objection is the tautological character of psychoanalytic writing. It is not unlike the individual who "proves" he has an invisible pet by saying, "you don't see him, do you!"

Perhaps the major objection—at least my major objection—to psychoanalysis is that it aims at restoring a homeostatic balance that precludes self-actualizing growth. It purports to take you out of the darkness, but not into the light. It is oriented toward identifying individual deficits within the individual, but fails to do more than explain and interpret them, thus leaving the patient with the same bag of worms he came in with—but understanding them better.

In short, the future of formal psychoanalysis as a treatment method seems limited, at best, even for those qualified to use it. For the counselor, it has some value as a means of describing observable behavior. No matter what your perspective is, you must talk about personality and behavior. Psychoanalytic terminology offers one vehicle. Nothing more.

REFERENCES

ABELES, N.   Psychodynamic theory. In H. M. Burks, Jr., & B. Stefflre, *Theories of counseling* (3rd ed.). New York: McGraw-Hill, 1979.

ALEXANDER, F. M.,   *Psychoanalysis and psychotherapy.* New York: Norton, 1956.

ALLEN, G. J.   *Understanding psychotherapy: Comparative perspectives.* Champaign, IL: Research Press, 1977.

AMERICAN PSYCHOANALYTIC ASSOCIATION,   *Standards for Training in Psychoanalysis.* New York: Author, 1980.

CARKHUFF, R. R., & BERENSON, B. G.   *Beyond counseling and therapy* (2nd ed.). New York: Holt, Rinehart, & Winston, 1977.

Dewald, P. A., *The psychoanalytic process: A case illustration.* New York: Basic Books, 1972.

FINE, R.   Psychoanalysis. In R. Corsini (Ed.), *Current psychotherapies.* Itasca, IL: F. E. Peacock, Publishers, 1973.

FREUD, A.   *The ego and the mechanisms of defense* (rev. ed.). New York: International Universities Press, 1966.

FREUD, S.   *New introductory lectures on psychoanalysis.* New York: W. W. Norton, 1933.

FREUD, S.   *On the history of the psychoanalytic movement, 1914.* Standard Edition, Vol. III. London: Hogarth Press, 1962.

LUBORSKY, L., & SPENCE, D. P.   Quantitative research on psychoanalytic therapy. In A. E. Bergin, & S. L. Garfield (Eds.), *Handbook of psychotherapy and behavior change* (2nd ed.). New York: John Wiley & Sons, 1978.

MACK, J. E., & SEMRAD, E. V.   Classical psychoanalysis. In A. M. Freeman, H. I. Kaplan, & H. S. Kaplan (Eds.), *Comprehensive textbook of psychiatry.* Baltimore: The Williams & Wilkins Company, 1967.

PRICE, R. H.,   *Abnormal behavior: Perspectives in conflict.* New York: Holt, Rinehart, & Winston, 1972.

RADER, G. E.   Psychoanalytic therapy. In D. C. Rimm, & J. W. Somervill, *Abnormal psychology.* New York: Academic Press, 1976.

ROSENZWEIG, S.,   *Freud, Jung, and the kingmaker: The visit to America, 1909.* St. Louis: Rana House, 1977.

STEWART, R. L., & LEVINE, M.   Psychoanalysis and psychoanalytic therapy. In A. M. Freeman, H. I. Kaplan, & H. S. Kaplan (Eds.), *Comprehensive textbook of psychiatry.* Baltimore: The Williams & Wilkins Company, 1967.

STRUPP, H. H.,   *Psychotherapy: Clinical, research, and theoretical issues.* New York: Jason Aronson, Inc., 1973.

TRAINING INSTITUTIONS APPROVED BY THE AMERICAN PSYCHOANALYTIC ASSOCIATION

Baltimore-District of Columbia Institute for Psychoanalysis, 821 North Charles Street, Baltimore, Maryland 21201

Boston Psychoanalytic Society and Institute, Inc., 15 Commonwealth Avenue, Boston, Massachusetts 02116

Chicago Institute for Psychoanalysis, 180 North Michigan Avenue, Chicago, Illinois 60601
Cincinnati Psychoanalytic Institute, 2600 Euclid Avenue, Cincinnati, Ohio 45219
Cleveland Psychoanalytic Institute, 11328 Euclid Avenue, Cleveland, Ohio 44106
Columbia University Center for Psychoanalytic Training and Research, 722 West 168th Street, New York, New York 10032
Denver Institute for Psychoanalysis University of Colorado School of Medicine, 4200 East 9th Avenue, Denver, Colorado 80262
Houston-Galveston Psychoanalytic Institute, 5300 San Jacinto, Suite 145, Houston, Texas 77004
Institute of the Philadelphia Association for Psychoanalysis, 15 St. Asaph's Road, P. O. Box 36, Bala-Cynwyd, Pennsylvania 19004
Los Angeles Psychoanalytic Society and Institute, 2014 Sawtelle Boulevard, Los Angeles, California 90025
Michigan Psychoanalytic Institute, 16310 West 12 Mile Road, No. 204, Southfield, Michigan 48076
New Orleans Psychoanalytic Institute, Inc., 3624 Coliseum Street, New Orleans, Louisiana 70115
New York Psychoanalytic Institute, 247 East 82nd Street, New York, New York 10028
Philadelphia Psychoanalytic Institute, 111 North 49th Street, Philadelphia, Pennsylvania 19139
Pittsburgh Psychoanalytic Institute, Suite 200, 211 North Whitfield Street, Pittsburgh, Pennsylvania 15206
Psychoanalytic Institute of New England, East Inc., P. O. Box 56, Arlington Heights, Massachusetts 02175
Psychoanalytic Institute, New York University Medical Center, Bellevue Psychiatric Hospital, 30th St. and First Ave., New York, New York 10016
St. Louis Psychoanalytic Institute, 4524 Forest Park Avenue, St. Louis, Missouri 63108
San Diego Psychoanalytic Institute, 817 Silverado St., Lajolla, California 92037
San Francisco Psychoanalytic Institute, 2420 Sutter Street, San Francisco, California 94115
Seattle Psychoanalytic Institute, 4029 East Madison Street, Seattle, Washington 98112
Southern California Psychoanalytic Institute, 9024 Olympic Boulevard, Beverly Hills, California 90211
Topeka Institute for Psychoanalysis, Box 829, Topeka, Kansas 66601
University of North Carolina—Duke University Psychoanalytic Training Program, Department of Psychiatry, University of North Carolina School of Medicine, 239 Old Nurses Dorm, Chapel Hill, North Carolina 27514
Washington Psychoanalytic Institute, 4925 MacArthur Boulevard, N. W., Washington, D.C. 20007
Western New England Institute for Psychoanalysis, 340 Whitney Avenue, New Haven, Connecticut 06511

CHAPTER THREE
INDIVIDUAL PSYCHOLOGY

Individual psychology has not received the attention it deserves. For many years, Adler was dismissed as "just" a disciple of Freud. He was not; he was a contemporary and colleague. Then he was reviled for his "socialist leanings," partly because of his interest in "social interest" and partly because his Russian wife was a friend of Leon Trotsky. In any case, Adlerian counseling has remained somewhat clouded—obscured. Pity.

Just a cursory glance at the pages that follow will show that Adler was, indeed, a man ahead of his time in more ways than one. A close examination of the other perspectives in this book will reveal that his influence on subsequent generations of theorists was far greater than is generally realized. Adler's own works, even in translation, are difficult to read. Even a man ahead of his time is a product of his century. But his ideas, interpreted and presented by his followers, make interesting, absorbing, even exhilarating reading.

HISTORICAL DEVELOPMENT

Personal Background

Alfred Adler was born on February 7, 1870, in Penzing, a suburb of Vienna. His father was a middle-class Jewish grain merchant; his mother was a fairly typical Viennese *hausfrau*. Few Jews lived in his community; thus, he never acquired a strong cultural identity. Although he attended a synagogue as a boy, as an adult he considered himself Christian. Alfred was the second son and third child in a family of six children (four boys and two girls). This fact was very significant for his life—and even his later theories—because he always seemed to live in the shadow of his older brother's successes. Though he was apparently fairly popular and a physically active child, Adler did not view his childhood as a particularly happy time of life.

Athough he had pleasant memories of his mother, he was not close to her and identified very strongly with his father. At the same time he felt overshadowed by his older brother and spent many hours trying to compete with him. Although he was only an average student, he managed to earn a medical degree from the University of Vienna in 1895. While in college, he joined a group of Marxist students, among whom he met a wealthy young Russian girl whom he married in 1897 (Rychlak, 1981).

Adler began practice as a generalist. Since his office was near an amusement park, many of his patients were performers, artists, and acrobats. From these patients Adler learned that many had developed their strength and abilities in reaction to childhood weaknesses or accidents (Furtmuller, 1964).

His initial contact with Freud seems to have resulted from a defense Adler made of Freudian theory in the public press. In 1902, Freud invited him to join him in a series of weekly meetings to discuss psychoanalysis. This group became the Vienna and then the International Psychoanalytic Association. Adler became the first president of the Vienna group in 1910. By late 1911, he had resigned his position and broken permanently with Freud. Contrary to popular opinion, Adler was not a disciple of Freud, but a peer who was already an established professional in his own right before joining Freud's circle (Rychlak, 1981).

After serving as a medical officer in World War I, Adler instituted several child-guidance clinics in Vienna public schools. In 1926, he made his first lecture in the United States and thereafter spent more and more time in this country, until, in 1935, he fled the Nazis and settled here. Adler died on May 28, 1937, of a heart attack while on a lecture tour at the University of Aberdeen in Scotland. Adler's children, Kurt and Alexandra, are both psychiatrists, practicing individual psychology as formulated by their father.

Adler was truly a man ahead of his time. He was the first to work publicly with clients by practicing group and family therapy in front of large audiences of doctors, teachers, parents, and others. He explained that neurotic symptoms were "safeguards" against threats to one's self-concept from the outside world, not from repressed drives. As early as the 1920s, Adler predicted that it would be two more generations before women achieved true equality. His real and active concern for equality for women is reflected in Danish sculptor Tyra Boldsen's plan for a monument to commemorate the enfranchisement of women. It was to be a large piece depicting many women and one man—Adler (Dinkmeyer, Pew, & Dinkmeyer, 1979).

Theoretical Background

There were many influences in Adler's theoretical background. Notable among these were famous writers—Dostoevsky, Goethe, and Shakespeare. The Bible and the Stoic philosophers also contributed to the formation of Adler's personality theory. More particularly, he drew from Karl Marx, Nietzsche, Henri Bergson, Immanuel Kant, and the Americans G. Stanley Hall, John Dewey, and William James.

In his youth, Adler became interested in the psychological and philosophical aspects of socialism. This accounts for his emphasis on social interest. His concern about creativity and equality for women is also derived from Marx. His ideas of inferiority-superiority derive from Nietzsche; except that, while Nietzsche's ideal was "Superman," Adler's was "Fellowman." The concept of purposeful memory came from the French Pragmatist Bergson. The notion of "common sense" as a criterion for sanity and "private logic" as a measure of insanity derived from reading the German philosopher Kant (Ansbacher, 1977).

Adler agreed with Freud that the meaning of pathological symptoms must be understood by the therapist, that knowledge of the patient's early experiences and dreams can shed light on these meanings, and that the patient's understanding of the relationship between early experiences and current behavior may result in significant improvement. On the other hand, fundamental differences in the thinking of Freud and Adler began to appear about 1908. Initially, these differences were related to Freud's interest in the etiology of neurotic symptoms and Adler's concern with their goal or purpose. They had a series of heated debates, which culminated in Adler's development of his own theory of personality. He redefined "conscious" and "unconscious" and rejected Freud's concept of the repression of instincts or drives as the cause of pathological symptoms. Adler left Freud's circle in 1911, and in 1912, coined the term "individual psychology" to describe his system (Ansbacher, 1977).

Adler's earliest personal contribution was a study of the effects of "organ inferiority"—often a congenital bodily defect—on personality formation. Later, other aspects of the developmental situation, such as pressures due to the attributes of parents and siblings, assumed greater importance than specific organic anomalies. Adler derived his psychology, not from the biological constitution itself, but from the attitudes that individuals adopted toward their defects. His view of the conditioning of psychological attitudes is quite simple: the infant is a helpless little creature surrounded by powerful adults. Humans—even adult humans—are puny in comparison with natural forces (earthquakes, floods, etc.). Thus, the basic feeling of any individual must be inferiority: each one starts life with a normal sense of helplessness. Developmental efforts are seen as a compensatory striving for socially useful power and superiority over the environment.

THEORY OF PERSONALITY

Definition of Terms

Basic mistakes. Basic mistakes are erroneous or distorted attitudes, which were once appropriate but are so no longer. They usually are unconscious and function to misdirect the life style.

Birth order. Birth order, or ordinal position, is the order in which a child is born into a family; i.e., firstborn, only child, second child, youngest child.

Discouragement. This term connotes both a state or condition and a process: it applies both to the person who is discouraged and to the process by which he or she became discouraged. The discouraged person cannot perceive the possibility of winning a battle, of solving his or her problems, or even moving toward a solution. The process of discouragement involves leading a person to expect such failure.

Early recollections. Early recollections are specific incidents that the person can remember in clear detail, including the thoughts and feelings at the time of their occurrence.

Encouragement. The essence of encouragement is to increase an individual's confidence in himself and to convey to him that he is good enough *as he is*, not just *as he might be*.

Family atmosphere. Family atmosphere or climate is the characteristic pattern established by parents and presented to their children as a standard for social living.

Family constellation. This is a term used to describe the socio-psychological configuration of a family group: the personality characteristics and emotional distance of each person, age differences, order of birth, the dominance or submission of each member, the sex of the siblings, and the size of the family.

Fictional goal. Each person develops, in early childhood, a fictional (not yet realized) image of what he or she would have to be like in order to be safe, to be superior, to feel belonging.

Individual psychology. Adler used the term "individual" to identify his system because he wanted to convey the concept of a unified community. This seems, at first blush, to be contradictory; but Adler used the term in its etymological sense of *indivisible.*

Inferiority complex. The inferiority complex is a deep conviction of one's inability to correct or improve what is wrong.

Organ inferiority. Organ inferiority refers to the fact that, in certain individuals, a particular organ or organ system functions as the point of least resistance. Consequently, that organ or system is likely to be the first to fail to function when the body is subjected to unusual stress.

Private logic. While common logic encompasses the similarity of values and the validity of experiences and connects one person with another, *private logic* is a private map by which the individual makes his way through life. It is not based on a psychological cause-and-effect relationship, such as resentment, frustration, drive reduction, or need-gratification. Rather, it is primarily dependent upon and consistent with the individual's goals and intentions.

Social interest. Social interest is a willingness to cooperate with others for the common good and an awareness of the universal interrelatedness of all human beings.

Style of life. An individual's life style, his style of acting, thinking, and perceiving, constitutes a cognitive framework within which he selects the specific operations that enable him to cope with life tasks.

Superiority. Superiority takes two opposite forms. Socially useless superiority involves an overwhelming need to be competent, right, useful, or to be a "victim" or "martyr." Socially useful superiority involves being master of one's environment.

Teleological. An adjective (from the Greek *tele*, meaning *far* or *distant*) that indicates the goal-directedness of human behavior.

View of Human Nature

The underlying assumption of Adlerian counseling is that humans are indivisible, social, goal-directed beings whose striving for significance explains their motivation.

Indivisible. A basic premise of individual psychology is the irreducible wholeness of the individual. In fact, this is why Adler called his system "Individual Psychology," basing it on the Latin term *individuum*, which means indivisible, complete, whole—a holistic rather than a reductionistic (e.g., Freudian) view of human nature. Such a view suggests that each of a person's actions be seen in the light of that person's chosen style of life. The way that people creatively organize themselves largely determines their response to the outside world. The practical consequence of this assumption is that we humans are influenced less by the facts than by our unique interpretations of those facts. Thus, for example, Adler would say that it is more important to know how a child feels about what happened than to know the details of what happened (Dinkmeyer et al., 1979).

Social interest. Another of Adler's basic premises is that humans are social beings; and, thus, human behavior can be understood only in its social context. Innate in each human being is the capacity to develop what Adler called *Gemeinschaftsgefuhl,* or "social interest"; i.e., the willingness to cooperate with others for the common good. Social interest includes not only an interest in others, but also an interest in the interests of others. Social interest is an assumed aptitude for cooperation and social living that can be developed through training. When it has been developed, it is expressed through substantive skills of cooperating and contributing, understanding and empathizing. Social interest, therefore, was Adler's criterion for mental health. "Social interest is the barometer of the child's normality" (Ansbacher & Ansbacher, 1956, p. 154). The degree to which an individual successfully shares with others, contributes through work, and forms a satisfying relationship with a member of the other sex manifests the individual's level of maturity and overall personality integration. Social striving is primary, not secondary. The search for significance and for a place in society are the basic objectives of every child and adult. Humans should be seen, then, not in isolation, but as socially interactive beings (Dinkmeyer et al., 1979).

Goal-directed.   According to Adler, all human behavior has a purpose. Apparently inexplicable or random behaviors become understandable in the light of their goal. "Individual psychology insists on the indispensibility of finalism for the understanding of all psychological phenomena. Causes, powers, instincts, impulses, and the like cannot serve as explanatory principles. The final goal alone can" (Ansbacher & Ansbacher, 1956, p. 92).

This teleological approach signifies that the goals of behavior are determined (Adler would say "created") by the individual, and not by early childhood experiences, as Freud would have it. Adler's emphasis on goal-directed behavior is based on his belief that humans are endowed with freedom of choice—a uniquely human characteristic, which he called the "creative power" of human nature. In Adler's view, we not only choose our own goals, but we use a "private logic"—personal, cognitive, and emotional abilities—to direct the pursuit of these goals. Thus, all behavior, including misbehavior, is a function of creative choice made in the process of selecting and pursuing personal goals (Dinkmeyer et al., 1979).

Perhaps the clearest examples of goal-directed behavior are children's misbehaviors (Dreikurs & Cassel, 1972). Children sometimes need attention so badly they will seek it by their annoying behavior. Children whose goal is power are out to show you that you can't win—and they are right! You can prevail, but you can't win. Children whose goal is revenge seek to ameliorate hurt feelings by being hurtful. They are like the football players who, behind by 89 to 0 at the two-minute warning, say, "we can't win, but we can break a few legs before it's over." Children whose goal is to display inadequacy are so discouraged they cannot believe they can be significant. They develop inadequacy as a protection so nothing will be demanded of them (Dinkmeyer et al., 1979).

Significance.   Adlerian psychology identifies the family as the first environment in which the individual seeks significance. The search begins when the person experiences the feeling of inferiority and then attempts to compensate for it. The striving for significance (superiority) is a movement toward achieving identity and belongingness—the motivating force behind all human activity. This, too, is seen as teleological rather than causal: a pull by a subjectively chosen goal rather than a push by some hidden drive.

Subjective perception. Early in life we acquire a perception of ourselves and of our world; a perception truly acquired, not imposed. We are proactors, not reactors. We tend to behave according to the way things appear to us. As our perceptions change, our behaviors change accordingly. Thus, for the Adlerian counselor, it is imperative that individuals be understood in the context of their unique perceptions and meanings (Dinkmeyer et al., 1979).

Freedom of choice. Freedom of choice means that we humans can and do choose for ourselves; we are not at the mercy of hidden drives, nor does either heredity or environment force us into specific or unchosen directions. We use both heredity and environment as stimuli for our own interpretations, and these unique interpretations are what gives significance to our day-to-day experiences. Our ability to interpret experience applies to our opinions of ourselves, as well as of the world. In both cases we make assumptions based on our unique perceptions of our experience. Some of these interpretations are not valid, but we act as if they were. Increasingly, the interpretations become dependent upon our characteristic pattern of response or style of life (Dinkmeyer & Dreikurs, 1963).

Style of life. Adler believed that humans need to frame their existence with meanings. Meanings, however, are not inherent in life experiences; rather, they are applied to life by each individual's unique interpretations. One of the earliest and most important meanings a person formulates is the *prototype*: the original form of an individual's adaptation to life. Between three and five years of age, the child evaluates his or her life circumstances and then develops a prototypical plan of action. Once the prototype is in place, the child continues to apply the meanings contained in it to his or her own life experiences. This is what Adler finally came to call "life style" or "style of life" (Rychlak, 1981). A person's life style is the cognitive framework within which that person selects the specific behaviors which enable him to cope with life. Thus, it expressess a central theme through which behavior can be interpreted (Mosak, 1971).

Types of life styles. Mosak has identified 14 *probable* behaviors associated with commonly observed life styles (1971, pp. 78–80):

1. The *getter* exploits and manipulates life and others by actively or passively putting others into his service. He may use charm, shyness, temper, or intimidation as methods of operation.
2. The *driver* is the person in motion: overconscientiousness and dedication to goals rarely permit rest. Underneath, such a person nurses a fear that he is a "zero."
3. The *controller* is either a person who wishes to control life or one who wishes to ensure that life will not control him. He generally dislikes surprises,

controls his spontaneity, and hides his feelings since all of these may lessen his control. As substitutes, he favors intellectualization, rightness, orderliness, and neatness.

4. The person who needs to be *right* elevates himself over others whom he manages to see as wrong. He scrupulously avoids error. Should he be caught in an error, he rationalizes that others are more wrong than he.

5. The person who needs to be *superior* may refuse to participate in any activity which he cannot "win."

6. The person who needs to be *liked* tries to please everyone all the time. Particularly sensitive to criticism, he is crushed when he does not receive universal and constant approval. He sees the evaluations of others as the measure of his worth.

7. The person who needs to be *good* prefers to live by higher moral standards than anyone else. Sometimes these standards are higher than God's, since he sometimes expects God to forgive "sins" in him that he cannot forgive in others.

8. The person who *opposes* everything, especially life's demands of him, really stands *for* something.

9. Everything happens to the *victim*, who may be characterized by feelings of nobility, self-pity, or resignation.

10. The *martyr* is similar to the victim except that whereas the victim merely "dies," the martyr "dies" for a cause. His goal is nobility and his vocation is injustice collector.

11. The *baby* finds a place in life through charm, cuteness, and exploitation of others.

12. The *inadequate* person acts as if he cannot do anything right. Through his default, he binds others to him as servants.

13. The person who *avoids feelings* may fear his own spontaneity because it might move him in directions he has not thoroughly planned.

14. The *excitement seeker* despises routine and repetitive activities, seeks novel experiences, and revels in commotion.

Structure of Personality

Adler's concept of the unity of personality renders dichotomized, reductionistic explanations of the structure of personality meaningless. Refusing to consider human nature as an aggregate of discrete parts, he preferred to study the total individual as a unified whole. Thus, for Adler, constructs such as "conscious" or "unconscious" are meaningless except as subjective experiences of the whole person: people behave *as if* the unconscious mind acted at cross purposes with the conscious mind. Refusing to reify such constructs, he used the terms "conscious" and "unconscious" as adjectives rather than as nouns. Whenever a conscious idea is no longer understood, it becomes unconscious; when an unconscious idea becomes understood, it is, by virtue of that fact, conscious. The individual, then, is not seen as a battleground of psychic forces at war with one another. Behavior has interpersonal, not intrapersonal, meaning (Dinkmeyer & Dreikurs, 1963; Mosak & Dreikurs, 1973; Papanek, 1967).

Development of Personality

We enter the world with certain genetic givens and find ourselves in specific human environments. After birth we not only react to stimuli, but also play an active role in influencing the world around us, especially the social world of significant others. We learn what works (meets our needs and theirs) and what doesn't work in relation to that world. Thus, each new event is met with a backlog of personal, subjective ways of interpreting that event. This backlog is what Adler calls the style of life.

Factors influencing personality development. There is no evidence to indicate that *genetic factors* influence personality development, and it is not possible to measure the effects of *physical defects*. However, Adlerian theory would suggest that, in any case, it is not the defect or abnormality itself that affects development, but the individual's perception of it. Cultural factors provide a developing personality with an organized and identifiable way of looking at the world. The organization and/or identification is not always beneficial to the full development of personality, but at least it is not chaotic or diffuse.

The most pervasive and influential of the influences on personality development is, of course, the family. *Birth order* is a factor, not because of ordinal position, but because of the way the child perceives—and is perceived—as a result of that position. For example, little Firstborn begins life as the only child among adults: frequently a very favorable position. When little brother or sister appears on the scene, Firstborn's position of preeminence is challenged, if not dissolved. This challenge has profound effects on Firstborn's view of self and the world. *Family constellation* is a collective term referring to the personality characteristics of each member of the family, the emotional ties between members, the birth order of siblings, the dominance or submission of various members, the age and sex of siblings, the number of siblings, and the presence of one or both parents. *Family atmosphere* refers to the social climate within the family. Dewey lists some two dozen "atmospheres," including rejective, authoritarian, inconsistent, suppressive, overprotective, and disorderly (cited in Nikelly, 1971). Finally, *early experiences*, like physical disabilities, are not, of themselves, causative factors, but become so through the individual's perceptions of those experiences (Dinkmeyer et al., 1979).

Life style. In Adlerian psychology, the term *life style* refers to one's basic orientation to life. It is a dynamic condition rather than a rigid, static state; and, it is therefore roughly equivalent to terms such as *personality, psyche, character,* or *ego*. Dinkmeyer (et al., 1979, p. 29) makes it quite clear: "The style of living is created in the course of an ongoing drama that takes place in the theater of the family, with parents and siblings all playing a part—a drama in which the child is his own director and whose last act he has already sketched out in broad outlines."

Each person's style of life is the net result of that individual's subjective interpretation of the factors influencing personality development (birth order, family atmosphere, etc.). How much each factor (or an interaction of factors) actually influences a given individual's development will depend upon that individual's creative weighting of those factors. For example, some people achieve despite a physical defect, others seem to overachieve because of the defect, while still others are relatively unaffected by it. In any case, within the first few years, children create their own highly subjective answers to the "big" questions: Who am I? What is life? What am I to do? What is good? What is bad? In the process of answering these questions they also develop a private logic that ultimately makes each one uniquely different from every other human being.

The style of living is created by each individual and remains internally consistent. Some are quite broad, providing a basis for the solution of most of life's problems: others are so narrow that they interface only with the most specific situations—and run the risk of being woefully inadequate. After the first years of life, the life style is pretty well in place, and new experiences are fitted into it rather than used to form it. In other words, the individual has, at an early age, created his own convictions about who he is, what he must become, and what he can expect from life. Mosak and Dreikurs (1973) have grouped these convictions into four categories: (a) the self-concept—convictions about who I am; (b) the self-ideal—convictions about what I should be or am obliged to be in order to have a place in the world; (c) the world-view—convictions I have about the world, other people, nature, life; and (d) ethical convictions—my personal code of right and wrong.

The basic structure of the life style is virtually set by the time the child is four or five years of age, and it remains essentially unchanged throughout life, unless challenged by some overwhelming experience or adjusted through therapy. This basic structure or foundation includes the individual's unique views on how security, belonging, superiority, perfection, or completion can be achieved. All aspects of personality serve to bring the individual to security, superiority, belonging. Thus all behavior is understandable if seen in the light of the individual's private logic—the key to that individual's life style (Dinkmeyer et al., 1977).

Development of Maladaptive Behavior

According to Alderian theory, humans are innately neither good nor bad: we become so through the process of psychological and social development. It is a fact of nature that a child is born, weak and helpless, into the world—a world of adults. Ordinarily, the child's awareness of this condition of helplessness abates and he finds his place among his peers and elders. On the other hand, if the child maintains feelings of uncertainty about himself in relation to his world and the people in it, he may resort to a private logic in order to distort or hide his fears and feelings of inferiority in that world. In this way, the child is able to maintain a subjective and unrealistic but superficially effective sense of superiority to compensate for his unconscious feelings of inferiority. He is now seen as maladjusted. Some of the causes of maladjustment are (Nikelly, 1971c, p. 21):

1. *Parental overprotection* tends to make a child feel inadequate and unaccepted by denying him the opportunity to become independent and responsible. He may attempt to compensate for these feelings of inadequacy through demonstrations of aggression.

2. *Parental pampering* develops an attitude of dominance in the child. When the child learns that he cannot always have what he wants, he is apt to become rebellious and hostile.

3. *Parental neglect* may cause a child to see others as demanding and unfriendly and to become incapable of social cooperation. Such a child may exhibit an excessive need for appreciation and love but be unable to elicit these from others.

4. *Parental partiality* often results in a power struggle between siblings.

5. *Physical unattractiveness or handicap*, whether actual, exaggerated, or imaginary, may dominate an individual's life pattern and cause him to rebel or to withdraw from others.

6. *Parental domination* may produce reactions similar to those generated by overprotection.

Adler viewed mental disorders as erroneous ways of living: a mistaken life style with mistaken opinions of the self and the world and mistaken goals—all permeated by underdeveloped social interest. Abnormality results when an individual develops massive feelings of inferiority in early childhood. Then, to compensate for the tension caused by these feelings, the child develops inappropriate patterns of behavior, frequently manifesting an unrealistic concern for personal superiority. Behavior then becomes self-centered, self-protective, and effectively precludes any chance of social interest or social interaction. In and of themselves, feelings of inferiority are not abnormal. It is only when the individual *acts as if* he were inferior that he can be labelled as having an inferiority complex.

Basic mistakes. Shulman (1973) pointed out that oversimplification, exaggeration, and mistaking the part for the whole are three common mistakes in logic that appear in many life styles. He categorizes them in six groups: (a) distorted attitudes about the self—"I am less capable than others"; (b) distorted attitudes about the nonself—"life is unpredictable" or "people are no damn good"; (c) distorted goals—"I must be perfect"; (d) distorted methods of operation—excessive competitiveness; (e) distorted ideals—"Boys don't cry"; and (f) distorted conclusions—"I am doomed to failure," or "Love conquers all," or "I am the only one who has the real truth."

Neurosis. A neurotic disposition stems from childhood experiences that are characterized by one of two polar opposites—overprotection or neglect—or some admixture of the two. As a result of these experiences, the child creates a self-image of helplessness and a conviction of inability to cope with life. This distorted view is frequently abetted by a hostile, demanding, punishing social environment. As a result, the child develops a deep discouragement, and, thus, a neurotic striving for personal superiority to compensate for the feelings of inferiority and anxiety. Behavior becomes self-centered and self-protective.

In summary, every neurosis can be seen as an attempt to free oneself from feelings of inferiority in order to gain a feeling of superiority. Unfortunately, the compensatory neurosis chosen by the individual, while consistent with the individual's private logic, is inconsistent with common sense, and, therefore only exacerbates the problem by carrying the individual further away from social interest.

Another way of viewing the development of maladaptive behavior associates it with discouragement. The discouraged person cannot perceive the possibility of winning a battle, of ever solving problems, or even of moving toward possible solutions. Such a person has no confidence in his own ability or in life.

Most difficult of all to tolerate is the assumption of being worthless, inadequate, a failure. Humiliation and disgrace, inferiority and deficiency are the most threatening dangers of all, since we often doubt our own value and do not realize that we have a place in society.

Adlerians see discouragement as a basic factor in all deviations, deficiencies, and failures, with the exception of brain damage and mental deficiency. People fail because they have first lost confidence in their ability to succeed. The deeply discouraged child will try to impress parents, teachers, and peers with his total deficiency so they will make no more demands (Ansbacher, 1977; Dinkmeyer & Dreikurs, 1963; Mosak & Dreikurs, 1973; Papanek, 1967).

THEORY OF COUNSELING

Rationale for Change

Adlerian therapy is based on the assumption that the client has projected and directed his or her life by a mistaken life style and so has failed to develop an adequate sense of social interest. The therapist's task, then, is to help the client achieve a more objective view of reality and to develop a more active social interest. As a result of therapy, the client not only understands his own behavior, but also realizes that he has the power to direct his own life in more satisfying ways. As his perceptions change, so do his actions (Mosak & Driekurs, 1973; Nikelly & Bostrom, 1971).

Process of Counseling

Adlerians recognize four stages in the process of counseling: (a) establishing an empathic relationship between counselor and client; (b) helping the client understand the beliefs and feelings, motives and goals that determine his or her life style; (c) helping the client develop insight into his or her mistaken goals and self-defeating behaviors; and (d) helping the client consider viable alternatives to the problem behavior or situation and make a commitment to change.

Relationship. Adlerian counselors see their relationship with their clients as a collaboration in which counselor and client are partners, working toward mutually agreed-upon goals. The relationship is sometimes spelled out in a written contract, which specifies the goals of the process and the responsibilities of each partner. The counselor then uses the relationship in a supportive way to emphasize assets rather than deficits, encouragement rather than analysis.

Understanding. Adlerians see the life style as a personal construct built upon one's perceptions, beliefs, and feelings. Therefore, the second phase of counseling involves developing and deepening—for both counselor and client—an understanding of the client's life style, and the counselor's, communicating that understanding to the client. The focus is always on the client's frame of reference, the client's goal. Once the counselor has reached an understanding of the client's life style, he or she is able to help the client understand how that life style has been influenced by basic beliefs and perceptions. It is the Alderian position that beliefs influence feelings, not vice versa: your belief about being shy creates your panicky feelings. This is why the Adlerian counselor discusses the beliefs that underlie the feelings, rather than just reflecting the feelings.

Insight. The Adlerian counselor, while empathic and accepting, is also confrontive. He or she will confront the clients with their basic mistakes, mistaken goals, self-defeating behaviors, and restrictive beliefs. These confrontations help clients resolve apparent contradictions and realign mistaken goals.

Alternatives. The final stage of counseling moves toward reorientation, in which insight is translated into action. Encouragement is the principal stimulus for the client's change. Another important factor is specificity;

concreteness of goals and purposes. These two, encouragement and specificity of goals, solidify the client's commitment to act upon new alternatives (Dinkmeyer et al., 1979).

Goals of Counseling

The psychoeducational process of Adlerian counseling has the following goals: (a) fostering social interest; (b) the decrease of inferiority feelings and the overcoming of discouragement; (c) changes in the person's perceptions and goals; (d) changing faulty motivation which underlies even acceptable behavior, or changing values; (e) encouraging the individual to recognize his equality among his fellow men; (f) helping him to become a contributive human being (Mosak & Dreikurs, 1973, pp. 53–54).

The psychologically healthy, or "normal," individual is one who has developed social interest and is willing to commit to life and life tasks without evasion or excuse. Another way to describe the healthy personality is as "courageous." The courageous person can look at a situation, task, or event in terms of possible actions and solutions rather than potential threats and dangers. The essential ingredients of courage seem to be confidence in yourself and your ability to cope, either with the particular situation at hand or with whatever situation may arise. What characterizes the courageous person is the conviction that solutions can be found, that any situation can be dealt with—not that he or she has all the answers. Courageous people are convinced that, as people of worth and integrity, they can take in stride whatever may happen, without feeling defeated or inferior, without giving up in despair (Dinkmeyer & Dreikurs, 1963).

Training of the Counselor

Training in Adlerian counseling may be obtained through several modalities. One way is through one of the several regional training institutes (see the list at the end of this chapter). Another form of Adlerian training is through a more-or-less traditional graduate program that emphasizes Adlerian principles and practices (see list). The North American Society of Adlerian Psychology approves all of the former and some of the latter (Kern, 1982).

The following, adapted from the 1981–1983 catalog of the Alfred Adler Institute of Chicago, will give you an idea of what is involved in training to become an Adlerian counselor.

The Institute, founded in 1952 by Rudolph Dreikurs, a student of Alfred Adler, teaches psychological theory and offers practice under the supervision of qualified faculty members. Students may enroll for studies leading to the award of a Master of Arts Degree or a Certificate, or for special courses without participating in a program. All of the training is clinically oriented. Planning for a doctoral program is in progress. The programs are conducted on a part-time basis; i.e., late afternoons and evenings, weekends, and some full days during the summer, to provide advanced training for the practicing professional and working lay person. Most courses are scheduled for two hours and are taught one evening a week for eleven weeks. One credit is offered by the Institute for each course successfully completed (1 Institute credit equals 1½ semester hours).

To be eligible for the Master of Arts program, an applicant must have an appropriate baccalaureate degree with a minimum of 18 credit hours of undergraduate or graduate work in counseling and/or psychology. The program consists of 21 courses, including a practicum, which consists of at least fifty contact hours with at least five clients. Practicum students receive a minimum of twelve hours of supervision from at least two different supervisors. In addition to the individual practicum, students must have at least thirty hours of small group supervision. All students must participate in two types of field experience: they must observe public family counseling and they must participate in, co-lead, or lead a parent discussion group or study group. Finally, prior to completion of the program, each student is required to have an individual and a group therapeutic experience.

Function of the Counselor

One of the fundamental assumptions of Adlerian psychotherapy is that the client is not a passive reactor to stimuli from outside, but is an active participant in life who reacts to others uniquely. Therapy is more effective, then, when the emphasis is on the individual's immediate and unique manner of perceiving and interpreting experiences, rather than on the nature of the experiences themselves. Unacceptable behavior cannot be understood as an isolated fragment; rather, it must be seen in terms of the client's total life pattern. Consequently, to understand and treat maladjustment, the therapist should deal directly with things as they are, not with things as they should or might be, nor with things as they were.

The client's difficulties always have a social meaning, and it is within this context that the therapist must understand the client's behavior. Maladjustment occurs when the individual has been prevented from experiencing and absorbing the elements of his social milieu and consequently depends upon an interactional process. The therapist must seek to discover what prevented the client from benefiting from experiences during development, what in the process of socialization diminished the client's sense of responsibility and social feelings, which are necessary for a successful adjustment to life (Nikelly, 1971a, p. 28).

The Adlerian counselor is, first, an active participant in the counseling process. The qualities of the therapist identified in the research literature are accepted as descriptive of an effective Adlerian therapist: empathy, warmth, and genuineness (Carkhuff, 1969; Frank, Hoen-Saric, Imber, Liberman, & Stone, 1978; Rogers, Gendlin, Kiesler, & Truax, 1967; Truax & Carkhuff, 1967). However, emphasis is given to more action-oriented dimensions such as interpretation, confrontation, and concreteness. In addition, Adlerian counselors must be aware of (a) their own beliefs and feelings, (b) their role as model for the client; and (c) of the conditions that are essential to the client's development; such as empathy; caring and concern, genuineness and openness, positive regard and respect, understanding and clarification of the meaning and purpose of the client's behavior, and action-oriented techniques (Dinkmeyer et al., 1979).

Having no allegiance to the medical model of therapy, the Adlerian counselor refuses to be cast in the role of the omnipotent, omniscient actor and is equally adamantly against viewing the client as a passive, submissive pawn who is acted upon. Therapy is designed to inform clients that they are creative beings who play significant roles in creating their own problems and are responsible for their own behavior (Mosak & Dreikurs, 1973).

PRACTICE OF COUNSELING

Major Techniques

Adlerians apply a variety of techniques, some of which are used throughout the entire course of counseling (e.g., attending and empathic responding), while others are used only in specific phases of the process (e.g., interpretations of early recollections).

Phase I: Relationship.   In order to facilitate movement toward the goals of this phase (development of mutual trust, goal alignment, development of tentative hypotheses about the client's behavior, and identification of the client's attitudes, ideas, and behaviors that may interfere with the relationship), the following techniques are used (Dinkmeyer et al., 1979):

1. Attending behavior and attentive listening includes good eye contact, a posture that is relaxed yet conveys involvement, and comments that follow directly from what the client is saying. Attentive listening involves learning not only the content of the client's words but also the feelings, intentions, and personal meanings that may be hidden in the message.

2. Goal alignment involves developing a contract—implicit or explicit—that clearly spells out the client's expectations and goals as well as the counselor's plan for helping. It may also involve realigning the client's goals with questions like, "Is this the person you want to be?" or, "What do you think will happen if you persist in this behavior?" Since therapy cannot take place unless

the counselor and client agree on the purpose and process of therapy, it is imperative that the counselor keep the client focused on the task at hand and not allow the therapeutic process to be sidetracked by the client's evasiveness or defensiveness or the counselor's vagueness.

3. Reflection of feelings—empathic understanding—involves capturing the essence of a person's communication and then communicating that understanding back to the person in terms of the feelings and meanings that are personally relevant to the person.

> Cl: I'm tired of being controlled by the group and forced to compromise. I can't function this way.
>
> Co: You are angry about the group's control and you want to be free to make your own decisions.

4. Productive use of silence means that the counselor accepts silence without becoming anxious. This facilitates the client's recognition of his or her responsibility for initiating topics and sharing concerns. After accepting the silence for a while, the counselor might ask, "What do you think is going on right now?"

5. Nonverbal communication—facial expression; body position; muscle tones; voice tone, pitch, and rate; and rate of breathing—may be as important as verbal communications. After observing several—not just one—nonverbal cues and drawing a unified inference from them, the counselor might say, "It seems very difficult for you to talk about this" or "Could it be that that thought makes you angry?"

Phase II: Assessing, understanding, diagnosing, and classifying the problem.   This phase has two major purposes: understanding the client's life style and seeing how that life style affects the individual's current functioning. There can be as many as ten different techniques used in this phase (Dinkmeyer et al., 1979).

The counselor usually begins this phase by exploring the current situation and the ways in which clients approach social relationships, work responsibilities, the sexual role, and their feelings about self. The total picture of clients' personalities may best be understood by penetrating into the depths of their thinking and uncovering their private logic which may be at the root of their maladjustment. To uncover this private logic, the therapist tries to discover what the clients tell themselves when they behave in a particular way. Once this private logic is shared with the therapist, it becomes less effective for the clients. They begin to see how they give up and bypass the consensual demands of reality and manufacture their own logic as a rationalization for their behavior (Nikelly, 1971d, p. 62).

Adlerians believe that determining a person's number one priority is a useful clinical method for quietly ascertaining short- and long-range goals and core convictions. In pinpointing the client's number one priority, the counselor might ask the person to describe in minute detail his typical day—what he does, why he does it, how he feels about it. The most common number one priorities are comfort, pleasing, control, and superiority (e.g., "Only when I am comfortable do I truly belong"). Other ways of determining the number one priority are to ask what the client must avoid at all costs and/or what feelings he or she consistently evokes in others.

The family constellation is understood by asking questions about the relationships between the client and parents and/or siblings, about family values, attitudes, and disciplinary procedures. The counselor is guided in this by the family constellation questionnaire. "The first step in eliciting a client's family constellation is to have him describe his siblings and their positive and negative attributes. The emotional relationships between siblings and between each child and the parents are then explored. Finally, the client is asked to express his or her own feelings and attitudes toward other members of the family and to mention people outside the family who influenced it" (Shulman & Nikelly, 1971, p. 39).

Early recollections (ER) are valuable because they are indices of present attitudes, beliefs, and motives and because people remember only those events of early childhood that are consistent with their present view of themselves and their world.

The use of ER's is one of many projective techniques which may be employed to help assess the dynamics of an individual's personality. The client is simply asked to "think as far back as you can and tell me your earliest memory from your childhood years." The unique emphasis given to these early recollections manifests the client's basic life style (Nikelly & Verger, 1971).

The summary of the family constellation and the interpretation of ER's enable the counselor to specify the client's mistaken and self-defeating perceptions—basic mistakes. Mosak and Dreikurs specified the following basic mistakes (1973, p. 57):

(a) overgeneralizations ("People are hostile"); (b) false or impossible goals of security ("I have to please everybody"); (c) misperceptions of life and life's demands ("Life never gives me any breaks"); (d) minimization or denial of one's worth ("I'm *just* a housewife"); (e) faulty values ("Be first even if you have to climb over others to do it").

In the course of pursuing the preceding macrotechniques, the counselor may use one or more of the following subroutines (Dinkmeyer et al., 1979):

1. Paraphrasing is the process of checking with the client to be certain that the counselor understands the client's meanings as the client intends them.

Cl: I don't know about him. At times he's very nice, but then again he can be very nasty.

Cl: You're not sure how he's going to act. He's hard to predict.

2. Confrontation involves the counselor's pointing out the clients' discrepancies between their intentions and behaviors, between their feelings and messages, insights and actions, or making clear to the clients their subjective views, mistaken beliefs and attitudes, private goals, or destructive behavior.

3. Interpretation shifts the focus from the client's frame of reference to the counselor's, thus providing a new perspective for understanding a situation.

In order to minimize resistances, the interpretation is usually expressed in a tentative format such as "Could it be that . . . " or "Is it possible that. . . . "

4. "The question" was developed by Adler to determine if the person's problem has an organic or functional basis. He would ask, "What would be different if you were well?" The answer would tell what the client is avoiding by having the physical symptom.

5. Perceiving and responding with concreteness encourages the client to communicate with specificity about personally relevant matters and situations.

> Cl: You don't know how some husbands might react.
>
> Co: You're not sure how Tom will react to your decision to return to school.

6. When the discouraged person seeks social significance, he or she uses various adaptive behaviors. Frequently such behavior disturbs others, and it is seen as maladaptive. The Adlerian therapist tries to identify for the client the goal of his (the client's) maladaptive behavior. The first goal involves the use of attention-getting mechanisms. When the attention-getting mechanisms fail, the child moves down to the next goal: power struggle. Seeking to win— particularly over powerful adults — becomes the child's primary motivation. When the child fails to prove his superiority over the adult(s), he will begin to seek revenge, the third goal. When even revenge fails him, the child adopts an attitude of hopelessness and will attempt to convince the adult of his total inadequacy (Lowe, 1971).

Phase III: Reorientation.   In this phase, counselor and client work together to consider new attitudes, beliefs, and actions in order to reeducate and remotivate the client to become more effective in his or her approach to living. Several specific strategies are employed in pursuit of this goal (Dinkmeyer et al., 1971).

1. Immediacy involves the counselor's expressing how he or she is experiencing the client in the present moment.

> Cl: I want to do something to get started, but it is no use. They are all ahead of me.
>
> Co.:   You say you want to get started, but I get the impression from your tone of voice and posture that you have already given up.

2. Paradoxical intention is a term which refers to a technique in which the client is encouraged to overemphasize symptoms (e.g., if a client bites her fingernails, encourage her to *imagine* nibbling her fingers to the elbow).

3. "Spitting in the client's soup" comes from the boarding school practice of getting someone else's food by spitting in it. Clinically, it involves modifying behavior by changing the meaning that it has for the client. The counselor determines the purpose and payoff of the behavior and then spoils the game by reducing the payoff in the client's eyes.

4. Problem solving and decision making are basic skills in the final phase of counseling. The counselor and client align goals, consider possible alternatives and their consequences, evaluate how these alternatives will help the cli-

ent meet his or her goals, and then implement the most effective course of action.

5. Task setting and commitment are the steps clients take to do something specific about their problems. To be effective, the task should be specific and chosen by the client. The step of setting specific tasks and developing commitments helps the client to translate new beliefs and feelings into effective action, to generate energy for the process; and it provides feedback by which progress can be evaluated (Dinkmeyer et al., 1979).

6. "Social interest or social feeling cannot be taught, but it unfolds through activity and communication between client and therapist. It is conveyed first by the therapist's verbal and nonverbal acceptance of the client." It is also fostered when the therapist serves as a role model for the client. Social interest is fostered in a third way as "the therapist helps the client recognize his value as a human being as well as the value of others." Social feeling is also fostered in the client by the therapist's self-disclosure. Finally, the client's social interest is developed when he or she becomes involved constructively in the lives of others (Nikelly, 1971b, p. 91).

Treatment Parameters

Adlerians function in every imaginable setting: private practice, in- and outpatient settings, jails, schools, and in community counseling and mental health programs. Ordinarily, the office does not contain any special furniture or equipment (such as a couch), since the Adlerian therapist sits facing the client during individual counseling or in a circle in groups. Some therapists use audio- or videotape sessions, while others do not; some use these tapes for client feedback, others for personal study and/or research, and still others for teaching. Many Adlerians, particularly the older, European-trained therapists, eschew psychological testing on the grounds that it only describes what a person has, not how he or she moves through life.

Adlerians are generally amenable to a variety of treatment modalities. Dreikurs and his associates introduced multiple therapy (one client with several therapists) and were among the first to use group counseling in private practice. Marriage counseling involving the entire family has long been a forte of the Adlerian approach, and Adler himself developed the first child guidance clinic.

In relation to many other therapies—particularly the psychoanalytic—the Adlerian approach is definitely short-term. When properly conducted, treatment should show some observable success within three months or less (Mosak & Dreikurs, 1973).

CASE STUDY   *The following case study is cited from Garfinkle, Massey & Mendel (1976, pp. 149–150).*

Charles S. was the older of two boys and was eight years old when he came to the attention of the counselor. What makes this an unusual case is that his younger brother had died at a very early age, and then Charles became an "only child." In such a situation, it is common for the parents to become overprotective and overconcerned about the remaining child. As a result, the child gets much more attention than he would under ordinary circumstances, which was true in Charles's case. At the time of counseling his parents were separated, and he was living with his mother.

As a reaction to his home environment Charles had drawn the following faulty conclusions: "I must get attention at all times, and if I don't, there must be something wrong with me. I must do all I can to get attention." In school he tried to get extra attention by calling out, getting out of his seat to walk around the classroom, showing disrespect for the teacher, and being antagonistic toward the other children. Moreover, he would get angry when he was not called upon to recite and would be surprised or hurt when he was told that he was doing something wrong. Last but not least, he always thought that he was not being treated fairly.

The effectiveness of using early recollections to gain an understanding of the individual's phenomenological view of life can be seen through the following illustrations. Charles's first recollection is as follows: "My mother and I were going downtown by bus to get a haircut. I had a little watch on my arm which I lost on the bus. My mother got angry with me, and she smacked me on my arm." When the counselor analyzed Charles's recollection, it was discovered he had an attitude which might be stated as, "Things often happen that make me get into trouble." The counselor realized that Charles's relationship with his mother was an important one.

The counselor looked at Charles's next recollection to see if the same themes were present. Charles related the following: "My mother took a picture of me, and I asked her why she took it, since I had my mouth open." The two recurring themes expressed in the first and second recollections are that things seem to happen to Charles and that he is concerned about his physical appearance (haircut, photograph).

A third recollection is helpful to get a more complete understanding of Charles' life style. "I remember me and my brother used to play, and he always used to beat me even though he was younger. Once he threw a box over my head. I couldn't do nothing. He put the box right over my head and sat on it. I couldn't get out. My mother took him off the box, so I could get out."

We begin to see the importance of Charles's relationship with his mother and the emergence of a new and important figure, his younger brother. Instead of Charles being the more powerful sibling, he sees his younger brother as always being able to overpower him. It is important for the counselor to understand that Charles is saying, "Everybody beats me, young (brother) and old (mother), and I cannot do anything abut it. Everything happens to me, so I need help from someone stronger."

During the counseling sessions, it became evident that Charles still held these same mistaken convictions of himself. It is interesting to note that at school when he gets into trouble, he never feels that he is at fault and often runs to the teacher for help in dealing with his peers. The teacher often hears him say in a whining voice: "Poor me, everything happens to me."

The primary focus in counseling with Charles was to arouse and build his feelings of social interest. This was done by encouraging Charles to make friends as well as by helping him to build greater confidence in himself. In order to do this, many sessions were spent in focusing on Charles's strengths and positive attributes.

Applications

In addition to the usual individual and group therapy applications, Adlerians have developed and/or used numerous treatment modalities. In his child guidance clinic, Adler used a group approach in which children were treated with observers present. This modality was originally used as a teacher training seminar, but it was soon found to be therapeutic for the children and is used today in many Family Education Centers. Adlerian counselors are active in other forms of group counseling: multiple counseling (several counselors with one client), family therapy, psychodrama, milieu therapy (therapeutic community), and educational group counseling. Furthermore, Adlerian principles and practice have been used in the classroom in parent education, social work, offender rehabilitation, industrial settings, geriatric counseling, leadership training, social movements, and self-help groups (Ansbacher, 1977).

CRITIQUE

Research Support

As were the psychoanalysts and most European clinicians, Adlerians were initially suspicious of statistical research methods. As a result, what research was done followed the clinical case study route. More recently, the statistical research that validates much of the Adlerian approach has been done by non-Adlerians.

Ellis (1957) compared the effects of psychoanalytic, eclectic, and rational-emotive therapy. The latter, devised by Ellis and based largely on Adlerian principles, was overwhelmingly more effective than the other two approaches. DiLoretto (1971), in a carefully controlled study, found that clients receiving rational-emotive (RET) group experiences showed appreciable improvement on measures of interpersonal anxiety and that these gains were maintained over a three-month follow-up. The most significant result of the experiment was that introverted RET clients began reaching out to others in socially appropriate ways far more than the placebo controls or the no-treatment controls. Furthermore, the RET group showed greater gains than either the systematic desensitization group or the client-centered group. Unfortunately, most other reports of research on Adlerian theory and practice have been of the testimonial type (Ansbacher, 1977), clinical observations of individual cases, or (as noted above) done by non-Adlerians (Allen, 1971).

Evaluation

When one views the contemporary world, it is difficult to find even one problem besetting us that is not a function of diminished—if not absent—social interest. From the family of individuals to the family of nations, each seems determined to "take my half out of the middle." Adler identified a lack of social interest as the major illness of mankind.

Freud locked us into a "lowest-common-denominator" approach to life—homeostasis—where the most to be hoped for is a more-or-less successful struggle to control the beast within. Adler pointed out that there is more to life than mere survival: through gaining mastery of one's environment, it is possible to achieve an ever improving slice of the quality of life.

By seeing human nature as "pulled from before" rather than "pushed from behind," i.e., as manifesting active rather than reactive behavior, Adler gave us the will and the means to determine ourselves, as well as the most effective framework to understand our own and others' behavior. One of the "spinoffs" of the teleological understanding of human behavior is the demystification of counseling and therapy. Instead of resorting to mythological explanations of behavior, you need only ask, "What are you getting out of it?" Another result is Dreikurs' and Cassel's (1972) illumination of the goals of children's misbehavior. These seem to be the major contributions made by Adler. Each has many implications and corollaries that are also contributions to psychology.

The major limitation seems to be that Adler and his disciples devoted too little time to a theory of, and guidelines for, therapy; and still less time to objective, empirical research into the practice of individual psychology. Fortunately, many modern Adlerians are beginning to fill that gap, and, *mirabile dictu,* they seem not the least defensive about acknowledging the contributions of non-Adlerians to the Adlerian system.

REFERENCES

ALLEN, T. W.,   The individual psychology of Alfred Adler: An item of history and a promise of a revolution, *The counseling psychologist, 3*(1), 1971, pp. 3–24.
ANSBACHER, H. L.   Individual psychology, in R. Corsini (Ed.), *Current personality theories.* Itasca, IL.: F. E. Peacock, Publishers, 1977.
ANSBACHER, H. L., & ANSBACHER, R. R. (EDS.)   *The individual psychology of Alfred Adler: A systematic presentation in selections from his writings.* New York: Basic Books, 1956.
CARKHUFF, R. R.   *Helping and human relations: A primer for lay and professional helpers* (2 vols.). New York: Holt, Rinehart, & Winston, 1969.
DILORETTO, A.,   *Comparative psychotherapy.* Chicago: Aldine, 1971.

68   Individual Psychology

DINKMEYER, D., & DREIKURS, R.   Encouraging children to learn. New York: Hawthorn Books, 1963.
DINKMEYER, D., PEW, W. L., & DINKMEYER, D. J.   Adlerian counseling and psychotherapy. Monterey, Calif.: Wadsworth, Inc., 1979. Reprinted by permission of Brooks/Cole Publishing Company.
DREIKURS, R., & CASSEL, P.   Discipline without tears (2nd ed.). New York: Hawthorn Books, 1972.
ELLIS, A.   Outcome of employing three techniques of psychotherapy. Journal of Clinical Psychology, 1957, 13, 344–350.
FRANK, G. D., HOEN-SARIC, R., IMBER, S. D., LIBERMAN, B. L., & STONE, A. R.   Effective ingredients of successful psychotherapy. New York: Brunner/Mazel, 1978.
FURTMULLER, C.   Alfred Adler: A biographical essay. In H. L. Ansbacher & R. R. Ansbacher (eds.). Superiority and social interest. Evanston, IL: Northwestern University Press, 1964.
GARFINKEL, M. I., MASSEY, R. F., & MENDEL, E.   Charles. Adlerian guidelines for counseling. In G. S. Belkin (Ed.), Counseling directions in theory and practice. Dubuque, IA: Kendall/Hunt, 1976. Used by permission.
KERN, R.,   Professor and Coordinator, Family Education Center, Georgia State University, Atlanta, Georgia. Personal correspondence, May 4, 1982.
LOWE, R. N.   Goal recognition. In A. G. Nikelly (Ed.), Techniques for behavior change. Springfield, IL: Charles C Thomas, 1971.
MOSAK, H. H.,   Life style. In A. G. Nikelly (Ed.), Techniques for behavior change. Springfield, IL: Charles C Thomas, 1971.
MOSAK, H. H., & DREIKURS, R.   Adlerian psychotherapy. In R. Corsini (Ed.), Current psychotherapies. Itasca, IL: F. E. Peacock, Publishers, 1973.
NIKELLY, A. G.   Basic processes in psychotherapy. In A. G. Nikelly (Ed.). Techniques for behavior change. Springfield, IL: Charles C Thomas, 1971a.
NIKELLY, A. G.   Developing social feeling in therapy. In A. G. Nikelly (Ed.), Techniques for behavior change. Springfield, IL: Charles C Thomas, 1971b.
NIKELLY, A. G.   Fundamental concepts of maladjustment. In A. G. Nikelly (Ed.), Techniques for behavior change. Springfield, IL: Charles C Thomas, 1971c.
NIKELLY, A. G.   Private logic. In A. G. Nikelly (Ed.), Techniques for behavior change. Springfield, IL: Charles C Thomas, 1971d.
NIKELLY, A. G., & BOSTROM, J. A.   Psychotherapy as reorientation and readjustment. In A. G. Nikelly (Ed.), Techniques for behavior change. Springfield, IL: Charles C Thomas, 1971.
NIKELLY, A. G., & VERGER, D.   Early recollections. In A. G. Nikelly (Ed.), Techniques for behavior change. Springfield, IL: Charles C Thomas, 1971.
PAPANEK, H.   Alfred Adler. In A. M. Freeman, H. I. Kaplan, & K. S. Kaplan (Eds.), Comprehensive textbook of psychiatry. Baltimore, Md: The Williams & Wilkins Co., 1967.
ROGERS, C. R., GENDLIN, E. T., KIESSLER, D. J., & TRUAX, C. B.   The therapeutic relationship and its impact. Madison, Wis: University of Wisconsin Press, 1967.
RYCHLAK, J. F.   Introduction to personality and psychotherapy: A theory-construction approach. (2nd ed.) Boston: Houghton Mifflin, 1981.
SHULMAN, B. H.   Contributions to individual psychology. Chicago: Alfred Adler Institute, 1973.
SHULMAN, B. H., & NIKELLY, A. G.   Family constellation. In A. G. Nikelly (Ed.), Techniques for behavior change. Springfield, IL: Charles C Thomas, 1971.
TRUAX, C. B., & CARKHUFF, R. R.   Toward effective counseling and psychotherapy. Chicago: Aldine, 1967.

ADLERIAN INSTITUTES

Region I—West

Alfred Adler Institute of Mountain States, Box 8225, Idaho State University, Pocatello, Idaho 83209 (208/236-3156)
Mountain Institute for Mankind Gold Hill Boulder, Colorado 80302
Western Institute for Research and Training in Humanities, 226 Stanford Avenue, Berkeley, California 94708 (415/524-4929)

Region II—Midwest

Alfred Adler Institute of Chicago, 159 N. Dearborn Street, Chicago, Illinois 60601 (312/346-3458)
Alfred Adler Institute of Fort Wayne, 1812 Fort Wayne National Bank Building, Fort Wayne, Indiana 46802 (219/422-9622)
Alfred Adler Institute of Minnesota, Suite 128, 5009 Excelsior Blvd., Minneapolis, Minnesota 55416 (612/926-6511)
Rudolf Dreikurs Institute for Social Equality, 1725 Emerson Ave. South, Minneapolis, Minnesota 55403

Region III—South

Adlerian Summer Workshops, c/o Francis X. Walton, 660 Townes Road, Columbia, South Carolina 29210
Institute for Creative Community Living, c/o Dr. Pattye Weaver Kennedy, 2243 West Alabama, Houston,Texas 77098

Region IV—Middle-Atlantic

The Adler-Dreikurs Institute of Human Relations, Harold V. McAbee, Director, Bowie State College, Bowie, Maryland 20715
Alfred Adler Institute of Cleveland, 14625 Detroit Ave., Suite 203, Lakewood, Ohio 44107
Alfred Adler Institute of Dayton, 122 E. Apple Street, Dayton, Ohio 45409 (513/274-6329)
Alfred Adler Institute of Toledo, c/o Keith Wiggins, 857 Maple Lane, Waterville, Ohio 43566

Region V—Northeast

Alfred Adler Institute of New York, 37 West 65th Street, New York, New York 10023 (212/874-2427)
Alfred Adler Institute of Ontario, 4 Finch Ave. West, Suite 10, Willowdale, Ontario Canada M2N 2G5

Alfred Adler Institute of Rhode Island, c/o Woonsocket Family and Child Service, 8
    Court Street, Woonsocket, Rhode Island 02895 (401/762-5656)
Alfred Adler Mental Hygiene Clinic, 37 West 5th Street, New York, New York
    10023

A PARTIAL LIST OF GRADUATE PROGRAMS
EMPHASIZING THE ADLERIAN APPROACH

PROGRAM	DIRECTOR (1983)
Bowie State University	Dr. Harold McAbee
Florida State University	Dr. Donald Kelley
Georgia State University	Dr. Roy Kern
Graduate Center of West Virginia	Dr. James Bitter
University of Arizona	Dr. Oscar Christianson
University of California	Dr. Richard Kopp
University of South Dakota	Dr. Frank Main
University of Idaho	Dr. Thomas Edgar
University of Nevada	Dr. William Marchant
University of Texas	Dr. Guy Manchester
University of Vermont	Dr. H. L. Ansbacher
West Virginia University	Dr. Michael Yura

CHAPTER FOUR
TRANSACTIONAL ANALYSIS

Most theories of personality and/or perspectives on counseling reflect the personality and characteristics of their originators. In the case of transactional analysis, it seems as though Eric Berne was telling us, "Do as I say and as I do, but don't be as I am!" He taught that others could change their "scripts" but believed he could not change his. He did not receive strokes well and was inept in giving them. He had an active Child—as is evidenced by his colorful language—but he died of a broken heart (literally) in 1970, an unfilfilled man (Steiner, 1974). It seems inexpressibly sad that a man so adept at analyzing the states and transactions of others, so expert at leading them to the light at the end of the tunnel, came to his end in the darkness, alone.

HISTORICAL DEVELOPMENT

Personal Background

Eric Berne was born Eric Leonard Bernstein in 1910 in Montreal, Canada. Following in his father's footsteps, Berne received his M.D. from McGill University in 1935 and entered a psychiatric residency at Yale University Hospital. Shortly after that, sensitive to the antisemitism in this country, he shortened his name to Eric Berne. At the same time, he became an American citizen, and in 1941, began training at the New York Psychoanalytic Institute. In 1943, he entered the army as a psychiatrist and began to experiment with group therapy techniques.

After his discharge in 1946, he established a private practice in San Francisco. He resumed his psychoanalytic training under Eric Erikson at the San Francisco Psychoanalytic Institute. Although he spent the first twenty years of his professional life seeking formal credentials as a psychoanalyst, he never made it. When his application for membership in the Psychoanalytic Institute was rejected in 1956, he gave up the paper chase. Steiner (1974) attributes the rejection to Berne's unorthodox (from a psychoanalytic point of view) group methods and to his insistence on active involvement with his patients. In any case, at this point, Berne began to formalize his own ideas about psychotherapy (Elson, 1979).

His first formal presentation of transactional analysis (TA) was at a professional conference in Los Angeles in 1957. In 1961, he published *Transactional Analysis in Psychotherapy,* in which he outlined the basic philosophy and major concepts of his perspective. Other books followed in quick succession: *The Structure and Dynamics of Organizations and Groups* (1963), *Games People Play* (1964), *Principles of Group Treatment* (1966), and *What Do You Say After You Say Hello?* (published posthumously in 1972). Berne's own contributions to TA were mainly philosophical and theoretical; his followers have augmented the perspective and refined the practice (Wollams & Brown, 1979).

Theoretical Background

Although Berne (1961) denied any intentional borrowing from Freud, given his long association with psychoanalysis, it is difficult to see the similarity of constructs as accidental—perhaps unconscious, but not accidental. Berne himself thought of psychoanalysis as "the core and transactional analysis as the apple" (Holland, 1973, p. 354). Berne (1961) insisted that Parent, Adult, and Child are all and only *ego* states. However, his description of their function at least obscures the distinction between them and Freud's superego, ego, and id.

Berne was also profoundly influenced by Adler. The most obvious parallel is between Adler's *life style* and Berne's *life script:* The Adlerian life style is a bit more general (Holland, 1973); Berne's script is somewhat more specific and organized. His concern with feeling "not-OK" is also very similar to Adler's worry about feelings of inferiority. Other similarities between TA and Individual Psychology include the social perspective that characterizes each and the similarity of treatment methods: in each, the therapist is more teacher than healer; the client, more student than patient (Corsini, 1977).

THEORY OF PERSONALITY

Definition of Terms

Activites. Work or other goal-oriented behavior is an activity. In activity, the individual sets up a situation in which the accomplishment of the task brings the needed strokes.

Adult ego state. The Adult ego state is best characterized as being concerned with facts: it acts as an assimilator of information. (When Adult, Parent, and Child are capitalized, they refer to ego states; when not capitalized, they refer to individuals.)

Child ego state. The Child ego state is composed of all the feelings and ways of behaving that were experienced during the early years of childhood.

Child, Adapted. The Adapted Child is formed as the individual interacts with parents and is, thus, more controlled.

Child, Little Professor. The part of the Child ego state that is the forerunner of Adult reasoning is known as the Little Professor.

Child, Natural. This part of the Child ego state contains the young, impulsive, untrained, emotionally expressive child.

Contamination. Contamination is one of two ego-state boundary problems. It occurs when the logical, clear thinking of the Adult is interfered with by the prejudicial or irrational ideas and attitudes of the Parent or by the archaic feelings of the Child.

Discounting. Discounting involves ignoring or distorting some aspect of internal or external experience. One may discount the existence of a problem, the significance of a problem, the change possibilities of a problem, or one's own personal abilities.

Drama triangle. The Karpman drama triangle is a triadic interaction in which one person acts as persecutor, another as rescuer, and the third as victim.

Ego state. The term "ego state" denotes states of mind and their related patterns of behavior as they occur in nature.

Exclusion. This boundary problem exists when one or more ego states are effectively prevented from operating.

Game. A game is a series of "duplex transactions," which leads to a switch and a well-defined, predictable payoff that justifies a not-OK or discounted position.

Injunction. Injunctions are a type of negative parenting behavior: edicts that require children to behave in certain prescribed ways. They are usually "don't" messages.

Intimacy. Intimacy is a candid, game-free relationship with mutual, free giving and receiving without exploitation.

Life position. Early in life, people experience a need to take a position regarding their own intrinsic worth and that of others. There are four life positions: (a) I'm OK, you're OK; (b) I'm OK, you're not OK; (c) I'm not OK, you're OK; and (d) I'm not OK, you're not OK.

Parent ego state. The Parent consists of a collection of tapes from significant others who had some kind of power relationship with the person.

Parent, Controlling. The controlling Parent (Critical Parent) is opinionated, powerful, strongly protective, principled, punitive, and demanding.

Parent, Nurturing. The Nurturing Parent is caring, concerned, forgiving, reassuring, permissive, warmly protective, and worried.

Pass time. A passtime is a semiritualized conversation in which people share opinions, thoughts, or feelings about relatively safe topics that don't require them to act.

Position hunger.   Position hunger refers to the need to have one's basic decisions about life confirmed constantly—decisions about the "OKness" of oneself and the world.

Racket.   A racket is an internal or external process (usually of complementary transactions) by which a person interprets or manipulates the environment to justify a not-OK or discounted position.

Racket feeling.   A racket feeling is a feeling that results from a discount.

Rituals.   Rituals are highly stylized and predictable ways of exchanging low-involvement, low-risk strokes, such as greetings.

Script.   A script is a personal life plan, which each individual forms by a series of decisions early in life in reaction to his or her interpretation of the important things happening in his or her world.

Stamps.   Stamps are feelings or strokes collected to justify some later behavior.

Stimulus hunger.   Stimulus hunger refers to the universal need for stimulation or stroking—recognition. According to Berne (1964), stroking is essential for life.

Stroke.   A stroke is a unit of attention that provides stimulation to an individual.

Stroke, conditional.   Conditional strokes are given for *doing* something. They are used to influence behavior.

Stroke, filtered.   Strokes that are distorted or contain nonrelevant information are called "filtered strokes."

Stroke, negative.   Negative strokes are painful, sometimes carry a "You're not OK" message, and may result in unpleasant feelings for the receiver.

Stroke, positive.   Positive strokes are pleasurable, carry a "You're OK" message, and usually result in good feelings for the receiver.

Stroke, unconditional.   Unconditional strokes are given for *being*. They pertain to conditions that occur naturally and do not require special effort.

Structure hunger.   Structure hunger refers to people's need to use their time in ways that maximize the number of strokes they can receive.

Symbiosis.   Symbiosis occurs when two or more individuals behave as though they form a whole person.

Transaction.   A transaction is an exchange of strokes between two persons, consisting of a stimulus and a response between specified ego states.

Transaction, complementary.   A complementary, or parallel, transaction is one in which stimulus and response vectors are parallel so that only two ego states are involved, one from each person.

Transaction, crossed.   A crossed transaction occurs when the vectors are not parallel, or more than two ego states are involved.

Transaction, ulterior.   An ulterior transaction is one that contains both an overt (social) and a covert (psychological) message. They may be either angular or duplex. An *angular transaction* involves three ego states and occurs when messages are sent simultaneously from one ego state of the initiator to two ego states of the respondent. A *duplex transaction* involves four ego states, two in each person. During the course of a duplex transaction, two sets of complementary transactions occur simultaneously, one on the social level and one on the psychological level.

Withdrawal.   Withdrawal is the most limiting and least rewarding way of structuring time. People who structure time by withdrawing live on strokes stored from the past or fantasized in the future.

View of Human Nature

Berne's view of human nature is neatly captured in his assertion that "people are born princes and princesses and then their parents kiss them and turn them into frogs" (Steiner, 1974, p. 2). This implies an optimistic view of people and a pessimistic view of parents. It also reflects the conviction that early experiences profoundly affect later behavior. Despite his pessimism regarding parental influence, Berne was convinced that the individual has the ultimate responsibility to make his or her own basic life decisions.

Berne eschewed the Freudian view of drives or instincts; but he did postulate several psychological needs or "hungers," the most important of which are "stimulus hunger," "structure hunger," and "position hunger." Berne taught that the satisfaction—in some measure—of these hungers is necessary for survival; and the way people have learned to survive (i.e., meet these needs) affects their transactions, interpersonal relationships, and even their basic outlook on life (Elson, 1979).

Stimulus hunger. According to Berne, acknowledgement, stimulation—*stroking* in TA language—is not just pleasant and desirable, it is essential for life. The need for strokes continues throughout life, although the strokes themselves gradually assume a more symbolic, less physical character over time. Strokes are basic units of social interaction and may be either positive (hugs, smiles, words of approval) or negative (slaps, frowns, words of disapproval). So strong is the need for stroking that an individual deprived of positive strokes will actually seek negative strokes. Strokes may also be conditional or unconditional: conditional for what you do ("You look nice today"), unconditional for what you are ("I like to be with you"); and each of those may be either positive or negative. Finally, strokes carry varying levels of power, with negative strokes being the more powerful. For example, "Hi" might carry one positive stroke and "I love you" 100 positive strokes. "Hi" (in a disinterested tone of voice) might carry one negative stroke, while a severe physical beating might rate 1000 negative strokes (Elson, 1979; Wollams & Brown, 1979).

Structure hunger. "What do you say after you say hello?" (Berne, 1972) is Berne's way of identifying the problem of structuring time: what do you do with twenty-four hours a day? Structure hunger is an extension of stimulus hunger, because it involves the way people use time in order to maximize the number of strokes they receive. Time can be structured in six different ways.

The most restricting and least rewarding way to structure time is by *withdrawal*. People who structure time this way cannot take risks, especially the risk of interpersonal communication. *Rituals* are the safest form of time structuring. When people engage in rituals, their transactions sound as if they were being read from a script ("Hi, how're ya doin'?" "I'm fine, how are you?"). Although rituals do provide some strokes, the yield is so low that the person who lives by ritual is likely to experience stroke-deprivation and loneliness. When people interact with each other, not to achieve a goal, but only to "talk about something," they are engaging in a *pass time*. Pass times are less predictable than rituals, but only slightly more rewarding. The typical passtime involves such non-goal-oriented discussions as the weather, sports, children, or food. The discussion is intended to exchange strokes, not to deal with issues. *Activities* include any goal-oriented behavior such as that related to work or hobbies. In *games,* safety and minimal involvement of the preceding four categories are replaced by excitement and drama. Games are essentially dishonest because they always have covert— possibly unconscious—motives. The payoff in games is a sought-for negative feeling, such as anger, jealousy, or guilt. The purpose of all of the foregoing means of structuring time is to inhibit or prevent intimacy.

Intimacy, the sixth method of structuring time, is the most risky and the most rewarding. It involves sharing feelings, thoughts, or experiences in a relationship of openness, honesty, and trust. It is characterized by a direct, spontaneous exchange of strokes in the present with no ulterior motives, no exploitation, and no other forms of time structuring involved (Elson, 1979; Wollams & Brown, 1979).

Position hunger. The third important need or motivator refers to the need to have one's fundamental decisions about life constantly validated. As developing children are confronted with messages such as "What a sweet child you are," or "You're a bad boy," they learn to identify themselves as "OK" or "not-OK"; and this becomes their own estimation of their intrinsic worth. This judgment, once made, brings some order into the child's confused, often chaotic world. As social contacts increase, a similar judgment is made about others: "You're OK," or "You're not OK." These two judgments, about self and about others, coalesce to form the individual's life position. Once the position is chosen, the way that individual structures time and the kind of strokes he or she seeks are fairly well determined (Elson, 1979; Harris, 1969; Wollams & Brown, 1979)

Structure of Personality

Berne (1961), like Freud, divided all personality into three parts (I could make a terrible pun about Caesar and "all gall," but I won't); but, unlike Freud's tripartite division, Berne's three divisions are all *ego* states. The Parent (P) ego state consists of the attitudes, thoughts, feelings, and behaviors the person has incorporated from parents or parent figures. The

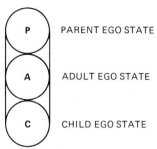

PARENT EGO STATE

ADULT EGO STATE

CHILD EGO STATE

FIGURE 4.1   The three ego states of a person (Wollams & Brown, 1979, p. 9).

Adult (A) ego state is a data processor that, computer-like, organizes information, estimates probabilities, and makes logical deductions. The Child (C) ego state consists of feelings, thoughts, and behaviors that are typical of children and spontaneous adults. The foregoing is known as a first-order analysis (Wollams & Brown, 1979).

A second-order analysis involves both structural and functional aspects of each ego state. Structural analysis looks at each ego state's developmental history and innate capacity for expression. Functional analysis describes how people use their ego states to relate to themselves and others.

Structural analysis of the Child ego state.   Bodily functions and reactions are of prime importance to the newborn infant; and, thus, the related behavior patterns and feelings may be called the *Somatic Child*. This part of the Child originates from the needs, wants, and feelings of the body and exists throughout life as the primary motivator of behavior. The Somatic Child also has memories of past experiences. In TA jargon, these memories are often called "tapes," since they may be "played back" at any time. The thinking part of the Child ego state is called the *Little Professor,* because this type of thinking allows the preverbal infant to perceive how others feel, and to get along with them. The Little Professor is available throughout life. Sometimes the Somatic Child becomes upset when parents react negatively to his spontaneous expressions. In response to these feelings, the Little Professor may try to discover which feelings and behaviors will gain parental approval. Those behaviors that are approved may be integrated into a course of action. They are called the *Parent in the Child,* because they have many characteristics of a parent (Wollams & Brown, 1979).

Functional analysis of the Child ego state.   The Child functions in two basic ways—the *Free* or *Natural Child* and the *Adapted Child.* The *Free Child* is spontaneous, without concern for the reactions of others. The *Adapted Child* behaves as if under the watchful eye of a parent and so is much more restrained than the Free Child. Both the Free Child and the Adapted Child may react creatively or through an old tape; the distinguishing factor is whether or not the behavior is an adaptation to others (Wollams & Brown, 1979).

Structural analysis of the adult ego state.   The Adult collects, keeps, and uses information from many internal and external sources; its recordings are essentially factual. This information is used to make factual judgments and to estimate probabilities. The Adult is often called the *Computer* because it computes data and makes assessments logically but without feeling. The Adult must be programmed with accurate information in order to function effectively (Wollams & Brown, 1979).

Functional analysis of the adult ego state.   Since the Adult functions as a probability-estimating computer, it seems not to be fully autonomous, but rather functions at the request of one of the other ego states. Thus, the Adult cannot maintain social control—make decisions about behavior and then carry them out—unless it receives cooperation from the Child.

Structural analysis of the parent ego state.   "The Parent consists of a collection of tapes from significant others who had some kind of power relationship with the person" (Wollams & Brown, 1979, p. 19). Parents are usually most important, followed by older siblings, grandparents, parental surrogates, teachers, religious leaders, etc. The parent can assimilate new information at any age; however, it is the Child who decides what is "taped." This decision is based on three criteria: (a) vulnerability of the self, (b) power of the parent figure, and (c) believability of the parent figure (Wollams & Brown, 1979).

Functional analysis of the parent ego state.   One of the main things that parents do for their children is teach them how to perceive and live in the world. Accordingly, the Parent ego state is replete with opinions, judgments, values, and attitudes (Wollams & Brown, 1979). The Parent assumes two major modalities: the *Nurturing Parent* and the *Controlling* or *Prejudicial* or *Critical Parent.*

Ego state advantages and disadvantages.   Each ego state has both positive and negative aspects. The Child is characterized by energy, spontaneity, joy, and assertiveness. The Child feels and manifests pleasant and happy feelings and experiences closeness, intimacy, and love. The Child also experiences sadness and fear and often feels small and weak. The ever present need for safety and strokes often results in unfortunate adaptations and script decisions. The *Adult* thinks, analyzes, and understands complex ideas. Its basic activity is to help the Child meet its needs and wants. On the other hand, the Adult is relatively weak and cannot use its store of information to influence an action directly. The *Parent* contains useful tapes about how to act and care for children and other people. Its primary purpose is to support and protect the Child. Unfortunately, parent tapes may also contain inadequate, incorrect, outdated, or otherwise harmful information, which is then given to the Child (Wollams & Brown, 1979).

Development of Personality

Personality development is a function of the child-rearing practices of parents. Healthy parenting practices will result in the child's having a positive view of self (I'm OK) and others (you're OK); negative parenting practices move the child in the opposite direction (I'm not OK and/or you're not OK). All children begin life with an attitude of basic trust; I'm OK, you're OK. The most important parenting skill is to help children decide to maintain this position.

If parents (note the small "p") encourage self-discovery and self-expression in their children, the messages recorded during infancy will include a full range of emotional experiences. These tapes can then be replayed in adolescence and adulthood without detriment to autonomy. During this time the individual's Parent ego state is also developing. Healthy parents (small "p") who operate in their Nurturing Parent (capital "P") will encourage appropriate spontaneity and autonomy in their children, thus paving the way for the development of a Nurturing Parent ego state in their children. The Adult ego state reaches full development in the early teens. If the teenager has been neither constrained nor pressured by parents, then he or she will be free to maintain the OK position. Normal personality development, then, is characterized by maintenance of the "I'm OK, you're OK" position, a game-free script, and sufficient permeability among the ego states so that the individual can use each when appropriate.

Development of Maladaptive Behavior

What observers may identify as emotional disorders are simply learned behaviors based on decisions made in early childhood. They represent the child's attempt to strike a compromise between his own needs and parental demands. According to Steiner (1974), poor parenting patterns leading to maladaptive behavior in children are typical of American culture. He calls child-rearing "basic training" because of its similarity to the vigorous, harsh experience of new inductees in the military (p. 125). Parents drill their children in the basics of how to get along in life in ways that often amount to a systematic attack on the child's potential for intimacy, awareness, and spontaneity. This is the process of transformation from princes and princesses into frogs.

The parental arsenal during this "basic training" consists of conditional and negative strokes, discounts, and injunctions. When children receive *only* conditional strokes ("I don't like your tone of voice"), they tend to conform to the condition, thus limiting exploration and free expression. They are, in a sense, forced to conform to parental demands. The cumulative effect is the erosion of the "I'm OK" position and the emergence of 'I'm not OK." Negative stroking also has a deleterious effect on the child's early decisions. If the child receives primarily negative stroking, he or she may conclude that this is the only kind available and thus choose a life position ("I'm not OK") and a life script that ensures a continuation of these strokes (Elson, 1979).

Although both conditional and negative stroking are harmful, even more devastating to the child's healthy development are parents' discounts (e.g., ignoring the child's needs for strokes). There are four levels of severity of discounting, and, within each level, three possible areas of discounting: self, others, and situation (Wollams & Brown, 1979, p. 103).

> 1. Discounting the *existence* of a problem (baby cries and parents go to sleep). This is a total discount and the most pathological. Since the awareness of the stimulus from the baby (others) is blocked, the problem cannot be defined or solved.
> 2. Discounting the *significance* of the problem (baby cries and parents say she is always fussy at that particular time of day). The baby and the cry are acknowledged as existing, but the situation is being discounted. Since the problem is not considered significant, the parents do not put energy into solving it.
> 3. Discounting the *change possibilities* of the problem (baby cries and parents claim that there is no way she will be satisified). The parents are aware of a problem, acknowledge that it is important, but believe that it has no solution. They do not look for optional ways of responding and so discount the baby (others).
> 4. Discounting *personal abilities* (baby cries, parents know that it is a problem, that it can be solved, and that others could handle it, but see themselves as incapable of dealing with it). In this instance, the parents are likely to get someone else to solve the problem, while discounting themselves.

Another type of destructive parenting behavior is the use of injunction. Injunctions are, typically, "don't" messages. They may be straightforward—even necessary—commands ("Don't touch the spider!") or they may be confusing, double messages ("Grow up!"). Injunctions frequently involve harsh, unreasonable orders enforced by physical punishment and fear.

Conditional and negative strokes, discounts, and injunctions from parents constitute the environmental input that pushes children to abandon their original "I'm OK, you're OK" position and to replace it with one of the three maladaptive positions. When children are neglected or severely abused, they tend to adopt the "I'm OK, you're not OK" position. This position is adopted principally as a defense against a more threatening feeling of not being OK themselves. This position is called the paranoid position since those who are in it are extremely distrusting.

The depressive position ("I'm not OK, you're OK") is the most prevalent in our society. When children's needs are not met, they frequently decide that it is their fault: "I am inferior inadequate, ugly, etc." People in this position experience depression, fear, guilt, and mistrust of others.

Finally, people in the "I'm not OK, you're not OK" position have decided that "everybody is no damn good." This is the futility position. Prisons, mental hospitals, and morgues are filled with people in this position (Wollams & Brown, 1979).

The adoption of one of these three positions leads to the time-structuring strategy of game playing. Although the necessity for games is created by taking an unhealthy life position, the specific games a person plays are taught by parents. The child learns that only certain transactions will garner the kinds of strokes and give rise to the types of feelings that are acceptable to parents. Over time, these simple transactions expand into the more complex and subtle manipulations of which games are made. Often, they originate in the classic child-parent struggles, such as feeding and toilet training, in which both participants attempt to gain the upper hand. Depending upon how these transactions are resolved, the child may learn to play games that lead to feelings of helplessness, anger, or mistrust. Eventually these games become a routine part of life and can then be described as a racket. Basically, they are designed to advance the life script and to confirm the life position of both participants in the game. As a result, both child and parent have a stake in continuing to play the game.

Negative parenting practices also contribute to ego-state boundary problems such as contamination and exclusion. *Contamination* occurs when ego-state boundaries break down so that the individual's Adult becomes contaminated by his or her Parent and/or Child. A Parent contamination has occurred when the person mistakes Parent information, prejudices, and slogans for fact ("Women are poor drivers"). A Child contamination has occurred when old experiences are incorrectly identified as current reality ("Spiders are scary"). A double contamination has occurred when the Adult is contaminated by Parent beliefs and Child experiences simultaneously (Parent: "All men are evil"; Child: "I feel evil"; Adult: "I am evil"). This is probably the most common form of contamination.

Exclusion occurs when one or two ego states dominate a person's behavior over an extended period of time. When only one ego state dominates behavior, that state is called "constant." For example, a constant Parent may be preachy or authoritarian; a constant Adult seems to have no feelings; a constant Child wants only to play or entertain others. On the other hand, some people use only two ego states, excluding the third. No exclusion is total, and the degree of exclusion varies from time to time.

As with the life decision about position, personality difficulties that are related to the malfunctioning of the ego states are a product of the quantity and quality of parental stroking and injunctions. Despite the powerful influence of parents on their children, it is the children who make the decisions in response to real or imagined parental attitudes, behaviors, and injunctions (Elson, 1979; Wollams & Brown, 1979).

THEORY OF COUNSELING

Rationale for Change

Whatever was once decided can be redecided, but what would lead a client to risk change? According to Wollams & Brown (1979, p. 171), motivation and safety are the principal change factors. Motivation is rooted in three sources: a dissatisfaction with present behavior, thinking, or feelings; a desire to behave, think, or feel differently; and a quest for strokes. A sense of safety is engendered by an awareness of personal power, an ability to handle stress, a mature thinking capacity, the availability of needed information, and a range of options. Harris (1969) suggested three other possibilities: enough hurt, ennui, and the sudden realization that change is possible.

Process of Counseling

Stage 1: structural analysis. The initial stage is highly didactic: clients are taught to identify their ego states and to be cognizant of their content and functioning. They are also indoctrinated in the concepts and encouraged to read the literature and to attend TA workshops and/or courses. Within the counseling session, the counselor makes frequent use of audiovisual devices to facilitate the clients' learning. In order to begin to free clients from the domination of parental rules and injunctions, the counselor will "give permission" to the client to express all ego states. This experience may be facilitated by borrowing techniques from other approaches, such as the Gestalt empty chair technique (Elson, 1979).

Stage 2: transactional analysis. While not nearly so didactic as the first stage, the second is still clearly insight-oriented. The counselor's main job here is to teach the clients the various forms of transactions and to help them understand their own transactions with others (Elson, 1979). There are three major types of transactions: complementary, crossed, and ulterior.

Complementary transactions may occur between any two ego states, but they must always meet two criteria: the response must come from the

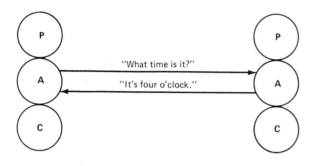

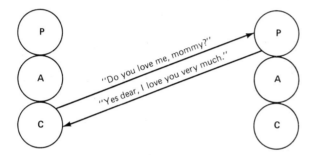

FIGURE 4.2 Complementary transactions (Wollams & Brown, 1979, p. 66).

same ego state to which the stimulus was directed, and the response must
be directed back to the ego state that initiated the transaction. "The first
rule of communication is that as long as transactions remain complementary, communication may continue indefinitely" (Wollams & Brown, 1979,
p. 66).

A crossed transaction occurs when one or both of the criteria for complementary transactions are violated. Any break in communication—sigh,
gulp, stammering—may indicate a crossed transaction. Since these breaks
may be almost imperceptible, the counselor needs great concentration to
perceive them. Of course, not all crossed transactions are that subtle; indeed, some are quite blatant! "The second rule of communication is: wher-
ever the transaction is crossed, a breakdown . . . in communication results
and something different is likely to follow" (Wollams & Brown, 1979, p.
66).

Ulterior transactions involve two messages (one social, the other psychological) and two ego states in either initiator, responder, or both. They
take one of two forms: angular or duplex. Angular transctions occur when
the sender sends a different message to each of two ego states in the respondent. Duplex transactions involve two ego states in both the sender

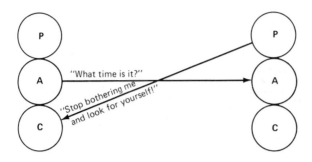

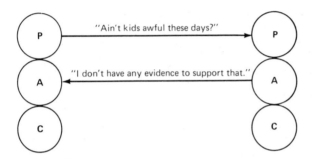

FIGURE 4.3   Crossed transactions (Wollams & Brown, 1979, p. 67).

and the recipient. In both cases there is a hidden game being played: with angular transactions, only the sender is aware of the game; but in duplex transactions, both sender and recipient are aware of the hidden messages. "The third rule of communication states: the outcome of the transactions will be determined on the psychological level rather than on the social level" (Wollams & Brown, 1979, p. 71).

Stage 3: game analysis.   When people communicate on two levels simultaneously, and when these transactions result in rackets, they are playing a "game." The game player will usually take one of the three positions of the Karpman drama triangle: persecutor, rescuer, or victim. Wollams & Brown have identified five different methods of understanding the dynamics of games (1979, p. 126).

1. *Formal game analysis*—analyzes the various "advantages" of a game.
2. *Drama triangle*—focuses on racket and game positions.
3. *Transactional game diagram*—involves the diagnosis of ego states, including emphasis on psychological level communication.
4. *Symbiosis diagram*—focuses on identifying the preferred ego states of each player.

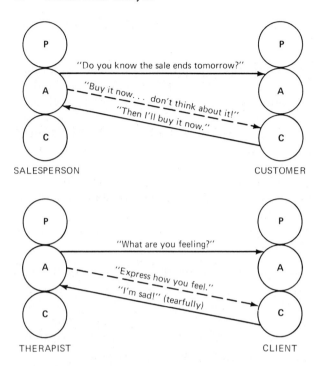

FIGURE 4.4   Angular transactions (Wollams & Brown, 1979, p. 70).

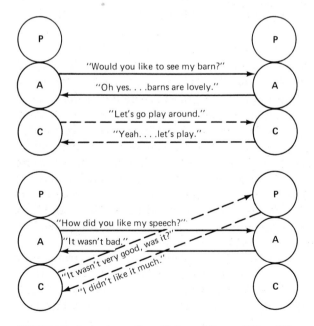

FIGURE 4.5   Duplex transactions (Wollams & Brown, 1979, p. 71).

5. *Formula G*—describes the flow of a game, outlining the steps it will take once the initial moves are begun.

Stage 4: script analysis.   Script analysis involves a detailed exploration of the decisions clients have made about their life positions. Although these decisions were made in childhood, they can be uncovered through techniques such as a script checklist (Berne, 1972), analysis of fairy tales (Karpman, 1968), or autobiography (James & Jongeward, 1971). Through script analysis, clients are enabled to understand their life positions and to make new decisions in order to adjust their scripts. New decisions based on new understanding usually rid them of the need for games and other self-defeating behavior and lead them toward autonomy, spontaneity, and intimacy.

Goals of Counseling

The goals of counseling have been stated in characteristic TA language: to obtain a friendly divorce from one's parents (Berne, 1964), to make losers into winners (James & Jongeward, 1971), to turn frogs into princes and princesses (Berne, 1972). These somewhat oblique expressions are based on the global goal of TA, which is to help clients achieve autonomy (Berne, 1964). In the TA view, "autonomy is characterized by *awareness* (a realistic understanding of the world), *spontaneity* (the ability to express emotions in an uninhibited, game-free fashion), and *intimacy* (the capacity to share love and closeness with others)" (Elson, 1979, p. 286).

Training of the Counselor

The International Transactional Analysis Association (ITAA) identifies three categories of membership. The first involves only "Interest memberships," which do not support any clinical function. The second category includes three sublevels that culminate in a clinical membership, which is the approximate equivalent of a master's degree. To be certified as a clinical member, the candidate must (a) hold a current regular membership; (b) complete a training program of not less than one year, which includes 50 hours of advanced TA training, 50 hours of supervision of direct clinical service, 150 hours of clinical application, and participation in various TA seminars and other presentations; and (c) pay dues and fees. The third level of membership culminates in a clinical teaching membership. To be certified as a clinical teaching member, a candidate must (a) hold a current clinical membership; (b) complete a training program of not less than two years in association with three sponsoring Teaching Members; (c) hold a graduate degree in "healing arts profession" or six years full-time experience in the field; and (d) pay fees and membership dues. (ITAA, note 1).

Function of the Counselor

Since the major goal of TA counseling is autonomy for the client, which by definition cannot be achieved through an agent, then it follows that a major function of the TA counselor is to teach clients the skills that will lead them to autonomy. These skills include structural analysis, transactional analysis, game analysis, and script analysis—all of which provide the client with the input needed to make new decisions.

PRACTICE OF COUNSELING

Major Techniques

Although not exactly a technique, the contract is one of the most important aspects of TA treatment. "A contract is an agreement between counselor and client which specifies the goals, stages, and conditions of treatment" (Wollams & Brown, 1979, p. 221). Clients usually work through a series of contracts: from those related to easily attained goals designed to inspire confidence, to more complex treatment contracts based on the client's individual learnings in therapy.

Berne (1966) outlined eight categories of therapeutic operations or techniques. The first four are simple interventions; the remaining four he called "interpositions," because they attempt to stabilize the Adult by placing something between it and the Parent or Child. Patterson (1980, pp. 408–410) clarified these terms.

Through *interrogation*, the therapist can obtain relevant information. It is important not to ask for too much information, since this could cause the client to play the "psychiatric history" game.

Specification is the therapist's attempt to help the client be responsible for what he or she has said. The therapist repeats the thoughts the client has been communicating.

The therapist uses *confrontation* when inconsistency needs pointing out. This assists the client to recognize discrepancies, and prevents him from playing the stupid game.

TA counselors use *explanation* when the client allows his Adult to listen. It is effective at that point when the client is vulnerable to facing reality.

By *illustration*, the therapist gives meaningful examples for the purpose of helping the client achieve new understandings.

Confirmation is given when the client manifests acceptance of the confrontations that have been made. If the client's Adult has been strengthened enough to keep the Parent from using the confirmation against the Child, then the therapist's reinforcement is effective.

While using *interpretaion*, the therapist's job is to decode and detoxify the messages of the pathological Child. Distortions must be corrected, and the client must be helped to reorganize his or her memory/perception of past experiences.

A *crystallization* occurs when the therapist clarifies the position of the client in the position of Adult to Adult. This means that the client can behave normally without the need of games. The Child will accept the crystallization if the Child and Adult are in accord. If the Parent, however, should resist the Child's growth toward health, then the therapist must deal with this resistance.

Treatment Parameters

TA is usually conducted in groups, although Berne sometimes worked with individual clients as well. The typical TA group numbers eight members and meets once a week for two-hour meetings. Meetings start on time and end as scheduled. Group members are seated so they can visually observe the entire body of each participant, including the therapist's (Holland, 1973). Lighting is also arranged with this end in mind, particular care being reserved for the visual needs of the therapist. Other equipment in the treatment room will usually include a blackboard and a tape recorder.

CASE STUDY *The following transcript is a condensed version of a TA group counseling session. In this segment, the focus is on Bob, a recent group member who has been complaining about problems at work. Bob established a contract that included as a major goal improving his work situation. He agreed to read Harris' (1969) book before he joined the group (Elson, 1979, pp. 290–292).*

Cl. 1: So, he did it to me again. He got his report to me too late to do anything with it and, of course, I'll get the blame.

Cl. 2: Bob, isn't that basically what happened at your job before you were transferred? You told us about that last week.

Cl. 1: No . . . No, that was just the opposite. Instead of expecting the impossible from me, my former supervisor used to take all the credit for my work. It was unbelievable! I knocked my brains out for that woman and never heard a word of appreciation from her. Everyone thought she was doing a great job, and she let them believe it was all her doing. No question that she rode my back to her promotion. If anyone was to get a promotion, it should have been me!

Cl. 2: But, isn't it the same thing going on now with your present supervisor?

Cl. 1: Not at all! My boss now always hands me too much work too close to the deadline. It's just impossible for anyone to do what he expects. I can't believe how I always seem to wind up with losers for bosses.

Cl. 2: Don't you think you might have something to do with how your bosses treat you?

Cl. 1: I don't see how . . . I have really tried to do my best. What do you mean anyway?

Cl. 2: Well, it may be that you're not aware of how you sabotage yourself at work, and you're not taking responsibility for yourself. You seem to be blaming your bosses for some of your own hassles.

Cl. 1: That is ridiculous. I can't help it if I get stuck with crummy people for bosses. I give my job my best shot . . . always have. As a matter of fact, if it weren't for them, I'd be in a much better position at work.

Cl. 2: Well, I'm not so sure . . .

Cl. 3: Wait a second, Mollie . . . You're really stretching things, aren't you? Let's go easy on Bob, huh? After all, he's new to the group.

Co: Let me interrupt here. Bob, what ego state were you just coming from?

Cl. 1: My Child . . . I think.

Co: Right! How about Mollie and Jim?

Cl. 1: Hmmmm . . . Well, Jim was definitely coming on Parent. Mollie . . . I'm not so sure.

Co: Was she being objective? Mostly asking for information?

Cl. 1: Yeah, I guess so.

Co: And that would be what ego state?

Cl. 1: Adult.

Co: Right. Now, I'd like to take a look at that interchange on the viedotape and see if there are any patterns here. (*Counselor plays videotape of above transactions.*)

Co: Anyone pick up anything?

Cl. 4: I agree with Mollie. I think Bob is trying to make excuses for the problems he's had at work.

Co.: Sara, would you give that feedback directly to Bob?

Cl. 4: Bob, it seems to me that you're avoiding your own responsibility in this thing with your supervisors. From what you said last week, and what I heard today, it's almost like you don't want to succeed at work, so you sabotage yourself and blame your bosses.

Co: Good feedback, Sara. Bob, how does that set with you?

Cl. 1: I suppose it's possible . . . I must say I was relieved not to be promoted.

Co: The added responsibility was kind of scary, huh?

Cl. 1: Yeah, for sure.

Co: Bob, I want you to consider the possibility that you're playing a variation of the "If it weren't for you" game. In fact, you used that very phrase earlier in referring to your bosses. Basically, it appears that you are blaming your superiors for your own lack of achievement at work. And, from comments you've made about your wife, it looks like this is a favorite game of yours. The stamps you collect in this game are ones of reassurance and resentment. You're saying to yourself, "It's not that I'm undeserving; it's that he's keeping me back." I'd say it's fairly convenient that your superiors have been so obliging!

Cl. 1:   Boy, that has a ring of truth to it.

Co: Bob, what do you remember your parents saying to you as a kid?

Cl. 1:   Well, my father died shortly after I was born, so I never knew him. My mother seemed to feel like I was a big bother. I remember she always had trouble finding a babysitter for me, and she used to complain about that a lot.

Co: How did she complain?

Cl. 1:   (*Smiling*) She would say, "If it weren't for you, I could go out at night."

Co: She was a fairly influential model, wasn't she?

Cl. 1:   Yeah, I guess she was . . . But, you know, I never really believed she would go out; she didn't have many friends.

Co: Did she seem afraid of social relationships?

Cl: I think so . . . She wouldn't let me bring my friends to the house.

Co: So she used you as an excuse to avoid social contacts.

Cl. 1:   It sounds like it, doesn't it?

Co: And you're doing the same thing now at work . . . blaming your boss for holding you back but really glad that you won't have to take the risk of more responsibility.

Cl. 1:   Yes . . . I guess that is true.

Co: Bob, I am going to give you permission to take the risk to do your best at work and to quit playing the "If it weren't for him" game.

In the weeks that followed, Bob was able to see the recurring pattern in his transactions with his boss. He became skilled at identifying his own and others' ego states, and he was able to interrupt the games he played and to use his Adult more frequently.

Applications

Although Holland (1973) indicated that TA has national and even international applications, its most realistic utility is in terms of the problems of individuals. According to Holland, TA lends itself well to dealing with marital and/or family problems, delinquent and criminal behavior, mental retardation, alcoholism, and schizophrenia. The value of TA is in providing new insights and new treatment approaches to these problem areas. In recent years, TA has received considerable attention in the popular literature, associating TA with everything and everyone from tots to bosses. However, as Steiner (1974) noted, it is TA—but is it therapy?

CRITIQUE

Research Support

Berne (1966) reported some early results. From September 1954 to September 1956, 75 clients were treated, 23 of whom were prepsychotic, psychotic, or postpsychotic. Of these 23, 2 (10%) were failures, 3 (12%) showed little or no change, and 18 (78%) improved. Of the 42 other clients, none were failures, 14 (33%) showed little or no change, and 28(67%) improved. From 1956 to 1960, about 100 people gave the treatment a fair trial (at least seven consecutive weeks); about 20 of these clients were severely disturbed. In the majority of cases, the treatment ended with the clients, their families, and the counselor all feeling better. Berne considers that these results compare favorably with other approaches.

To date, there have been no objective empirical research studies of TA—only case studies. *The Total Handbook of Transactional Analysis* (Wollams & Brown, 1979) doesn't list the word "research" in its index.

Evaluation

Berne's system is highly complex and difficult to master—two facts obscured by the rampant popularity of TA. The picturesque descriptions couched in a man-on-the-street vocabulary have led to the widespread popularity of the approach and have misled its untrained supporters to believe it to be a simple communication style. It is not. Berne's love of colorful language and his frequent use of myths and metaphors opened the way for abuse and misuse of his perspective by those not trained to understand it. Although Berne claimed the TA vocabulary had basically only five words (Parent, Adult, Child, game, and script), *Principles of Group Treatment* has a glossary of 127 terms and there are nearly 100 listed in *What Do You Say After You Say Hello?* TA may claim no technical terminology (even that is not quite accurate), but it certainly does have and use an extensive lexicon of jargon.

While Berne's language is unique, at least among psychotherapeutic systems, I find little new in his concepts. Whether or not Parent, Adult, and Child are *ego* states, they serve the same purpose as Freud's superego, ego, and id. Whether or not "scripting" is conceptually different from Adler's "life style," it serves the same function. This is not to say that those concepts are not valid or useful—only that they are not new or unique.

According to Patterson, "there is no evidence that Transactional Analysis is more effective or more efficient than any other therapy. Berne appears to have been an effective therapist, but there is no way to demonstrate that this was because of his theory" (1980, p. 425).

What, then, are the contributions of transactional analysis? People usually feel better when they can explain their behavior according to some system or logic, regardless of whether the system or logic is valid. TA teaches people the concepts and labels—in easy-to-remember terms—that they need to explain their behavior and thus to feel secure that, at least, they know.

REFERENCES

BERNE, E.   *Transactional analysis in psychotherapy.* New York: Grove Press, 1961.
BERNE, E.   *Games people play.* New York: Grove Press, 1964.
BERNE, E.   *Principles of group treatment.* New York: Oxford University Press, 1966.
BERNE, E.   *What do you say after you say hello?* New York: Grove Press, 1972.
CORSINI, R.   A medley of current personality theories. In R. Corsini (Ed.), *Current personality theories.* Itasca, IL.: F. E. Peacock Publishers, 1977.
ELSON, S. E.   Recent approaches to counseling: Gestalt, transactional analysis, and reality therapy. In H. M. Burks & B. Stefflre (Eds.), *Theories of counseling* (3rd ed.). New York: McGraw-Hill, 1979.
HARRIS, T. A.   *I'm OK—you're OK: A practical guide to transactional analysis.* New York: Harper & Row, 1969.
HOLLAND, G. A.   Transactional analysis. In R. Corsini (Ed.), *Current psychotherapies.* Itasca, IL.: F. E. Peacock, Publishers, 1973.
INTERNATIONAL TRANSACTIONAL ANALYSIS ASSOCIATION, INC.   Classification of memberships. ITAA, 1772 Vallejo St., San Francisco, CA, 94123. January, 1981.
JAMES, M., & JONGEWARD, D.   *Born to win: Transactional analysis with gestalt experiments.* Reading, MA.: Addison-Wesley, 1971.
KARPMAN, S. B.   Fairy tales and script drama analysis. *Transactional Analysis Bulletin,* 1968, 7, 39–43.
PATTERSON, C. H.   *Theories of counseling and psychotherapy* (3rd ed.). New York: Harper & Row, Publishers, 1980.
STEINER, C. M.   *Scripts people live: Transactional analysis of life scripts.* Copyright © 1974 by Claude Steiner. New York: Grove Press, 1974.
WOLLAMS, S., & BROWN, M.   *The total handbook of transactional analysis.* Englewood Cliffs, N.J.: Prentice-Hall, 1979.

CHAPTER FIVE
RATIONAL-EMOTIVE THERAPY

When the American Personnel and Guidance Association met in Dallas in 1977, one of the main speakers was Albert Ellis. Imagine, if you will, an enormous, round lecture hall, bulging at the seams with several thousand wide-eyed counselors seated in hushed expectation. The curtain is parted, revealing a cavernous stage. Enter stage left: Socrates! A slightly built man with a pleasant smile, etched in the lower third of a large head. Except for the blue business suit, he does look like Socrates. We sat, waiting for the mellifluous tones. He opened his mouth to speak—instantly, the entire setting was transformed into a New York street corner; the voice was a taxi driver's, barking at the traffic. It took a good five minutes for the shock to wear off. As it did, we began to hear, not just the tone of voice, but the meaning of his words. Southern Baptists just aren't used to that kind of language! The 500 or so of us who remained were treated to an engrossing—and substantial—discourse on rational emotive therapy. Albert Ellis is a man of many parts—all of them unique.

HISTORICAL DEVELOPMENT

Personal Background

Albert Ellis was born in Pittsburg, on September 27, 1913. He earned a B.B.A. degree at the City College of New York in 1934 and an M.A.

(1943) and Ph.D. (1947) from Columbia University. After careers as a free-lance writer (1934-1938) and personnel manager (1938-1948), Ellis became senior clinical psychologist at the New Jersey State Hospital at Greystone Park. At the same time, he was instructor in psychology at Rutgers University. In 1949, he took the post of chief psychologist with the New Jersey State Diagnostic Center in Menlo Park. Concurrently with these appointments, Ellis had been engaged in private practice since 1943, specializing in psychotherapy and marriage counseling. During this time, he became interested in psychoanalysis. He obtained training in this field and undertook a three-year personal analysis. Following this, he practiced classical psychoanalysis and psychoanalytical psychotherapy for several years.

During the middle 1950s, he began to move away from psychoanalysis and toward emphasizing his newly discovered rational-emotive therapy (RET). In 1958, he established the Institute for Rational Living and in 1968 the Institute for Advanced Study in Rational Psychotherapy. Ellis, a prolific writer, is the author of many popular books dealing with sex and several other, more scholarly discussions of sexuality and homosexuality. He has also written numerous works presenting, explaining, and/or defending his position on RET (Belkin, 1980; Ellis, 1979).

Theoretical Background

Ellis traces his theoretical ancestry back to the Stoic philosophers (ca. A.D. 500), particularly Epictetus: "Men are disturbed not by things, but by the view which they take of them" (*Enchiridion*). Even Shakespeare is in the family tree: "There's nothing either good or bad but thinking makes it so" (*Hamlet*). Alfred Adler (1964, p. 70) is a more recent precursor: "The individual . . . does not relate himself to the outside world in a predetermined manner . . . [but] always according to his own interpretation of himself and his present problem."

Initially, Ellis saw his function as delivering factual information to his clients, but he soon became aware that many clients needed much more than objective data. He tried psychoanalysis as the vehicle to meet those needs. He was a practicing analyst for several years but grew dissatisfied with both the theory and practice of psychoanalysis. He moved from classical psychoanalysis to a neo-Freudian approach and then to learning theory all the while becoming more active, more directive as a therapist. His own rational approach began to crystallize about 1951.

Based on his reading of the ancient philosophers and his own experience with his patients, Ellis was convinced that people persisted in irrational behavior because they continually reindoctrinated themselves to do so. His logical conclusion was that therapy must consist of convincing people that they must stop indoctrinating themselves with old, irrational ideas and teaching them to think rationally about themselves and the world. Rational-emotive therapy was born from these insights.

THEORY OF PERSONALITY

Definition of Terms

RET is remarkably free of jargon and uniquely defined constructs and terms. In fact, there seem to be only two.

Rational. The term "rational" is not defined in an absolute or dogmatic way. People choose to live by values, purposes, or goals. Once they choose such values, it is *then* rational for them to think, feel, and act in ways that help them to achieve their goals and live by their values. It is *then* irrational for them to think, feel, or act in ways that interfere with their goals or values.

Musturbating. When people tell themselves that they *must, should, ought* to do (or not do) something, they are, according to Ellis, "musturbating." He has classified these tendencies into a "musturbatory ideology."

View of Human Nature

Ellis (1979) makes certain assumptions about human nature that seem more a personal belief than a necessary support for RET.

1. Humans are only human, and are neither angels, nor devils, nor "dumb" animals. They have certain physical and/or psychological restrictions or limitations, which they may overcome to a degree, but it is doubtful that they will ever transcend their humanity and achieve higher states of consciousness or being.

2. As far as is now known, all humans are mortal—we all die—and there is no evidence of immortality or life after death. (This is a scientist's acknowledgment of the lack of empirical evidence, not necessarily an atheist manifesto.)

3. The main goal of life, for most humans, is survival in a relatively happy (i.e., painless) state. Other goals can be chosen, but humans are *biologically* predisposed toward survival and happiness.

4. Happiness—hedonism—is a valid choice; but long-range rather than short-range goals seem a wiser, more rational choice. On the other hand, there are certain assumptions about human nature that clearly support the theory and practice of RET (Ellis, 1979).

5. Human behavior is, to some extent, determined by strong biological and social forces. RET embraces a "soft determinism"; i.e., humans experience strong pressures, which they can (only with great difficulty) resist; but they also have a strong element of free will, which they can control.

6. RET takes an existentialist position that people by-and-large create their own worlds, and they tend to view those worlds phenomenologically and subjectively.

7. When human beings are born, they have conflicting tendencies within them. They have a strong tendency to be reasonable and to find fulfillment; but at the same time, they are drawn to act irrationally and to thwart their own growth.

8. One of the strongest innate tendencies of humans is to be influenced by family, by immediate associates, and by culture.

9. All normal humans think, feel, and act; and their thoughts profoundly affect (and sometimes effect—create) their feelings and/or behaviors. But, by the same token, feelings affect thoughts and behaviors, and behaviors affect thoughts and feelings.
10. RET holds that virtually all serious emotional disturbances stem, not from events or experiences, but from the view people take of them.

Structure of Personality

RET does not subscribe to the concept of libidinous instincts as an explanation for human behavior. Human beings are not seen as possessing the Unconscious as it is understood by Freudians or Jungians. Instead, we have a certain unawareness of many of our feelings or our thoughts.

Development of Personality

According to RET theory, the normal individual develops in terms of personal desires, wishes, and preferences; therefore, each person is different from every other person. On the other hand, in many ways, we humans are remarkably similar: we all eat, sleep, move, breathe, and grow older.

Most normal growth and development occurs with some regularity, but seldom with the lock-step regimentation assumed by many theorists. Most of Freud's psychosexual stages seem to have been projections of his own fears or desires, rather than objectively observed phenomena. Other "spinoffs" from the Freudian theme are also largely overgeneralizations. RET has not developed such theories of development, and, in Ellis' view, should never do so (Ellis, 1979). He sees RET as emphasizing *redevelopment* and suggests that there is little relationship betweeen personality theory and a theory of personality change.

Development of Maladaptive Behavior

We really do not know a great deal about the origin or the development of maladaptive behavior. Furthermore, what little we do know is frequently obfuscated by some of the existing theories that overemphasize one or two special incidents; such as the "Oedipus complex," birth trauma, or primal pain. Ellis finds little evidence for the existence of such events and still less for their importance.

According to Bard, RET considers psychopathology to be indicated by (1980, p. 23):

> 1. any frequently reported actions which tend to shorten the span of enjoyable living (e.g., abusing the body by drugs, cigarettes, etc.);
> 2. any frequently repeated actions which generate immediate and unnecessary discomfort and pain (e. g., making oneself anxious when there is no real danger);

3. failure to cultivate innate capacities for different satisfactions, thus subjecting oneself to frequent periods of boredom, inertia, or dissatisfaction;
4. preoccupation with short-range enjoyment obtained at the cost of long-range satisfactions; and
5. a pattern of avoidance of those opportunities to acquire knowledge which increases the individual's power to maximize future enjoyment.

RET puts its emphasis on pathology rather than etiology, but a careful reading of several sources indicates some organization of thought in this regard. Almost all humans, according to Ellis, have an innate tendency to disturb themselves. Some are more vulnerable than others, but all, to some degree, needlessly upset themselves. In addition to disturbing themselves, most people continually repropagandize themselves with irrational ideas. Ellis (1962) originally listed 11 irrational ideas, but more recently Ellis and Grieger (1977) have grouped 27 irrational ideas under three major "musturbatory ideologies." A small sampling will give the flavor (pp. 12–14).

Musturbatory ideology 1:

I *must* do well and win approval for my performance or else I rate as a rotten person. (a) I must have sincere love and approval almost all the time from all the people I find significant. (b) I *must* prove myself thoroughly competent, adequate, and achieving, or at least have real competence or talent at something important.

Musturbatory ideology 2:

Others *must* treat me considerately and kindly in precisely the way I want them to treat me; if they don't, society and the universe should severely blame, damn, and punish them for their inconsiderateness.
If others behave incompetently or stupidly, they turn into complete idiots and ought to feel thoroughly ashamed of themselves.

Musturbatory ideology 3:

Conditions under which I live *must* get arranged so that I get practically everything I want comfortably, quickly, and easily, and get virtually nothing I don't want. (a) I *must* find correct and practically perfect solutions to my problems and others' problems; if I don't, catastrophe and horror will result. (b) People and external events cause practically all my unhappiness and I have to remain a helpless victim of anxiety, depression, feelings of inadequacy, and hostility unless these conditions and people change and allow me to stop feeling disturbed.

Disturbability about disturbances. Because humans are self-conscious creatures, they observe their disturbance and then make themselves disturbed all over again about being disturbed. Frequently the metadistrubance becomes more important—and more disturbing—than the original problem. The original dysfunction is usually circumscribed in some way, limited to one set of circumstances. The secondary symptoms, on the other hand, frequently become quite pervasive and may disrupt the individual's entire life. Finally, even with unusually clear insight into their problems, people experience great difficulty in changing their behavior because dysfunctionality is based on innate tendency (Ellis, 1979).

Thus, RET holds—though, of course, not dogmatically—that the real causes of human disturbance are rooted in two uniquely human characteristics: (a) the general propensity to think crookedly, emote inappropriately, and act dysfunctionally; and (b) an individual's specific tendencies to behave self-defeatingly. Ellis (1979) insisted that both of these characteristics are mainly biologically based—innate. He demonstrated the effects of these propensities with the A-B-C theory.

A-B-C theory.

RET holds that virtually all serious emotional problems with which humans are beset directly stem from their magical, superstitious, empirically unvalidatable thinking. . . . According to RET theory, no matter how defective an individual's heredity may have been and no matter what "traumatic" experiences he may have been subjected to during his early or later life, the main reason why he is *now* overreacting or underreacting to noxious stimuli . . . is because he *now* has some dogmatic, irrational, unexamined beliefs. (Ellis, 1973, p. 172).

For example, at point A something occurs (the Activating Event)—you get fired from a good job. Your reaction to getting fired is to feel depressed, to be furious at your former boss, to hang around the house (or the bar), and avoid looking for a job (emotional and behavioral Consequences—point C). Getting fired (point A) *caused* the emotional and behavioral consequences (point C) right? Wrong! C, the emotional and behavioral consequence follows, not from A—the Activating Event, but from B, your irrational Belief about that event. The irrational belief (s) would be based on your "musturbating ideology." For example, you might tell yourself, "I *must* have *that* job" or "I *must* have a good job in order to respect myself." If you had told yourself, "I liked that job; I wish I hadn't gotten fired," you would no doubt experience some emotional consequences; but they would not be the disturbing, debilitating kind.

THEORY OF COUNSELING

Rationale for Change

In light of the above, it follows that in RET change in behavior is brought about by change in thinking—by moving from irrational to rational. Ellis acknowledges the contributions of Freud, Adler, Rogers, and others to the understanding of human nature, but rejects their approaches to curing the ills of human nature. He does acknowledge the contributions of the behaviorists as facilitating the change from unreason to reason; but the rationale for change is just that: learning to think rationally.

Many times RET counseling has a heavily cognitive orientation, which is based on several assumptions (Ellis, 1979).

1. Humans tend to cause or create their feelings by the way they think (and vice versa). When these feelings or emotions are disordered, they can be changed by examining, disputing, and reconstructing the thinking that underlies them.

2. Peoples' philosophies or beliefs about their experiences have a much more profound effect on their emotions and behavior than do the experiences themselves. Therefore, effective psychotherapy is aimed at helping clients change their irrational beliefs.

3. People frequently create their disturbances by their own expectations of what "should" happen or how others "should" behave toward them. When these unreasonable demands are surrendered, behavior changes for the good.

4. Disturbed people attribute negative motives, reasons, and causes to others and to outside events. When they change their attributions, they frequently feel better and act better.

5. Disturbed and unhappy people tend to rate themselves (rather than their performance) and frequently to rate themselves negatively. When they are taught to give up the self-rating, their disturbance dramatically decreases.

6. Finally, when people are taught to abandon their musturbatory ideals and their irrational beliefs, they return to more satisfying lives.

Process of Counseling

The RET counselor's job is to help clients rid themselves of illogical, irrational ideas and replace them with logical, rational ideas. This process begins by showing the clients that they are irrational and illogical. Ellis (1973) calls this Insight No. 1. It occurs when the clients recognize that their present disturbance has antecedent causes, but those antecedent causes are their own irrational beliefs and attitudes, not some past or present event.

The second step in the process (Insight No. 2) involves convincing the clients that they maintain their disturbance by reindoctrinating themselves with the same irrational ideas. In step three (Insight No. 3), the clients are led to a full acknowledgment that the only way to rid themselves of their disturbances is to challenge their belief systems, and through the challenge, to arrive at a new, rational belief system (Ellis, 1973).

A last step deals with specific irrational tendencies and proposes a philosophy of life designed to avoid additional irrational ideas. The result the RET counselor desires is that the clients progress toward a rational way of living by exchanging their irrational beliefs for reasonable beliefs. If this happens, then self-defeating behaviors disappear and emotional disturbances decrease (Patterson, 1980).

Goals of Counseling

RET is sometimes thought to be "anti-emotional." On the contrary, it sees emotion as essential to human living: without strong feelings people would surely not be happy and probably could not survive. RET does try to divest clients of their inappropriate feelings, such as anxiety, depression, despair, or hostility. In addition, RET counselors attempt to help their clients achieve specific goals (Ellis, 1979).

Responsibility. Assuming responsibility for their own lives, healthy people can work out their own problems. Even though they may want others to help them, they are not distraught without such help. They are able to direct their own lives. They can be true to themselves and at the same time, they can be aware of others.

Tolerance of others. Clients who are functioning well without emotional disturbance can allow others to be wrong. They do not condemn other people because they march to a different drummer. They can dislike the behavior of others without degrading them as people.

Acceptance of self. Emotionally stable people are able to accept the reality of who they are. The value they attribute to themselves does not depend upon their exterior actions or rely upon the opinions of others. They are comfortable with themselves. As a result of this, they have the courage to take risks.

Openness. People who are healthy are open to change. They can objectively use the scientific method to explore life. They can use the laws of logic as they interpret themselves as well as their own interpersonal and intrapersonal relationships with others.

Commitment. People who are not disturbed and are tending toward self-fulfillment are also interested in people and things. They are able to turn their efforts outward and to become absorbed in other-directed pursuits.

Acceptance of Chance. Mature people deal with uncertainty and chance with calmness. They realize that the world does not offer certainty, that absolutes do not exist. They do not expect that humans will be free of all frustration and unpleasantness. Therefore, one of the goals of RET is to lead clients to the realization that they do not have to live in a perfect world in order to be mentally healthy.

Training of the Counselor

In addition to the usual brief workshops and demonstration programs of professional meetings, RET offers five levels of training through the Institute for Rational-Emotive Therapy (Ellis, 1982):

1. The *Primary Certificate* may be earned by completing one of two options: (a) attending one five-day Primary Certificate Practicum or (b) attending four one-day Primary Certificate workshops and receiving five sessions of individual supervision. Candidates electing either option are also required to complete assigned readings and written and oral examinations. The Primary Certificate Program is open to psychologists, counselors, social workers, physicians, nurses, and full-time graduate students. Minimum qualification for certificate candidacy is a master's degree in psychology or counseling, an M.S.W., M.A., or R.N.

2. The Intermediate Certificate Program provides training for Primary Certificate holders who are not eligible for, or do not wish to, participate in the Associate Fellowship Program. Candidates will further their knowledge of RET principles, theoretical foundations, and clinical applications during these training sessions. Featured in the program is RET supervision involving cases from the participants' professional case loads. Candidates are required to complete (a) four training workshops in addition to those required for the Primary Certificate, (b) and eight hours of individual supervision of therapy cases by an Institute training faculty member beyond the supervision required for the Primary Certificate, (c) or one five-day Associate Fellowship program.

3. The Associate Fellowship Program provides practitioners the opportunity to broaden their rational-emotive and other cognitive-behavioral therapeutic techniques. The Associate Fellowship Program is open to certified psychologists, physicians, registered nurses, M.S.W.'s, clergy with graduate training and counseling experience, and holders of master's degrees carrying case loads of clients in supervised institutional settings. Candidates are required to complete (a) two practica; (b) 24 sessions of individual case supervision within a 12-month period, and (c) a tape-recorded session to be submitted for evaluation by the International Training Standards and Review Committee.

4. The Fellowship Program is the most comprehensive program of study offered by the Institute. During this two-year part-time course of study, participants receive in-depth training in rational-emotive and allied cognitive behavioral psychotherapeutic techniques. Fellowship candidates treat clients, receive weekly supervision, colead public education workshops, and participate in research.

5. In addition to the program of the Institute, RET-oriented training can be obtained through the Department of Clinical Psychology at Hofstra University.

Function of the Counselor

In order to straighten out irrational ideas, RET therapists are directive. They are actively involved in assisting clients in depropagandizing themselves. Frequently this is accomplished through homework assignments. For example, a young women is afraid to ask for a much-deserved raise. She may be assigned the task of making the appointment to see her boss and of following through in asking for the salary increase. If it is necessary, the therapist persuades the client to do the homework assignment and even orders that it be done.

RET therapists are more verbally active than many other therapists. This is especially true in the first sessions of the counseling relationship. Confrontation may be used in the first session in order that the client have the opportunity to face his or her illogical thinking and the irrational behavior that follows from such thinking. Therapists use argument and persuasion; they even attack their clients' self-defeating behaviors.

The RET approach is deliberately didactic. It may appear to be more of a philosophical disputation than psychological therapy or counseling. The therapists often assign readings and spend time in discussion of clients' understandings—and misunderstandings—of the material. The RET therapist frequently wears the professor's cap and gown as well as the clinician's coat (Ellis & Greiger, 1973).

On the other hand, the RET therapist does not spend much time on the clients' "activating events"—the gory details of who did what to whom. These details are seen as a smokescreen, hiding the real material of therapy: the emotional consequences and the irrational beliefs that generate them. Furthermore, RET therapists avoid the typical psychodynamic techniques of free association, dream analysis, establishment of a transference relationship, analysis of Oedipal or other psychodynamic complexes, and explanation of present symptoms in terms of past events.

In summary, RET involves the counselor's taking a fairly rapid-fire, active, directive, persuasive, disputational stance. Much of the time is spent confronting and challenging the clients' irrational beliefs and directing them toward more satisfying, less self-defeating behavior (Ellis, 1979).

PRACTICE OF COUNSELING

Major Techniques

Cognitive methods. In the process of leading clients to see their disturbances (ABCs) and in disputing their irrational ideas (D), the RET counselor uses many cognitive therapeutic techniques. Among these are logical and philosophical analysis, teaching, disputation about magical thinking, suggestions, deliberate distractions, and even thought-stopping exercises. The counselor requires the client to prove that it is "awful" to be angry and to show how getting angry makes a person worthless (Ellis, 1979).

For example, in order to discover your irrational beliefs (IBs), Ellis (Ellis & Greiger, 1977, p. 10) recommends the following:

1. Look at your awfulizing. Ask yourself, "What do I think of as awful in connection with my (feeling) about _____ ?"
2. Look for something you think you can't stand. Ask yourself, "What about A (activating event) do I think I can't bear?"
3. Look for your musturbating. Ask yourself, "What *should* or *must* I keep telling myself about this situation?"
4. Look for your damning of yourself and others. Ask yourself, "In what manner do I condemn or put down anyone in connection with _____ ?"

In addition, RET counselors teach their clients logical and semantic accuracy, show them how to fill out the Rational Self-Help form, and provide them with interpersonal skills, such as assertiveness (Ellis, 1979).

Emotive-evocative methods.   RET advocates unconditional acceptance of the client, regardless of his or her behavior. As described by Ellis (1979), this seems to be very similar to Rogers' (1951) "unconditional positive regard"; however, Ellis' mode of communicating acceptance would seem to be somewhat different from Rogers' mode of communicating regard. The RET counselor also makes use of role-playing, modeling, exhortation, humor, shame-attacking exercises, and a variety of encounter exercises such as risk-taking, opening-up exercises (Ellis, 1979).

Behavioral methods.   RET advocates *in vivo* behavioral homework assignments: *behavioral* because the client must do something, not just read about it; and *in vivo* because it is done in the real world, not in imagery. Operant conditioning techniques, especially in the form of self-help procedures, are used extensively by RET counselors. Relaxation and other kinds of tension-reducing procedures are often used in conjunction with cognitive and emotive methods. Finally, rational-emotive imagery (Maultsby, 1971) combines cognitive, emotional, and behavioral methods.

Treatment Parameters

The setting in which RET takes place is similar to that of most other modern approaches. Most individual sessions take place in the therapist's office. For the RET therapist, this is a relatively informal environment: both the room and the therapist are usually informally "dressed." The only special equipment is a tape recorder (the client is frequently encouraged to bring his or her own tape recorder to the session).

CASE STUDY (Ellis, 1977, pp. 258–265)

"But why," asked Jim at one point in the fourth session, "shouldn't I want things to go my way? Why *shouldn't* I try to get what I want?"

Therapist: No reason at all. To want what you want when you want it is perfectly legitimate. But you, unfortunately, are doing one additional thing—and that's perfectly illegitimate.

Patient: What's that? What's the illegitimate thing?

Therapist: You're not only *wanting* what you want, but *demanding* it. You're taking a perfectly sane desire—to be able to avoid standing trial for your crimes in this instance—and asininely turning it into an absolute *necessity*.

Patient: Why is that so crazy?

Therapist: For the simple reason that, first of all, *any* demand or necessity is crazy. Wanting a thing, wanting any damned thing you happen to crave, is fine—as long as you admit the possibility of your not being able to get it. But as soon as you demand something, you turn it into a necessity, you simply won't be able to *stand* your not getting it. In that event, either you'll do something desperate to get it—as you usually have done in your long history of antisocial behavior—or else you'll keep making yourself angry, exceptionally frustrated, or anxious about not getting it. Either way, *you* lose.

Patient: But suppose I *can* get what I want?

Therapist: Fine—as long as you don't subsequently defeat your own ends by getting it. As in this case. Even assuming that you could skip bail successfully—which is very doubtful, except for a short while—would you *eventually* gain by having to give up everything and everyone you love here to run, let us say, to South America?

Patient: Perhaps not.

Therapist: Perhaps? Besides, let's assume for a moment that you really could skip bail and that you wouldn't get caught and wouldn't live in perpetual fear. Even then, would you be doing yourself a great favor?

Patient: It seems to me I would! What more could I ask?

Therapist: A lot more. And it is just your *not* asking for a lot more that proves to me at least that you are a pretty sick guy.

Patient: In what way. What kind of crap are you giving me? Bullshit!

Therapist: Well, I could get highly "ethical" and say if you get away with things like that, with rifling vending machines, jumping bail, and such things, that you are then helping to create the kind of a world that you yourself would not want to live in. For if you can get away with such acts, of course, others can too; and in such a pilfering bail-jumping world, who would want to live?

Patient: But suppose I said that I didn't mind living in that kind of world—kind of liked it, in fact?

Therapist: Right. You might very well say that. And even mean it—though I wonder whether if you really gave the matter careful thought, you would. But let us suppose you would. So I won't use that "ethical" argument with a presumably "unethical" and guiltless person like you. But there is still another, and better argument, and one that you and people like you, generally overlook.

Patient: And that is?

Therapist: That is—your own skin.

Patient: My own skin?

Therapist: Yes, your own thick and impenetrable skin. Your guiltless, ever so guiltless skin.

Patient: I don't get it. What the hell are you talking about?

Therapist: Simply this. Suppose, as we have been saying, you are truly guiltless. Suppose you, like Lucky Luciano and a few other guys who really seem to have got away scotfree with a life of crime, really do have a thick skin, and don't give a good goddamn what happens to others who may suffer from your deeds, don't care what kind of a world you are helping to create. How, may I ask, can you—you personally, that is— manufacture and maintain that lovely, rugged impenetrable skin?

Patient: What difference does it make how I got it, as long as it's there?

Therapist: Ah, but it does!—it does make a difference.

Patient: How the hell does it?

Therapist: Simply like this. The only practical way that you can get guiltless, can maintain an impenetrable skin under conditions such as we are describing, where you keep getting away with doing in others and reaping criminal rewards, is by hostility—by resenting, hating, loathing the world against which you are criminally behaving.

Patient: Can't I get away with these things without hating others? Why can't I?

Therapist: Not very likely. For why would a person do in others without hating them in some manner? And how could he not be at least somewhat concerned about the kind of dog-eat-dog social order he was creating unless he downed his potential concern with defensive resentment against others?

Patient: I don't know—why couldn't he?

Therapist: Have you?

Patient: Have I, you mean, managed not to—?

Therapist: Exactly! With your long history of lying to others. Leading them on to do all kinds of things they didn't want to do, really, by your misleading them as to your feelings for them. The girls you got pregnant and deserted, for instance. The partners in crime you double-crossed. The parents whose help you've always run back for after breaking promise after promise to them? Would you call that love you felt for these people? Affection? Kindliness?

Patient: Well—uh—no, not exactly.

Therapist: And the hostility, the resentment, the bitterness you felt for these people—and must keep perpetually feeling, mind you, as you keep "getting away" with crime after crime—did these emotions make you feel good, feel happy?

Patient: Well—at times, I must admit, they did.
Therapist: Yes, at times, but really, deep down, in your inmost heart, *does* it make you feel good, happy, buoyant, joyous to do people in, to hate them, to think that they are no damned good, to plot and scheme against them?
Patient: No, I guess not. Not always.
Therapist: Even most of the time?
Patient: No—uh—no. Very rarely. I must admit.
Therapist: Well, there's your answer.
Patient: You mean to the thick skin business? You mean that I thicken my skin by hating others—and only really hurt myself in the process.
Therapist: Isn't that the way it is? *really* is? Isn't your thick skin—like the lamps made of human skin by the Nazis, incidently—built of, nourished on little but your own corrosive hatred for others? And doesn't that hatred mainly, in the long run, corrode you?
Patient: Hm. I—You've given me something to think about there.
Therapist: By all means think about it. Give it some real thought.

After 22 sessions of this type of rational therapy, the patient finally was able to admit that for quite a long time he had vaguely sensed his self-defeatism and the wrongness of his criminal behavior, but that he had been unable to make any concerted attack on it, largely because he was afraid that he couldn't change it. The therapist then started to make a frontal assault on the philosophies behind these defeatist feelings.

Applications

Ellis and Greiger (1977) have brought together a number of applications of the RET approach: sex therapy; marital therapy; group therapy; assertion training; treatment of psychotics, neurotics, and depressives; child psychotherapy; and education. Ellis acknowledges that RET is not for everybody, but the only exclusions are people for whom no psychotherapy would be useful (e.g., schizophrenics).

CRITIQUE

Research Support

RET has generated considerable research activity. The results of this research, as well as a growing body of literature in related areas, provide support for the efficacy of the RET approach. Specifically, the research does suggest that (a) RET is more effective than client-centered therapy with introverted people (DiLoreto, 1971); (b) it is more effective than systematic desensitization in the reduction of general or pervasive anxiety (Kanter, 1975); (c) a combination of cognitive therapy and behavior therapy appears to be the most efficacious treatment for depression (Rush,

Khatami, & Beck, 1975); and (d) the relative effectiveness of RET versus assertiveness training is inconclusive, due to limited and unfounded research (Tiegerman, 1975; Wolfe, 1975).

While practitioners of RET agree that it is more effective with high socioeconomic status (SES) clients (all therapy is), it is possible that it may be more effective with low SES clients than other forms of therapy. Research has shown that low SES clients often drop out of therapy because of the nondirective, non-goal-oriented behaviors of therapists (Heitler, 1976). Furthermore, low SES clients expect therapists to be active and directive. Thus, it may be hypothesized that such clients may do better—or drop out less frequently—with RET. Such speculation awaits systematic research.

Although RET has generated a substantial amount of research much of it suffers the methodological limitations that characterize much of the outcome and process research in psychotherapy—inadequate (or nonexistent) control groups, lack of comparison with other forms of therapy, inadequate numbers of subjects, poorly defined variables, psychometrically poor instruments, short duration of treatment, inadequate training of therapists (usually graduate students), and the use of a single therapist. While results are positive and hopeful, they are far from conclusive (Di Giuseppi & Miller, 1977; Mahoney & Arnkoff, 1978).

Evaluation

I can't recall a single client with whom I have worked who did not suffer from some measure of superstitious and/or absolutistic thinking and some form of blame—self-blame or other-blame. I know of no case of successful counseling in which these forms of "crooked thinking" were not at least mitigated, if not eliminated. However, I do have some reservations about the way Ellis rids his clients of these woes. Argumentation usually results in resistance, not compliance; and in therapy, compliance is not good enough. As Patterson (1980) pointed out, Ellis' success with his clients is probably due more to his evident concern than to his disputations, more to his relationship than to his ABCs.

I think it is very important for a counselor to be aware of his or her client's "crooked thinking" and "musturbatory ideology." I think it is important for people to think "straight" and to govern their own lives. I think that, in the long run, it is not important—and not very effective—to try to argue people out of one and into the other.

REFERENCES

ADLER, A. *Social interest: A challenge to mankind.* New York: Capricorn Books, 1964.
BARD, J. A. *Rational emotive therapy in practice.* Champaign, IL.: Research Press, 1980.

BELKIN, G. S.   *An introduction to counseling.* Dubuque, IA.: Wm. C. Brown, 1980.
DIGIUSEPPI, R. A., & MILLER, N. J.   A review of outcome studies on rational-emotive therapy. In A. Ellis & R. Greiger, *Handbook of rational-emotive therapy.* New York: Springer Publishing Co., 1977.
DILORETTO, A.   *Comparative psychotherapy.* Chicago: Aldine, 1971.
ELLIS, A.   Rational-emotive therapy. In R. Corsini (Ed.), *Current psychotherapies.* Itasco, IL.: F. E. Peacock, Publishers, 1973, chap. 5.
ELLIS, A.   The treatment of a psychopath with rational psychotherapy, in S. J. Moore & R. I. Watson, *Psychotherapies: A comparative casebook.* New York: Holt, Rinehart, & Winston, 1977, Chap. 14.
ELLIS, A.   The rational-emotive approach to counseling. In H. M. Burks, Jr., & B. Stefflre, *Theories of counseling* (3rd. ed.). New York: McGraw-Hill, 1979.
ELLIS, A.   Personal correspondence, April 14, 1982.
ELLIS, A.   *Reason and emotion in psychotherapy.* New York: Lyle Stuart, 1962.
ELLIS, A., & Greiger, R.   *Handbook of rational-emotive therapy.* New York: Springer Publishing Co., 1977.
HEITLER, J. B.   Preparatory techniques in initiating psychotherapy with lower-class, unsophisticated patients. *Psychological Bulletin,* 1976, *83,* 339–352.
KANTER, N. J.   *A comparison of self-control, desensitization, and systematic rational restructuring for the reduction of interpersonal anxiety.* Unpublished doctoral dissertation, State University of New York at Stoney Brook, 1975.
MAHONEY, M. J., & ARNKOFF, D. B.   Cognitive and self-control therapies. In S. L. Garfield & A. E. Bergen (Eds.), *Handbook of psychotherapy and behavior change* (2nd ed.). New York: John Wiley and Sons, 1978, Chap. 18.
MAULTSBY, M. C., JR.   Rational-emotive imagery. *Rational Living,* 1971, 6 (1), 24–26.
PATTERSON, C. H.   *Theories of counseling and psychotherapy* (3rd ed.). New York: Harper & Row, 1980, Chap. 2.
ROGERS, C. R.   *Client-centered therapy.* Boston: Houghton Mifflin, 1951.
RUSH, A. J., KHATAMI, M., & BECK, A. T.   Cognitive and behavioral therapy in chronic depression. *Behavior Therapy,* 1975, *6,* 398–404.
TIEGERMAN, S.   *Effects of assertive training and cognitive components of rational therapy on the promotion of assertive behavior and the reduction of interpersonal anxiety.* Unpublished doctoral dissertation, Hofstra University, 1975.
WOLFE, J. L.   *Short-term effects of modeling/behavior rehearsal, modeling/behavior rehearsal plus rational therapy, placebo, and no-treatment on assertive behavior.* Unpublished doctoral dissertation, New York University, 1975.

CHAPTER SIX
REALITY THERAPY

Like most of the individuals whose perspectives are reviewed in this text, Glasser is a student of psychoanalysis; but his perspective—reality therapy—is probably less rooted in psychoanalysis than any of the others. Glasser is a man who leads an active life, physically, emotionally, and intellectually. It shows in his perspective on counseling: he is concerned about what you do, about being emotionally involved with you, and with your awareness of the real world.

On first reading, reality therapy may seem too simple to be substantial, too easy to be effective. But soft! Read on. You do live in a real world. Your actions do have consequences. You are—or can be—master or mistress of your own life. Whether you like it or not, two plus two always equals four. A system of insight and action built upon these and other realities can be substantial, can be effective.

HISTORICAL DEVELOPMENT

Personal Background

William Glasser was born in Cleveland, Ohio, in 1925. He spent all of his childhood and adolescent years there and, in fact, all of his schooling. He received a bachelor's degree in chemical engineering, a master's in clinical psychology, and an M.D. (1955), all from Case Western Reserve University in Cleveland. He was married while still in college, then moved to UCLA for his residency in psychiatry.

His last year of residency was spent at the West Los Angeles Veterans Administration Hospital. He found the program to be a classic example of custodial psychiatry evidenced by a discharge rate of about two patients a year. Glasser began to try new procedures. Although he was encouraged by his supervisor, his colleagues at UCLA were not pleased, and this cost him a teaching position at UCLA.

About this same time (1957), Glasser was offered the position of chief psychiatrist at a new state facility for juvenile delinquent girls at Ventura, California. He saw this as an opportunity to implement the ideas he had developed at the VA hospital. His program included placing responsibility for their condition on the girls themselves. Consequences of unacceptable behavior were spelled out ahead of time, excuses were not accepted, and punishment was eliminated. It worked. The girls began to behave more responsibly, and the recidivism rate was cut to 20 percent. Glasser helped his former supervisor implement a similar program at the VA hospital. Results were equally dramatic: a discharge rate of two patients per year increased to nearly 100 percent within four years.

In 1961, Glasser published the initial formulations of reality therapy in the first book, *Mental Health or Mental Illness?* These concepts were honed, expanded, and republished in *Reality Therapy* (1965).

Shortly after publication of the 1965 book, Glasser founded the Institute of Reality Therapy, which was geared to train reality therapists. As his work became better known, schools invited his consultation; and he was able to adapt his procedures to educational settings. As a result of these experiences, he published *Schools Without Failure* (1969) and established the Educator Training Center, through which teachers receive training in his approach. He has since published several more books. *The Identity Society* (1972), *Positive Addiction* (1976), and *Stations of the Mind* (1981) are the major works. Glasser is currently president of the Institute for Reality Therapy in Los Angeles and spends most of his time lecturing at the Institute and in workshops around the country (Elson, 1979).

Theoretical Background

Glasser's most immediate theoretical predecessor was Paul Du Bois, a Swiss physician, who developed a procedure he called "medical moralizing" (Glasser & Zunin, 1973). He would teach his patients a philosophy of life that accented thoughts of health, rather than preoccupation with disease. Many of Glasser's ideas are similar to those of Adler and the Americans Adolph Meyer and Abraham Low. However, their influence was indirect since, by 1965, Glasser had not read their works. Also influential—and just as indirectly—were the contemporary writers O. H. Mowrer (whose integrity therapy involves some moralizing), Thomas Szaz (a physician who wants to abolish the "myth of mental illness"), and Norman Vincent Peale (the preacher who advocates the "power of positive thinking"). Although Glasser was influenced by these and other writers, he insists that reality therapy is a unique and independent system (Glasser & Zunin, 1973).

THEORY OF PERSONALITY

Definition of Terms

Autonomy. The ability to let go and relinquish environmental support and substitute individual internal psychological support, the ability of an individual to psychologically stand on his own two feet, is known as "autonomy."

Commitment. After a client has made a value judgment about his behavior and a plan to change it, the reality therapist asks him to make a commitment to the therapist to carry out the plan.

Identity. "Identity" includes the need to feel separate and distinct from every other living being. According to Glasser, it is the single basic psychological need that all people in all cultures possess from birth to death.

Identity, failure. People who have not established close, personal relationships with others, who do not act responsibly, and who feel helpless, hopeless, and unworthy have a failure identity.

Identity, success. People who (a) define themselves as basically competent, capable, and worthwhile; (b) who have the power to influence their environment and the confidence to govern their own lives; and (c) who have met the need to love and be loved, are seen as having a success identity.

Involvement. In Glasser's usage, "involvement" is essentially the same as empathy, except that involvement includes the communication of empathy, not just its presence.

Love. Consistent with his emphasis on behavior, Glasser defines love by what people do, rather than by what they feel. "Love is unrelenting concern and involvement" (Reilly, 1973, p. 17).

Reality. Reality is the world as it is including one's current behavior. Glasser does not take a phenomenological view of reality.

Responsibility. Glasser defined responsibility as the ability to fulfill one's needs and to do so in a way that does not deprive others of the ability to fulfill their needs. Reality therapists equate responsibility with mental health.

Right. Glasser believes that there is an accepted standard or norm against which behavior can be measured. The behavior is right if it meets this standard, wrong if it does not.

Self-worth. Also called self-respect and self-esteem, self-worth requires that individuals evaluate their behavior and work to correct it when it is not up to standard.

Value judgment. Reality therapy asks that each person make a value judgment about whether his or her behavior is responsible. If it is not, then a plan is developed to change the behavior.

View of Human Nature

"Reality therapy is based upon the premise that there is a single psychological need that all people in all cultures possess from birth to death, that is the need for an identity; the need to feel that we are somehow separate and distinct from every other living being on the face of this earth" (Glasser & Zunin, 1973, p. 292).

Glasser's view of human nature is, perhaps, most evident in his approach to education. Traditional education, according to Glasser (1969), has seen the student as a sort of empty bucket into which the teacher is supposed to pour an unending stream of facts. That many of those "facts" are largely irrelevant in the lives of the students is itself an irrelevant fact. In the traditional system, the emphasis is on the teacher, not the student. In Glasser's system, on the other hand, the teacher is seen as a facilitator of learning rather than a dispenser of facts (Rogers, 1969); and the emphasis is on the student and the student's development of relevant problem-solving and critical-thinking skills. Like Rogers (1969), Glasser believes that humans (specifically students) have the capacity to make use of their own potential for learning and growth. Each person is ultimately self-determining. If people would depend more on their decisions than on their situations, they would be more likely to live responsible, successful, satisfying lives. According to Glasser, people are what they do, and they do what they decide to do. If their lives are unsatisfactory, they can redecide to do differently (Elson, 1979).

Since we are what we do, then each of us must create a sense of who we are. We must define ourselves as unique, separate individuals. It must be kept in mind, however, that when Glasser emphasizes a separate and unique identity for each individual, he does so in the context of what Adler has called "social interest." The identity that Glasser advocates is not opposed to the rest of mankind, but is instead a unique self-concept that facilitates involvement with others. This need for identity exists in all cultures.

Glasser distinguishes two kinds of identity: a success identity and a failure identity. People with success identities define themselves as capable, competent, and worthwhile; they see themselves as having power over their environment and the confidence and ability to govern their own lives. People with failure identities see themselves as incapable, incompetent, and powerless (Glasser & Zunin, 1973).

Glasser (1972) sees society as becoming identity-oriented. "Less anxious than formerly about fulfilling *goals* to obtain security within the power hierarchy, people today concern themselves more and more with an independent *role*—their identity" (p. 5; italics mine).

Structure of Personality

Taking a holistic view of personality, Glasser eschews Freudian concepts of the division of the psyche into structural elements. By the same token, he rejects the notion of unconscious drives. The need for identity is inherited (Glasser & Zunin, 1973).

Glasser identifies two basic needs: "the need to love and be loved and the need to feel worthwhile to ourselves and to others" (1965, p. 9). Although the two needs are separate, they are usually interrelated: a person who has satisfied one need is more likely to have satisfied the other. However, whether or not a person is loved, in order to feel worthwhile, he or she must maintain a satisfactory standard of behavior. This involves correcting the behavior when it is wrong and crediting oneself when it is right (Glasser, 1965).

Development of Personality

Personality develops out of the individual's attempt to meet his or her basic needs. Those who learn to fulfill these needs develop normally and identify themselves as successful. Those who are unable to meet their basic needs become irresponsible and identify themselves as failures. This personality or identity development comes about through involvement with others. Glasser does not see personality development as occurring in stages, but he does stress the importance of two periods in the life of a child: the years between five and ten, because of the beginning associations at school.

Because we are not born with the ability to fill our own needs, it falls principally to parents to teach the skills necessary for this task. It is essential that parents teach their children to be responsible through appropriate discipline; i.e., enforcing reasonable rules in a deliberating consistent manner. Punishment should be abandoned completely as a parenting modality because it typically is arbitrary, capricious, and ineffective (Driekurs & Grey, 1968; Glasser, 1972).

The most important aspect of parenting is the parents' involvement with their children ("parents" include parent surrogates). Barring unusual circumstances, the only chance children have to learn to give and receive love and to develop a sense of self-worth is in intimate contact with their parents—a contact that includes satisfying physical, emotional, and intellectual interaction.

The salutary involvement assumes, of course, a loving relationship in which the parents actively teach their children, democratically discipline (not punish) them, and allow them to learn by their own (the children's) experience. Such parenting will create a growth environment that will enable the children to establish success identities.

Glasser emphasizes that teachers must also get involved with their students, make education relevant, and provide many success experiences. Teachers have enough influence that, if a child's parents have provided poor learning experiences at home, a positive school experience can help the child to salvage a success identity.

Given the proper home and school environment, a person will develop normally. Normal development leads to maturity—the ability to stand on one's own two feet psychologically. Mature individuals identify themselves as successes and take responsibility for who they are, what they do, and what they want. They are also able to develop responsible plans to achieve these goals and to meet their needs (Elson, 1979; Glasser, 1965; Glasser & Zunin, 1973).

Development of Maladaptive Behavior

When people are unable to satisfy one or both of their needs for love and worth, they experience psychological pain. The pain—anxiety—signals a problem and alerts the person to the need to do something about it. According to Glasser (1965), people instinctively seek to alleviate this pain through involvement with others. If they are successful in establishing and maintaining involvement with others, the pain will diminish. If not, the pain increases.

Failure to become involved initiates the failure cycle: lack of involvement leads to an inability to meet one's most basic needs; this, in turn, leads to a denial of those needs, which leads to a denial of responsibility, which distances one even further from involvement with others, which, finally, leads to what Glasser (1972) calls "self-involvement"; i.e., seeking within oneself relief from the pain of failure. Becoming involved with oneself takes the form of a psychological, social, or physical symptom: such as depression, phobias, antisocial behavior, alcoholism, and even some physical illnesses. "I believe *every* psychologically diagnosable condition is an example of involvement with one's own idea, behavior, symptom, or emotion, or some combination of them" (Glasser, 1972, p. 47). Because these self-involvements, these symptoms replace involvement with others, Glasser calls them "companions." Self-involved people identify themselves as failures; they have not learned to act responsibly; they have not learned to meet their needs in realistic ways (Elson, 1979).

Formation of a failure identity seems to occur about the age of four or five—the age at which most children enter school. Before that time, most children see themselves as successful because they have generally been allowed to do what they can do. In school, the child is made to do what others ask of him, frequently without their revealing its relevance (if it has any); and when the child does not master the task, he is labeled a failure.

Glasser   acknowledges   that   others—particularly   parents   and teachers—may have some responsibility for an individual's initial failure to learn to meet his or her needs, but they bear no responsibility for that person's present failure to learn. Whether the problem began in childhood or only yesterday, is not important. What is important is that the person is failing *now*. "In almost every case we have the symptom now because we are lonely and failing now" (Glasser, 1972, p. 56). All people must take responsibility for their present behavior, look at it honestly, and determine whether it contributes to fulfilling their needs (Glasser, 1965, 1969, 1972; Glasser & Zunin, 1973).

THEORY OF COUNSELING

Rationale for Change

Reality therapists believe that maladaptive behavior can be changed, that people can become involved with others. People come to counseling seeking change because their denial of reality, self-involvement, and irresponsibility have not relieved their pain.

Glasser teaches that people want to see themselves as successful, to be responsible, and to enjoy meaningful interpersonal relationships. The suffering associated with a failure identity cannot be dispelled without a change in identity; i.e., a change in how one thinks, feels, and behaves. The effort to change is rooted in meaningful involvement with others. The change in identity will endure only if the change in behavior is maintained over a significant period of time. As counseling proceeds the counselor must make it clear that counseling does not make people happy: responsible behavior does. Only the client can make himself happy, and it will "take" only if he is willing to face reality and take responsibility for himself (Elson, 1979; Glasser, 1976; Glasser & Zunin, 1973).

Process of Counseling

Glasser (1965) sees therapy as a sort of corrective recapitulation of the original parenting process: the therapist does now what the parents should have done then. The principles of reality therapy serve as a guide to the process and a catalogue of procedures (Evans, 1982; Glasser, 1972; Glasser & Zunin, 1973). As you will see, these "principles" do not clearly describe the process of counseling, but their order of presentation approximates such an outline.

Involvement. For reality therapy to work, the counselor must become involved with the clients. He or she must communicate empathy, concern, and care for the clients. In a school context, involvement means this school (class) is a place where this child wants to be. "The ability of the therapist to get involved is the major skill of doing reality therapy" (Glasser, 1965, p. 22).

Current behavior. No one can achieve a success identity without being aware of his or her current behavior. Along with constant efforts at involvement, the counselor also consistently works at helping the clients to become aware, consciously and in detail, of their own behavior in the present. The emphasis is on "what *are you* doing," not on "what *did* you do."

Value judgment. In the third place, the clients look at their behavior and judge it in the light of their goals and the exigencies of the real world.

The counselor asks them to judge their behavior on the basis of whether it is good for them and the significant others in their lives. The clients also judge whether or not the behavior is socially acceptable.

Planning responsible bahavior. Once the clients have made a value judgment about their behavior, the counselor must help them formulate a realistic plan to execute the judgment. Part of the counselor's job is to be sure the plan is not beyond the clients' ability and motivation to carry it out. If a given plan doesn't work, it should be discarded and another developed.

Commitment. Having a good plan does not ensure that clients will carry it out, so the reality counselor asks for a commitment. Initially, this commitment is to the counselor; but eventually, after the clients gain a sense of self-worth, they make the commitment to themselves.

No excuses. When clients do not fulfill their commitment, their value judgment must be reexamined. If that is still valid, the plan must be checked. If the plan is reasonable, the clients must either recommit to it or reject it. If they reject it, then they either make a new plan or they leave therapy. If they don't reject it, then the counselor must hold them to the commitment and accept no excuses for failure to follow the plan.

No punishment. Punishment is any treatment of another person that causes that person physical or mental pain. The intent of punishment is to change the punishee's behavior; the actual goal is to let the punisher "get even" for a real or imagined wrong. In either case, punishment destroys any chance for involvement. On the other hand, reasonable and mutually-agreed-upon consequences of irresponsible behavior are not punishment and do not interfere with involvement.

Goals of Counseling

The major goal of reality therapy is to help clients become responsible and, through personal responsibility, to achieve a success identity. However, Glasser insists that identity must come as a by-product of responsible action. In addition to the global goal of responsibility, clients establish more immediate goals; such as weight control or improving a particular interpersonal relationship. In a broader sense, reality counselors attempt to teach their clients an approach to life, a system for living (Glasser & Zunin, 1973).

Training of the Counselor

The Institute for Reality Therapy was founded in Los Angeles in 1967 to teach the theory and practice of reality therapy in one-week intensive seminars. Since then, the Institute has expanded to teach the seminars throughout the United States and Canada. The seminars consist of an introductory lecture and question-and-answer period lasting part of one day. The rest of the week is spent in groups of seven to eleven trainees and one instructor. This provides the opportunity for a great deal of role playing and personal attention. For those who wish to train further, a supervised practicum of six months is required. If the individual wants reality therapy certification, the first practicum is followed by a second intensive seminar and a second six-month practicum. If the final practicum is completed successfully, the supervisor recommends the trainee for certification. At the present time, certification is done only in Los Angeles under the direct supervision of Dr. Glasser.

Advanced reservation is necessary for the seminars because enrollment is limited. The fee includes instruction, materials, lunch each day, and one supper. It does not include other meals or lodging. For further information, write Institute for Reality Therapy, 11633 San Vincente Blvd., Los Angeles, Calif. 90049 (Glasser, 1982).

Function of the Counselor

Reality counseling is a learning process that emphasizes rational dialogue between client and counselor. The counselor is quite didactic, asking many questions about the client's current life. The questions are focused on leading the client to greater awareness of behavior, making value judgments about that behavior, and then planning more responsible behavior. Reality counselors are verbally active in other ways, too. For example, they do not hesitate to engage clients in interesting and enjoyable conversations that seem unrelated to therapy; they use humor (never sarcasm) and even heated discussion; verbal confrontation frequently occurs when the counselor will not accept a client's excuse (Elson, 1979). It is not exactly a Socratic dialogue, but it does approach that mode of communication.

The reality counselor is essentially a teacher. "It is difficult to tell a starving man that he can have only a little food when he believes there is so much more. The therapist's job is to convince the patient that he has chosen starvation and that there is plenty of food around if he will go out and look for it; the therapist is not the only one with food" (Glasser, 1972, p. 79).

In explaining the importance of involvement, Glasser (1965) outlines the characteristics he wanted in reality therapists. First, the therapists must be responsible: tough, interested, human, sensitive. They must be able to meet their own needs and be willing to share their struggles with others, especially clients. The therapists must experience and communicate empathy for and acceptance of the isolated, failure-identity client. Finally, and most important, the therapists must be able to become emotionally involved with each client. This involvement, of course, is facilitative, not exploitative. Reality counselors are teachers, leading their pupils from weakness and irresponsibility to strength and responsibility, from pain to pleasure, from unfulfillment to fulfillment.

PRACTICE OF COUNSELING

Major Techniques

Beyond viewing counseling as a special kind of learning situation, Glasser does not say much about specific techniques. What few suggestions he makes are usually associated with the eight principles of process phases discussed above. Glasser and Zunin (1973) offered a number of specific suggestions to help the counselor become involved. They suggested the use of personal pronouns ("I," "we," "you"; never "he," "she," "they"). Self-disclosure is encouraged, as well as a friendly, optimistic demeanor. The counselor should talk with clients on a wide range of subjects. Particular attention should be paid to what the client's interests and successes are— what he or she is doing right.

The reality therapist focuses on behavior. In dealing with clients who say, "I'm very unhappy," the reality counselor does not ask them to elaborate on the feeling. Instead, he asks, "What are you doing to make yourself unhappy?"

Reality therapy focuses on the present. If the past is discussed at all, it is in relation to the present. Glasser and Zunin (1973) suggested that the reality counselor may find it useful to describe character-building experiences from the client's past, possible alternative choices, success—rather than failure—experiences.

Reality therapy leads clients to evaluate their own behavior in the light of their own goals. The therapist never makes this judgment for the client, but rather asks, "Did this behavior help you to meet your needs?" If the client answers, "I don't know" or "It made me feel better," the counselor presses the question: "Did the behavior do you any good?" If the client evaluates the behavior as wrong, the counselor must not condone it. On the other hand, if the client evaluates the behavior as good under the circumstances, the counselor should not debate the point. Only the client can make value judgments about his or her behavior. However, the counselor may lead the client to see the behavior in a wider context—such as its effect on others.

The value judgment must be followed by a realistic plan to carry out that judgment. The counselor might begin this phase by asking, "What is your plan? Do you have any ideas about how you can avoid this problem?" The plan should not attempt too much, because it would probably fail and thus reinforce the present failure. On the other hand, it should be ambitious enough that some change can be observed. Plans are never final. If one does not work, successive or alternative plans can be arranged.

Once the plan is developed, the client is asked to make a commitment to carry out the plan. The commitment is more likely to succeed if the client makes the commitment to the counselor rather than to self: "I'll do it for you."

The reality therapist doesn't accept excuses; therefore, "why?" is an irrelevant question. The therapist simply says, "Are you going to fulfill your commitment or not? If so, when?" Or "This plan didn't work, let's make another."

Critical statements and sarcasm are never a part of reality therapy, because they are punishing. While developing the plan, the counselor, together with the client, develops natural or logical consequences that will follow from the client's failure to implement the plan. Setting limits is an important function of a reality therapist: setting limits not only to the therapeutic situation but also the limits life places on the individual. The contract discussed earlier is a type of limit setting (Elson, 1979).

Arguing constructively or discussing intelligently may be therapeutic for some clients. Humor, too, can and should be a part of the counselor's approach. Confronting is used, especially when excuses are not accepted. Generally, the reality therapist tries to get involved in the client's real life (Glasser & Zunin, 1973).

Treatment Parameters

The counselor and client are seated so that each can see the other. Most reality counselors see their clients once a week, although (rarely) twice-weekly sessions may be used for a brief time. The duration of each session is usually flexible but is generally in the vicinity of 45 to 60 minutes. No specific fee is recommended—a "sliding scale" is the usual practice (Glasser & Zunin, 1973).

CASE STUDY   *The following case study is cited from Elson (1979, pp. 308–311).*

Norman is a 14-year-old first-year high school student whose grades have plummeted. To help him improve his academic performance, Norman's parents have tried to implement several homework and study plans with his junior high school counselor. So far, none has worked. Because they are frustrated and feeling helpless, his parents have referred Norman to a reality therapist in private practice. At the initial interview with Norman's parents, the counselor learns that Norman is doing poorly at home, too. He often refuses to do his chores, speaks disrespectfully to his parents, fights with both his older and younger sisters, and has twice stayed out all night without permission. Subsequently, the counselor has met once with Norman and his parents and twice with Norman alone. In this third session, most of the conversation has revolved around Norman's growing interest in cooking.

Co: So, because you've enjoyed the home ec. class so much the last couple of weeks, you think you might like to be a chef someday?

Cl: Yeah! I think it would be interesting . . . I hear chefs get paid pretty good, too, don't they?

Co: I don't know, but we could sure find out. What do you have to do to become a chef, do you know?

Cl: Naw . . . I'm not sure . . . I guess go to cook's school or something like that.

Co: Hmmm, I think you're right. How do you get into cook's school, anyway?

Cl: I don't know.

Co: Do you have to finish high school?

Cl: I don't know . . . I think so.

Co: What do you think about that part of it? Finishing high school, I mean.

Cl: I don't know . . . probably impossible for me.

Co: But, if you did graduate from high school, you would want to go to cook's school, huh?

Cl: Yeah, I think I would. How come you have to finish high school to go? That's ridiculous.

Co: I'm not sure. I suppose they want to make sure their students can read and follow directions . . . and add and subtract and things like that.

Cl: Well, I can do all that. How come I have to graduate?

Co: I don't know, Norman . . but it sounds like that's how it is.

Cl: Boy, I might as well throw in the towel then. I just got my grades for the quarter.

Co: You did? How did you do?

Cl: Not so hot.

Co: What exactly did you get, Norman? I'd like to know.

Cl: I got a B in home ec., D's in art and music, and an F in English, and F in math, and an F in social studies.

Co: So home ec. is definitely your best subject. How about gym?

Cl: Well, I was working out with the swim team instead of going to gym. I made the team last month.

Co: Great. I had forgotten that. You like swimming too, huh?

Cl: Yeah . . . yeah.

Co: What did you mean, *was* working out with the swim team?

Cl: Coach told me last Friday that I'm off the team until I pull up my grades. I guess I can't have three Fs and be on a school team.

Co: Boy, that's rough.

Cl: I'll say.

Co: Norman, let me see if I understand this. You want to be a chef, and that means graduating from high school; and you want to be on the swim team, and that means you've got to do better in school . . . yet, you don't like school.

Cl: That's about it.

Co: What are you doing that makes you not like school?

Cl: Nothing . . . it's those lousy teachers.
Co: Tell me what you're doing anyway. What's your toughest class?
Cl: English. I hate it.
Co: So, what happens in English class? What did you do today?
Cl: Huh? I just went, that's all.
Co: Did you get there on time?
Cl: Yeah . . . I don't know . . . I guess I was a little late.
Co: After the bell rang?
Cl: Yeah, I guess so.
Co: Then what?
Cl: Well, I sat down and . . .
Co: Where? What part of the room?
Cl: In the back, I think.
Co: Who did you sit next to?
Cl: Huh? George was on one side and Mary . . . I think it was . . . was on the other side.
Co: What kind of work do they do in English? George and Mary, I mean.
Cl: Not very good . . . like me, I guess.
Co: Then what?
Cl: Well, nothing . . . just sat there and fooled around.
Co: Did you ask any questions? Did you do your work?
Cl: Naw. I hate that class.
Co: Norman, let me ask you something. You want to swim on the team; you want to go to cook's school. Both require that you do better in school. Would you be doing better if you thought it was possible for you to do better?
Cl: Yeah, but it is hopeless. The teachers will never give me better grades.
Co: Well, you're right about that. They won't give them to you. Do you think you could somehow do better work and change the teachers' minds?
Cl: I doubt it.
Co: Let's think about that for a minute. Let's see . . . you arrived at class late . . . does that help you to do better work or hurt your work?
Cl: Probably hurt.
Co: I think so, too. How about sitting in the back of the room with George and Mary?
Cl: Probably hurt.
Co: How about never raising your hand . . . never acting interested?
Cl: Probably hurt.
Co: Yep, I'll ask you again, Norman. Do you want to change and do better work?
Cl: Yes, I do.
Co: What's the plan? How can we help you?
Cl: Well, I guess I could change what you were talking about.
Co: You mean come to class on time? What else?

> Cl: I could change my seat and act more interested.
> Co: Great! We've got a three-point plan. What say we write it down?

After writing down the plan, the counselor asked Norman to agree to carry it out in the coming week. Although Norman fulfilled his commitment in the first week, he failed when the plan was extended to include his math class. The counselor refused to accept his excuses for failure, but the plan was modified; and as Norman kept his commitment, it was slowly expanded to include all his classes. Success led to success. Norman was reinstated on the swim team, and his behavior at home began to improve. Before they terminated, Norman and his counselor explored several chef training programs.

Applications

Problems such as anxiety, maladjustment, marital conflicts, perversions, pyschoses, and delinquency have all been treated successfully with reality therapy. On the other hand, "since it is a highly verbal, rational approach, reality therapy is not effective with autistic or severely retarded persons" (Elson, 1979, p. 312).

Apart from therapy, the principles of reality therapy can be used effectively by parents with children, teachers with students, ministers with parishioners, and employers with employees (Glasser, 1976). However, its most direct—and probably successful—application is the Schools Without Failure Program (Glasser, 1969).

CRITIQUE

Research Support

As far as I have been able to determine by computer database (DIALOG) search, there have been no long-term significant studies of reality therapy as a therapy. There have been several studies of reality therapy principles and techniques in school settings. These efforts have produced mixed results.

English (1970) and Hawes (1971) noted positive results in reducing disciplinary problems, increasing school performance, and increasing belief in self-responsibility. Mink and Watts (1973) reported success in using reality-based counseling strategies with nontraditional students in a community college. They found that students in the program made a significant shift from externality to internality (Rotter, 1966) with a concomitant improvement in grade-point average. They also found that these students tended to remain in school significantly longer than most community college students. Browning (1979) found that junior high school teachers with twenty hours of training in reality therapy principles significantly improved their attitude toward student discipline and the school environment. However, there were no significant changes in the students' attitude toward themselves or in the students' misbehavior. Other studies (Brannon, 1978; Gang, 1975; Laspina, 1976; Shearn & Randolph, 1978) produced minimal or no results.

Most of these studies suffer from design and/or methodological problems (e.g., small N or insufficient treatment application).

Evaluation

Glasser's focus on commitment and action are a welcome relief to a field overburdened with the notion that insight is a necessary and sufficient condition for change. Elson (1979) has noted that its major limitations include the following:

The success of reality therapy will probably depend on the verbal and cognitive abilities of its clients. Glasser seems to emphasize behavior to the exclusion of feelings. It is not possible to communicate empathic understanding without some response to the client's feelings. Without deep empathy, how does a counselor develop and maintain involvement? There seems to be a lack of specific change technology—specified therapeutic procedures—which lack could severely limit the range of effectiveness of less creative counselors. Finally, there is some confusion in the use of terms such as "responsibility" and "right."

However, these limitations are insignificant when compared to the strength and potential contributions of reality therapy and, which is a short-term treatment that builds on the client's strengths and teaches him or her how to minimize, if not eliminate, weaknesses. Perhaps even more remarkable, Glasser has developed an effective, short-term, simple (not simplistic!) training program for practitioners of reality therapy.

I believe the business about "not emphasizing feelings" has been overblown and perhaps based on a misunderstanding of Glasser's intentions. Some counselors (no counseling perspective that I know of) seem to think that all a counselor has to do is reflect feelings. Glasser is saying go ahead and reflect feelings to establish involvement; but since feelings follow behavior, you cannot help a client change his or her life situation without dealing with the behavior that led to the feelings.

Reality therapy's most significant strength, however, is its applicability to preventive mental health, focusing on building strengths rather than attempting to eliminate weaknesses. Its positive philosophical base, which emphasizes personal responsibility and human concern, is an approach to life that could have enormous benefits for individuals and society.

REFERENCES

BRANNON, J. M.   The impact of teacher stage of concern and level of use of a modified reality therapy discipline program on selected student behaviors: A discriminant analysis approach. Doctoral dissertation, University of Mississippi, 1978. *Dissertation Abstracts International*, 1978, *38* (7-A), 4037.

BROWNING, B. D.   Effects of reality therapy on teacher attitudes, student attitudes, student achievement, and student behavior. Doctoral dissertation, North Texas State University, 1979. *Dissertation Abstracts International*, 1979, *39* (7-A), 4010–4011.

DREIKURS, R., & GREY, L.   *A new approach to discipline: Logical consequences.* New York: Hawthorn Books, 1968.

ELSON, S. E.   Recent approaches to counseling: Gestalt therapy, transactional analysis, and reality therapy. In H. M. Burks & B. Stefflre, *Theories of counseling* (3rd ed.). New York: McGraw-Hill, 1979.

ENGLISH, J.   *The effects of reality therapy on elementary-age children.* Paper for the California Association of School Psychologists and Psychometrists, Los Angeles, CA., March, 1970.

EVANS, D. B.   What are you doing? An interview with William Glasser. *Personnel and Guidance Journal*, 1982, *60*, 460–465.

GANG, M. J.   Empirical validation of a reality therapy intervention program in an elementary school classroom. Doctoral dissertation, University of Tennessee, 1975. *Dissertation Abstracts International*, 1975, *35* (8-B), 4216.

GLASSER, W.   *Reality therapy: A new approach to psychiatry.* New York: Harper & Row, 1965.

GLASSER, W.   *Schools without failure.* New York: Harper & Row, 1969.

GLASSER, W.   *The identity society.* New York: Harper & Row, 1972.

GLASSER, W.   Reality therapy. In V. Bender, A. Bender, & B. Rimland (Eds.). *Modern therapies.* Englewood Cliffs, N.J.: Prentice-Hall, 1976.

GLASSER, W.   Personal correspondence, April 12, 1982.

GLASSER, W., & ZUNIN, L. M.   Reality therapy. In R. Corsini (Ed.), *Current psychotherapies.* Itasca, IL.: F. E. Peacock, Publishers, 1973.

HAWES, R. M.   Reality therapy in the classroom. Doctoral dissertation, University of the Pacific, 1971. *Dissertation Abstracts International*, 1971, *32*, 2483–A.

LASPINA, A. V.   The effect of applied reality therapy methods upon creative thinking and behavior. Doctoral dissertation, University of Southern Mississippi, 1976. *Dissertation Abstracts International*, 1976, *37* (4-A), 1981.

MINK, O. G., & WATTS, G. E.   *Reality therapy and personalized instruction: A success story*, 1973. (ERIC Document Reproduction Service No. ED 115323).

REILLY, D.   Glasser without failure. *Human Behavior*, 1973, *2*, 16–23.

ROGERS, C. R.   *Freedom to learn.* Columbus, OH.: Charles E. Merrill, 1969.

ROTTER, J.   Generalized expectancies for internal vs. external control of reinforcement. *Psychological Monographs*, 1966, *80*, 1–28.

SHEARN, D. F., & RANDOLPH, D. L.   Effects of reality therapy methods applied in the classroom. *Psychology in the schools*, 1978, *15* (1) 79–82.

CHAPTER SEVEN
BEHAVIOR THERAPIES

Each of the perspectives examined in this text so far has had one individual who was primarily responsible for its establishment and development—with the exception of the behavior therapies. Actually, even this is not a departure from the norm because there is not one behavior therapy; there are several. Because it is not possible to give a personal history of one "founder" of behavior therapy, and because to review the personal histories of all the behaviorists would fill a small library, I have decided to depart from the usual chapter outline in this instance. Instead of presenting a personal history, I will try to summarize the developmental history of behaviorism as a therapy. This will, of course, necessitate some treatment of the people responsible for that development.

HISTORICAL DEVELOPMENT

People have been concerned about behavior and behavior change as long as there have been people. Cave men, although driven by necessity to eat, surely found some foods more palatable than others and tended to return to the tastier foods. If so, they were following the principles of operant conditioning, even though there was no B. F. Skinner to tell them so. As psychology matured through the end of the nineteenth century and into the twentieth, a certain dissatisfaction with current modes of psychotherapy arose. Psychologists became aware of the need to bring greater precision to the study of personality and behavior change. Scientists such as Ivan Pavlov in Russia and E. L. Thorndike, John B. Watson, Edward Tolman, George Guthrie, Clark Hull, and B. F. Skinner in the United States began to experimentally study the laws of learning and the application of those laws to behavior.

The history of behavior therapy must begin with John B. Watson (even though Pavlov began his experiments before Watson's work), who coined the term "behaviorist" because he focused on observable behavior. During the period between the World Wars (1920 to 1940), behavioral psychology began to grow in America while dynamic psychology—especially psychoanalysis—flourished in Europe. Following World War II, the demand for mental health services dramatically increased; and, as a result, more and more scientifically trained clinical psychologists were allowed to practice psychotherapy (prior to that, they were permitted to do diagnostic testing only). This influx of scientific methodology together with a growing dissatisfaction with the methods and cost of dynamic therapies facilitated the growth of behavior therapy (Morse & Watson, 1977).

Thoreson and Coates (1978) make an intriguing analogy comparing the development of behavior therapy to the development of a human being. They point out that the adolescence of behavior therapy was punctuated by five major publications: Lindsley's (1956) use of operant conditioning with neurotic and psychotic patients, Wolpe's (1958) extension of classical conditioning to psychotherapy by reciprocal inhibition, Bandura's (Bandura & Walters, 1959) studies of the effects of vicarious learning on aggression, Eysenck's (1960) studies of alternative models of abnormal behavior, and Krumboltz's (1966) argument for behavioral objectives as the goals of counseling and psychotherapy.

Although all forms of behavior therapy are based on theories of learning and scientific methodology, it sometimes seems as if the only agreement is on the scientific methodology. There is widespread disagreement on which learning theory to apply when and precisely how the scientific method is best served. Despite this confusion, there emerged two major modalities, each with several subdivisions: classical conditioning and operant conditioning.

Theoretical Background

Classical conditioning. Ivan Pavlov (1849–1936) discovered what is now called classical or respondent conditioning through an unplanned event in an experiment. Using dogs as the experimental animals, he set out to study the physiology of the secretion of digestive fluids (he was a physiologist, not a psychologist). After presenting food to the dogs on several successive days, he discovered that the dogs began to salivate even before they saw, much less tasted, the food. At first he called these secretions "psychic" because he believed the dogs were *thinking* about the food. Being a true scientist, he neither accepted nor rejected this explanation without further evidence. In the course of gathering that evidence, he learned that after he had presented the food to the dogs several times, they associated the taste with his presence and finally with the sound of his footsteps! In modern terms, he had conditioned the dogs to salivate (response) to the sound of his footsteps (conditioned stimulus) as they would to the food itself (unconditioned stimulus). He then devised an experiment to test his hypothesis. He presented the food (unconditioned stimulus—UCS) to the dogs and, of course, they salivated (unconditioned response—UCR). Then for several times (trials), while presenting the food, he also rang a small bell (conditioned stimulus—CS). After the bell had been "paired" with the food over several trials, the dogs would salivate (conditioned response—CR) at the sound of the bell even though no food was presented. It has taken you less than three minutes to read about Pavlov's experiments. It took him thirty years to complete them!

The success of the classical conditioning procedure can be measured in either of two ways: the magnitude of the response (e.g., how much saliva was secreted), or the length of the latency period (e.g., how soon salivation occurs after the sound of the bell). Another aspect of classical conditioning discovered by Pavlov was that, after conditioning had been achieved, if the CS were not paired with the UCS, the magnitude of the response would gradually diminish until it disappeared entirely. He called this effect "extinction." Pavlov found that the process of extinction seemed to inhibit reconditioning. Finally, he discovered that other stimuli similar to the CS will also produce the CR. This effect is known as stimulus generalization.

Although it was now known that much of Pavlov's neurophysiological speculation was unsophisticated and even incorrect, the importance of his monumental work on classical conditioning cannot be minimized as one basis for behavior therapy (Morse & Watson, 1977).

Operant conditioning.   Operant or instrumental conditioning really begins with E. L. Thorndike (1874–1949) and his "law of effect." This law states that if a behavior is followed by rewarding consequences, then it is more likely that the behavior will be repeated. Operant conditioning takes place only through strengthening behaviors that have already occurred; it cannot be used to elicit totally new behaviors.

There are four basic principles of operant conditioning: reward (positive reinforcement), punishment, escape (negative reinforcement), and omission. A reward, or positive reinforcement, tends to increase the probability that the behavior it follows will recur because the reward is positively valued by the organism (Thorndike's law of effect). Punishment decreases the probability that the response will recur because the response is followed by painful or aversive stimuli. Negative reinforcement or escape increases the probability that the response will recur because it is followed by the removal of, or escape from, aversive stimuli. Omission decreases the probability that the response will recur because a reward usually present in the environment is absent after the response.

B. F. Skinner (1904–) and his students have made the major contributions to the study of operant conditioning. He prefers the term *operant conditioning* because he calls those responses that seem to have a common effect on the environment *operants*. Of equal importance with the concept of operant conditioning is his discovery of contingencies of reinforcement. Skinner and his students discovered that when behavioral responses (operants) were followed by varying stimuli (reinforcers) in varying patterns of presentation, they produced differential effects on learning. For example, the reinforcer might follow the operant every time, or every second, third, or "nth" time. This procedure is called a fixed ratio schedule. When the reinforcer is presented at the same specified interval, it is called a fixed interval schedule. A third method is the variable ratio schedule in which the reinforcement is varied from every "xth" time to every "yth" time and then back to every "xth time. Skinner's investigation of different schedules of reinforcement led to the discovery that the schedules themselves have a direct effect on learning.

There are some important distinctions between classical and operant conditioning. In classical conditioning, the reinforcement (US) is always presented by the experimenter, regardless of the behavior of the subject. The preconditions are that the UCS be paired with the CS and that both precede the response (CR). In operant conditioning, the reinforcement is presented *only* after the desired behavior has been emitted by the subject. In this case, the precondition is the environmentally determined relationship between reinforcement and response. If the desired behavior (or an approximation to it) is not emitted by the subject, no reinforcement is given (Morse & Watson, 1977).

Social learning theory. Albert Bandura, Walter Mischel, and Julian Rotter have attempted to integrate cognitive psychology principles with traditional learning theory in a system they call social or observational learning theory. The traditional theories (e.g., Pavlov, Skinner) explain learning through action: an individual—human or animal—learns because some action that he took has consequences for him and he is aware of both his action and the consequences. Bandura and his associates found that in addition to learning by action, we also learn by observation. It is much more efficient to teach a high school baseball player to hit effectively by watching films of Hank Aaron than by reinforcing successive approximations. According to Bandura (1969), the main effects of social learning are (a) the acquisition of new response patterns, (b) increased probability of the observer's performing (or eliminating) the observed behavior, and (c) previously learned responses are more likely to recur.

THEORY OF PERSONALITY

Definition of Terms

An **anxiety hierarchy**   is a list of stimuli on a theme, ranked according to the amount of anxiety they produce. The hierarchy provides the therapist with a graded set of anxiety-producing stimuli to present to the client in conjunction with a counterconditioning agent in order to remove the anxiety attached to the stimuli.

Assertiveness training   is a semistructured training approach that is characterized by its emphasis on acquiring assertiveness skills through practice. Assertiveness skills enable one to stand up for one's rights and beliefs more effectively.

Behavior rehearsal   is a therapeutic technique that consists of acting out short exchanges between client and counselor in settings from the client's life. The aim of such rehearsing is an effective preparation for the client to deal with a real "adversary," so that the anxiety that the latter evokes may be reciprocally inhibited.

Behavior therapy   is a therapeutic approach involving the application of principles of learning to change behavior. While behavior therapy and *behavior modification* are frequently used interchangeably, the former is associated principally with classical conditioning, while the latter is associated with operant conditioning.

Conditioning, aversive.   This is a behavioral technique involving the association of the client's symptomatic behavior with a painful stimulus until the unwanted behavior is inhibited. The aversive stimulus is typically a mild electric shock or an emetic mixture, such as antabuse.

Conditioning, classical.   Classical, or respondent, conditioning is a theory of learning derived from the work of Ivan Pavlov. Basically, it operates on the principle that a conditioned stimulus evokes a conditioned response similar to the unconditioned response, when that conditioned stimulus is paired with the unconditioned stimulus.

Conditioning, operant.   Operant, or instrumental, conditioning is a theory of learning derived from the work of B. F. Skinner. The essential difference between operant and classical conditioning is that, in operant conditioning, the unconditional stimulus follows some predetermined behavior when that behavior occurs spontaneously. In this procedure, the unconditioned stimulus is called a reinforcer.

Counterconditioning is a technique in which the experimenter (or therapist) presents an unconditioned stimulus that elicits an unconditioned response that is incompatible with the conditioned response and thus inhibits the conditioned response. For example, relaxation (UR) is incompatible with fear (CR).

Desensitization is a behavioral technique through which anxiety may be reduced by using relaxation as the counterconditioning agent. Graded anxiety-producing stimuli (in the anxiety hierarchy) are repetitively paired with a state of relaxation, until the connection between those stimuli and the response of anxiety is eliminated.

Discrimination is a learning process in which the relationships between stimuli and responses that have been generated through the process of generalization are broken down separately by combining extinction with reinforcement.

Extinction is the process of removing an unwanted response by failing to reinforce it.

Flooding is a therapeutic technique in which repeated presentation of the conditioned stimulus without reinforcement brings about extinction of the conditioned response. It differs from desensitization in that no counterconditioning agent is used.

Generalization operates on the assumption that a reinforcement that accompanies a particular stimulus not only increases the probability of that stimulus' eliciting a particular response, but also spreads the effect to other, similar stimuli. This process of generalization is extremely important, because no two stimuli or stimulus situations are exactly the same.

Imitative (social) learning is a process whereby an observer learns a particular response by watching some other person (the model) in the environment perform the response.

Neurotic behavior is any persistent habit of unadaptive behavior acquired by learning in a physiologically normal organism. Anxiety is usually the central constituent of this behavior, being invariably present in the causal situation.

Punishment is an interactional behavior involving the application of an aversive event as a result of the individual's engaging in a particular behavior. Punishment is applied only to those behaviors that are to be eliminated.

Reciprocal inhibition is the elimination or weakening of old responses by new ones. When a response is inhibited by an incompatible response and if a major drive-reduction follows, a significant amount of conditioned inhibition of the response will be developed.

Reinforcement is any specified event that strengthens the tendency for a response to be repeated.

Reinforcement, negative. This is a form of conditioning involving the removal of an aversive event as a result of the appearance (or disappearance) of the target behavior.

Reinforcement, positive. This is a form of conditioning in which the individual receives something pleasurable or desirable as a consequence of his behavior.

Response shaping is the process of moving from simple behaviors that are approximations of the final behavior to a final complex behavior. Through this process, certain behaviors that are close approximations of the desired behavior are reinforced, while other behaviors are not reinforced. At each stage of this process, a closer approximation of the desired behavior is required before reinforcement is given.

View of Human Nature

Behavioral theory holds that most human behavior is learned. Humans are basically neither "good" nor "bad," but begin life with a "clean slate," or *tabula rasa,* upon which nothing has been written. We are, however, reactive beings: we respond to environmental stimuli. Behavior—patterns of behavior—is learned through this interaction with the environment. Some behavior is at least in part determined by heredity or by the interaction of heredity and environment; but since this is beyond direct control, it is not of clinical interest to the behavioral counselor.

Unlike animals, humans are capable of cognition, which allows them to create new responses to the environment. We are not bound—as are animals—to past conditioning but are able to plan for and evaluate our responses to the environment. The behavioral counselor believes that all that can be known about human nature can be learned only from behavior and that learning is useful only if the behavior is operationally defined and the data quantified (Hosford, 1969).

Structure of Personality

Behaviorists show little interest in theory of personality, because, in their view, the hypothetical constructs that are the bases of such a theory offer no help in the development of techniques to change behavior. Some scorn personality theory because, they say, the clinician tends to fit the person and/or behavior to the theory, rather than adjusting the theory to conform to observed reality. In any case, behaviorists are interested in identifying, predicting, and (when appropriate) changing behavior, not in labeling individuals or inventing hypothetical constructs to explain what can be observed.

Development of Personality

Since the behaviorists are not interested in personality constructs, they have little to say about the development of personality as an entity in itself. They think rather in terms of behavior and behavior patterns, and they are much more interested in predicting behavior than in describing personality. According to learning theory, the individual learns, by "being there," that he or she is rewarded or punished by the quality of the psychological situation or environment. The quantity and quality of the reward or punishment—indeed, whether it be reward or punishment—varies from individual to individual. Thus, each individual learns through experience to perceive situations as satisfying (rewarding) or dissatisfying (punishing) and then reacts to that situation on the basis of his or her unique perception of it.

Development of Maladaptive Behavior

Operant behavior therapists generally view maladaptive behavior as not essentially different from any other behavior. Somehow, the individual has been conditioned by the environment to respond in a way considered inappropriate or maladaptive by society. Specifically, adaptive behaviors have not been learned and maladaptive behaviors have (Rychlak, 1981). In other words, maladaptive behavior is behavior that either no longer brings satisfaction to the individual or brings him or her into conflict with the environment.

The three initial questions for the behavior therapist are (a) "What behavior is maladaptive and with what frequency does it occur?" (b) "What aspects of the situation or environment are supporting and maintaining the symptom?" (c) "What situational or environmental events are amenable to manipulation?" It is important to note that there is no assumption concerning pathological processes in the client and no employment of the usual diagnostic categories and techniques.

THEORY OF COUNSELING

Rationale for Change

Behavioral counseling addresses itself to overt maladaptive behaviors or to internal processes directly related to such behaviors (e.g., anxiety or phobias). All of the behavior therapies are based on one or more theories of learning. According to those theories, all behavior—adapative and maladaptive—is learned through interaction with the environment. Thus, the same laws of learning that gave rise to a particular behavior can be applied to eliminate and/or replace that behavior. Treatment goals are quite specific, and procedures are "here-and-now," no-nonsense applications of scientific learning theory. This direct, limited-goal, focused-process approach to treatment gives behavioral counseling the appearance of a "band-aid" therapy. The behaviorists' response to such criticism is, in essence, "Judge us by our results, not by our appearance." Because of the behaviorists' scientific bent, direct assessment of results and revalidation of process are constant features of their therapy. Therefore, an empirically validated awareness of whether or not "it's working" is a part of the process (Rimm, 1977).

Process of Counseling

Behavioral counseling conceptualizes the counselor-client process variables as part of the learning environment and therefore as vital to counseling's effectiveness. While the various behavior therapies have a variety of steps in the process, four basic stages are common to all: assessment, goal setting, technique implementation, and evaluation-termination. Each of the four stages is considered necessary to the process, and all are interrelated. Each stage is concerned with both internal and external factors and with the relationships among them (La Fleur, 1979).

Assessment. The purpose of this initial stage of counseling is diagnostic: what is the client doing now, before treatment. It is a benchmark against which the effectiveness of treatment will be measured. This first assessment focuses on strengths and weaknesses in seven areas: (a) analysis of behavior problems as presented by the client, (b) analysis of the context in which the problem behaviors occur, (c) motivational analysis, (d) analysis of developmental history, (e) analysis of self-control, (f) analysis of social relationships, and (g) analysis of the social-cultural-physical environment (Kanfer & Saslow, 1969).

Since behaviors are not viewed as symptoms, diagnostic tests are not primary tools of assessment. Information is gathered from data provided by the client and possibly by others. The information is taken from interviews and questionnaires, survey and schedule responses, the client's records, rating scales, and direct observations of the client.

Goal setting. Using the information gathered and analyzed in the assessment phase, the counselor and client set mutually acceptable goals for counseling. The goals establish targets for both the counselor's and the client's actions. The goal-setting phase is composed of three steps: (a) helping clients to see their problems in terms of relevant and reachable goals: (b) considering clients' goals in terms of possible environmental constraints and in terms of developing reachable and measurable learning objectives; and (c) breaking down the objective into subobjectives and appropriately sequencing the subobjectives (La Fleur, 1979). Krumboltz (1966) identified three criteria for goals in behavioral counseling: (a) the client must desire the goal, (b) the counselor must be willing to help the client attain the goal, and (c) it must be possible to assess the degree to which the goal was attained. In order to meet these criteria, the goals must be stated as behavioral objectives: *who* will do it, *what* will they do, under *what circumstances* will it be done, and what is the *minimum level of performance* acceptable.

Technique implementation. In the next stage, the counselor and the client decide what are the best learning strategies or counseling techniques to implement in order to bring about the desired behavior change. The techniques chosen are fitted to the client's specific goal and are based on the information gathered during the assessment and goal-setting phases. Selection of the appropriate technique is based on the client's current internal and external environment—the factors that elicit and maintain the client's behavior. The counselor's task is to select techniques that focus on a given client's individualized learning (La Fleur, 1979).

Evaluation-termination.   In behavioral cunseling, evaluation is a continuous process, rather than one that occurs only at the end of therapy. The evaluation is made in terms of the client's current behavior. The specific client actions that form the basis for evaluation are the behavioral objectives detailed in the goal statements for each client.

Termination is more than just a cessation of counseling. It is a phase of counseling that includes (a) examination of the client's current behavior relative to the goal behaviors and desired levels of behavior; (b) exploration of the need for additional counseling; (c) helping the client transfer what was learned in counseling to other behaviors; and (d) providing a means for continued monitoring of the client's behaviors (La Fleur, 1979).

Goals of Counseling

Behavioral counseling goals are individualized behavioral goals for each client—there are no stated global goals for all clients. The goals are thus highly personalized so that the treatment "zeroed in" on a specific goal, may also be highly personalized. Examples of goals based on specific problems were presented by Krumboltz and Thoresen (1976) and summarized neatly by La Fleur (1979).

1. Even when the problem is the behavior of another party, the counselor must view it as the client's problem. In this case, the client has three options: (a) help the other person change behavior, (b) learn to live with it, or (c) withdraw from contact with that person.
2. If the problem is expressed as a feeling, the counselor can help the client learn new behaviors which are incompatible with the problem feeling.
3. When the problem is lack of a goal, the counselor can first help the client focus attention on specific behavioral goals and then acquire the skills needed to attain those goals.
4. When the client's stated goal is, in fact, undesirable, counselors can help their clients evaluate the consequences of achieving the stated goal and aid in the search for a possible alternative.
5. When clients are unaware that their behavior is inappropriate, their counselors can teach them how to seek and make use of feedback from the environment.
6. When the client is beset by a conflict of choices, the counselor can teach him or her systematic decision-making skills.

Training of the Counselor

According to Hollis & Wantz (1980), behavioral counseling ranked third behind eclectic and phenomenological orientations in terms of the number of training institutions identifying their "philosophical" orientation. In 1969, Woody lamented the fact that training opportunities for behavioral counselors were limited. By 1982, that limitation had been all but eliminated. Because of the diversity among behavioral counselors and therapists, it is not possible to point to any one organization or institution as the epitome of training in behavioral counseling. On the other hand, the leaders in the field are generally associated with graduate training institutions: Joseph Wolpe at Temple, Ray Hosford at the University of California at Santa Barbara, John Krumboltz and Carl Thoresen at Stanford, and Arnold Lazarus at Rutgers, to name only a few.

Function of the Counselor

From a learning theory framework, the counselor has the major responsibility for deciding on the particular course of the counseling: that is, what particular techniques will be used. Once the concern has been defined and agreed upon by both counselor and client, the counselor controls the process of counseling and accepts the responsibility for its outcome. It is the counselor's responsibility to launch the client on a course of action that will eventually help the client reach a resolution of his or her difficulty. In order to accomplish this end, the counselor must control the process. This is not an arbitrary, manipulative control that goes against the client's wishes; it is a control specifically designed to meet the goals of the c lient and is done with the client's full consent. The behavior therapist, then, assumes an active, directive role in treatment. He or she functions as a teacher, director, and expert in identifying maladaptive behavior and in prescribing curative procedures.

As early as 1958, Wolpe emphasized the need for the therapist to be accepting and empathic and to be nonjudgmental. Krumboltz (1966) also stressed the need for empathy and warmth. These counselor attitudes must be communicated to the client. The counselor must be warm and empathic and hold each individual in high regard. If these conditions are not present, it will not be possible to determine the client's difficulty or to gain the necessary cooperation of the client.

As a result of his thorough review of the literature, Krasner (1967) argued that the role of any psychotherapist, regardless of theoretical alliance, is really that of a "reinforcement machine." Whatever the therapist might think he is doing, he is basically involved in doling out social reinforcements. He further contended that, although most therapists are uncomfortable in the role of "controller" or "manipulator" of behavior, these terms accurately describe what the therapist's role actually is. He cited evidence showing that, by virtue of the therapist's role, the therapist has the power to influence and control the behavior and values of other human beings. For the therapist not to accept this situation and to be continually unaware of the influencing effects of her or his behavior on the clients would itself be "unethical" (p. 204).

Another important function is the therapist's role-modeling for the client. Bandura (1969) developed the point that one of the fundamental processes by which clients can learn new behavior is through imitation or the social modeling provided by the therapist.

PRACTICE OF COUNSELING

Each client has a unique reaction to the environment. Therefore, the counseling procedures differ from client to client, since each problem demands a specific technique. Most behavior is a response to environmental stimuli. Behavioral change requires the modification of the aspects of the environment that sustain the undesired behavior. The behavioral counselor derives his or her techniques from research in learning, not from theories of learning (Hosford, 1969). Rimm (1977) has neatly categorized behavioral techniques under the various learning theories upon which they are based.

Techniques: Operant Procedures

Self-control. Self-control problems fall into one of two categories: a surfeit of self-defeating behaviors (overeating, smoking, gambling, etc.) or a deficit of desired behaviors (e.g., study habits, exercises, social skills, etc.). A fundamental characteristic of both types of self-control problems is that there is *immediate* feedback for the undesirable behavior, whereas the reinforcement for changing the behavior is *delayed*—if it comes at all (e.g., when a student eats, talks, or naps instead of studying). The following are brief outlines of self-control programs applicable to each category of problem (Rimm, 1977):

A self-control program for the treatment of obesity might be as follows:

1. Establish a base line: record the frequency, amount, and type of food eaten and the circumstances surrounding the eating behavior.
2. Introduce the various procedures, usually one or two per week:
    (a) *Stimulus narrowing.* Eating at the dinner table *only*, and *only* at certain prescribed times; eating while engaging in other activities such as reading a newspaper or watching television is forbidden.
    (b) *Eating slowly*, savoring each mouthful, perhaps putting the eating utensils down for a few moments until the food is swallowed.
    (c) Removing food that requires *no preparation* from the house.
    (d) *Providing immediate self-reinforcement* (e.g., praising oneself, watching television) for appropriate eating behavior and also for engaging in activities that make eating impossible, such as going for a walk. The principle of immediate reinforcement for appropriate behavior is of the utmost importance in any self-control program.

The therapist and client meet once a week for several months. Once the long-term goal has been reached, they meet once a month or once every two months in order to ensure that good eating habits are maintained.

As a second illustration, consider the following brief outline of a self-control program designed to increase study behavior.

1. Establish a baseline.
2. Introduce the procedures, usually one or two per week:
   (a) *Changing the stimulus environment.* Find a place to study that is free of distractions.
   (b) *Cue strengthening.* Once a study area has been selected, the student should perform *no other activity* there, such as writing letters or reading for pleasure.
   (c) *Shaping and self-reinforcement.* The client is instructed to begin by studying for relatively brief periods of time, to stop *before* experiencing fatigue or boredom, and to provide some immediate reinforcement. Shaping refers to gradually increasing study time from day to day, perhaps only by a few minutes a day.
   (d) *Improving study efficiency.* Develop effective study habits, e.g., SQ3R.

Token economies.   Token economies can be applied to shape behavior when approval and other intangible reinforcers do not work. Under this system, appropriate behavior may be reinforced with tangible reinforcers (tokens) that can be later exchanged for desired objects or privileges. Tokens can be used to obtain candy, cigarettes, and toys, or to participate in certain programs. The use of tokens as reinforcers for appropriate behavior has several advantages: (a) tokens do not lose their incentive value, (b) tokens can reduce the delay that may exist between appropriate behavior and its reward, (c) tokens can be used as a concrete measure of motivation of a person to change certain behaviors, (d) the person receiving the tokens has the opportunity to decide how to use them, and (e) tokens tend to bridge the gap between life in an institution and in the real world (Ayllon & Azrin, 1968).

Biofeedback.   Biofeedback procedures are based on operant conditioning principles. Blood pressure, pulse rate, tension level, body temperature, and other quantifiable indicators of physical functioning are measured and presented to the client via gauges (meters) or lights or other visual and/auditory display. The client learns to control the level of the function by controlling the level of the light, sound, or meter.

Techniques: Classical Conditioning Procedures

Wolpe (1958) developed a system of "therapy by reciprocal inhibition," or counterconditioning, which involves developing a conditioned response incompatible with the existing, undesirable response. The two techniques most often associated with Wolpe are systematic desensitization and assertiveness training.

Systematic desensitization.   This technique is most effective against irrational fears or phobias. First, the therapist must determine whether the client's fears are, in fact, irrational. If it is established that the fear is indeed irrational, the therapist then decides whether the client has many or few major, phobias. This is necessary because there is evidence that desensitization is less effective with clients who are besieged by many phobias. The therapist next determines whether the client is able to vividly visualize scenes of his phobia and is able to experience anxiety while he imagines them. The client is then taught deep muscle relaxation in order to bring about a state of complete relaxation and absence of tension. The therapist talks the client through the exercise, which usually requires about 45 minutes, until the client learns to relax himself. When he has learned which of his muscles need relaxing and which do not, he may accomplish the task in as little as ten or fifteen minutes. Following relaxation training, the therapist and the client develop the client's anxiety hierarchy—one for each phobia (see Table 7.1).

Desensitization occurs when the client imagines the scenes of the hierarchy in realistic detail while in a state of relaxation. Behaviorists assume that relaxation is incompatible with anxiety, and thus, that fear will be deconditioned. They also assume that this deconditioning of fear will generalize to actual situations in the real world. The therapist begins with the scene evoking the least anxiety and works up the hierarchy until the client is able to imagine the most fearful scene without experiencing anxiety (Rimm, 1977).

Assertiveness training.   To be assertive means to stand up for your rights and beliefs without infringing on the rights and beliefs of others. The main method of assertiveness training is *behavior rehearsal;* i.e. practicing, with the help of the therapist, behaving more assertively (Rimm, 1977). The therapist begins by explaining the difference between assertive-

TABLE 7.1 Anxiety Hierarchy for a Snake Phobia (least to most fear)

See the word "snake" in a book
See a picture of a snake in a book
Hear someone talk about snakes
See a live snake in the zoo
See a dead snake as you walk down the road
See a live snake as you drive down the road
See a live snake as you walk down the road
Touch a dead snake on the road
Touch a live snake held by someone else
Hold a dead snake
Hold a live snake

ness, aggression, and nonassertiveness. Then he points out some of the reasons why people act in one of those three ways, emphasizing that the last two are ineffective and dissatisfying. The therapist and client then begin with the behavior rehearsal, in which they role-play "assertive situations," and the therapist offers feedback regarding the client's performance and models effective assertive behavior.

Most of the literature on assertiveness training (Alberti & Emmons, 1970; Jakubowski & Lange, 1978; Lange & Jakubowski, 1976) deals with problems associated with timidity. However, assertiveness training is also effective in assisting individuals who are either verbally or physically abusive. For example, the therapist might use assertiveness training to help a client express anger or resentment in an appropriate way, before it becomes uncontrollable (Rimm, 1977).

Aversive conditioning. Operant conditioners define punishment (negative reinforcement) as the removal or denial of a positive reinforcement. Classical conditioners, on the other hand, define punishment—they prefer the terms "aversive conditioning" or "avoidance conditioning"—as association of the symptomatic behavior with a painful stimulus until the unwanted behavior is inhibited. The aversive stimuli typically include punishment with an electric shock or emetic mixtures. Frequently, aversive or avoidance conditioning is more effective when combined with other procedures, such as assertiveness training and/or operant conditioning (Rimm, 1977).

Techniques: Social Learning Procedures

Bandura (1969) was the first to recognize the utility of models for social learning. Models can be used for three general client goals: (a) learning a new behavior, (b) weakening or strengthening a behavior already learned, or (c) response facilitation (perfecting a behavior). The effectiveness of the modeling procedure can be enhanced by using a model who is seen by clients as competent, prestigious, and similar to them. In addition, the client should be given an opportunity to practice the observed model behaviors following the presentation. This opportunity to imitate the modeled behavior will allow the client to receive feedback about the practice (La Fleur, 1979).

Techniques: Flooding and Implosive
Therapy Procedures

Systematic desensitization is done in a graduated fashion. In flooding, the client is asked to imagine the most fear-provoking scene until his fear response has been extinguished. In other words, the client is overwhelmed—flooded—with fear. Since, in flooding, relaxation is not used (as it is in desensitization), the fear is drained off by overuse. Implosive therapy also has the client imagine extremely fear-provoking scenes in the absence of relaxation. The difference between flooding and implosive therapy relates to the content of the scenes the client is required to imagine. Implosive therapy stresses the importance of psychoanalytic themes, such as unconscious fears relating to infantile rejection, sexuality, aggression, and such (Rimm, 1977; Stampfl & Levis, 1968).

Treatment Parameters

The treatment setting is very much like that of traditional psychotherapies, in that there are usually weekly sessions of 50-60 minutes in the therapist's office. Instead of a couch, behavior therapists like to have the client use a recliner, and the room lighting is controlled by a dimmer switch.

CASE STUDY

Because behavior therapy is unique to each client and because of the variety of techniques available for application to a given client problem, a typescript of one or two individual sessions or excerpts of a series of sessions would not be particularly instructive. However, in order to get some idea of the sequence of procedures, the following is presented (Fitchett & Sanford, 1976, pp. 139–140).

Mr. Jones was a thirty-one-year-old married man who had been convicted of "theft as a servant" ($27,200) and who had no previous convictions. He had embezzled his firm's money to pay debts he acquired through betting on horses. At the time the treatment program was begun, he had spent nine months in prison; and during that period he had received verbal psychotherapy, which had not weakened his interest in gambling. Although there was less opportunity to listen to races and to place bets in prison, he had taken part in illegal sweepstakes, listened to racing broadcasts when he was able, and placed two illegal bets. He approached one of the authors, who was a member of the prison classification board, because he was concerned about the possibility of his gambling's again becoming a problem when he was released.

An analysis of Mr. Jones' gambling behavior showed that he did not attend race meetings, but listened to the races on the radio. It was decided to focus treatment on this behavior. Base-line data collection included finding out how many times each week he listened to the races on the radio. This figure was expressed as a percentage of the total number of times that he could have listened in a week, because race broadcasts are not constant from week to week. The percentage of illegal prison sweepstakes in which he took part each week was also recorded.

To simulate "listening to a race broadcast," several such broadcasts were taped on twin-track tape. An old radio case with the knobs still attached was used to simulate a "working" radio. When the client switched the "radio" knob one way he heard the tape of the broadcast; switching the knob the other way allowed him to hear the other tape track.

The client had told us that his relationship with his wife was very important to him, and that, being in prison many miles from his home town, he missed her very much. We thus considered that a treatment program might be more effective if we could arrange for his wife to participate in it. One of the authors was able to interview her and gained her agreement to assist us in the treatment program. We recorded her telling her husband that she loved him and also being upset and saying, "Please don't bet on the races." Mr. Jones had also told us that he found the sound of a woman screaming very aversive, and this sound was simulated by a colleague and recorded.

Session 1. Preparation for the first session involved inserting the wife's aversive comments and the woman's scream into the tapes of the race broadcasts. Placement of these aversive stimuli was random so that the client could not learn to predict when the aversive stimuli were going to occur. There was one session of five practice trials, during which the client listened to the race broadcasts and the aversive stimuli. He was not allowed to turn the radio off or to leave the room.

Sessions 2-6. During the second part of treatment Mr. Jones could escape the aversive stimuli by turning off the racing broadcast, which automatically turned on the other tape track, from which he heard light music and at random intervals his wife's voice telling him that she loved him. Thus he was positively reinforced for turning off the race broadcast. There were five sessions during this stage, and each session consisted of five practice trials.

Session 7. Session 7 was similar to the preceding ones, except that not all the escape responses were reinforced. This stage consisted of one session of five trials.

Prison-staff members were asked to observe whether or not Mr. Jones listened to any race broadcasts outside treatment sessions. He was also asked to make a report on his own "listening to races" behavior. To compare progress with base-line data, we translated the information received from staff and Mr. Jones into a percentage of "racing broadcasts listened to."

Applications

Which behavior therapy—as well as which behavior therapy technique—is chosen by a given therapist or counselor will depend on that individual's behavioral orientation and on the nature of the client's problem. For example, with a phobic client, one counselor might use systematic desensitization, while another might prefer modeling implosive therapy or a cognitive-behavioral method. A similar diversity of treatment is available to the school counselor working with classroom discipline problems, the marriage counselor treating sexual dysfunction, the therapist shaping the behavior of mental hospital inpatients, or a parent attempting to get a teenager to (you fill in the blank).

CRITIQUE

Research Support

While there have been thousands of controlled investigations of the various behavior therapies, what follows is a small sample of some of the more prominent studies supporting each of the techniques.

Self-control. Bandura and Perloff (1967) indicated that even with preadolescent children, self-reward is an effective means of strengthening certain responses: the subjects "worked" for their rewards rather than rewarding themselves for doing nothing. To date, most self-control programs have dealt with obesity or smoking. In general, the results have been positive (Hall, 1972; Mahoney, Moura, & Wade, 1973). Subjects in such weight programs typically lose about one pound per week. Other studies suggest that self-control procedures may be effective in the reduction of cigarette smoking (Sachs, Bean, & Morrow, 1970).

Token economies. There is clear evidence that institutionalized mental patients behave more appropriately under token economies (Ayllon & Azrin, 1968). Token economies have also been shown to be successful in controlling the behavior of delinquent and predelinquent boys (Phillips, Phillips, Fixen, & Wolf, 1971). Unfortunately, there is no assurance that the appropriate behavior shaped by such a system will generalize to the natural environment.

Systematic desensitization. The vast majority of investigations have supported the value of this method. Among the classic studies are those of Paul (1966) dealing with the fear of public speaking; Davison's (1968) investigation of snake phobias; and Emery and Krumboltz's (1967) of test anxiety. Not all data have been supportive. There is some controversy over which elements of systematic desensitization are truly essential for fear reduction. Although most writers agree that desensitization is an effective therapeutic tool, precisely *why* it works is not yet resolved (Kazdin, & Wilcoxon, 1976).

Assertiveness training. Controlled studies of this technique have only recently been made (Hersen, Eisler, & Miller, 1974; McFall & Lillesand, 1971; McFall & Twentyman, 1973). Occasionally, negative results are obtained. For example, Young, Rimm, and Kennedy (1973) found that reinforcement for improved assertiveness failed to enhance the assertive behavior of their subjects; and McFall and Twentyman (1973) showed that modeling added little to assertiveness as a therapeutic procedure. In view of the power of reinforcement and modeling in the control of human behavior, it is clear that additional research examining these factors in assertiveness training is needed. On the other hand, assertiveness training lends itself readily to group treatment, and there is evidence suggesting that it is effective in such a setting (Hedquist & Weingold, 1970; Rathus, 1972; Rimm, Hill, Brown, & Stuart, 1974). The Rimm (et al.) study is particularly interesting in that the subjects were aggressive rather than timid.

Participant modeling. The results of participant modeling studies are generally quite impressive, especially for fear of specific animals (Bandura, Blanchard, & Ritter, 1969; Rimm & Mahoney, 1969). When the phobic stimuli are limited and specific, this technique is perhaps the most potent and rapid means of fear reduction.

Flooding and implosive therapy. Experiments employing flooding procedures have produced mixed results. De Moor (1970) found little difference between flooding and desensitization, although there was some indication at a later follow-up test that desensitization was more effective. Rachman (1966) found flooding to be totally ineffective, while Blanchard (1975) obtained positive results with it. The results for implosive therapy are also mixed. Positive results were reported by McCutcheon and Adams (1975), whereas negative results were obtained by Hodgson and Rachman (1970). The results are conflicting, although no studies yet show implosive therapy to be superior to systematic desensitization. Most authors agree that both of these techniques should be used only by highly skilled practitioners under controlled conditions.

Avoidance conditioning. Avoidance conditioning (often including anxiety-relief conditioning) has been used with some success in the treatment of homosexuality (Feldman & MacCulloch, 1971); and Blake (1965) reported somewhat positive findings with alcoholics, although the study was poorly controlled. Sexual deviations such as transvestitism and fetishism have been treated with some success using aversive control procedures (Lavin, Thorpe, Barker, Blakemore, & Conway, 1961).

Cognitive approaches. Several experimental investigations (Meichenbaum & Goodman, 1969; Rimm & Litvak, 1969; Russell & Brandsma, 1974) have provided evidence that cognitive activities, such as self-verbalizations, do exert some control over the way people feel and behave. The work of Meichenbaum and his associates (Meichenbaum & Cameron, 1973) and Rimm (Rimm, Saunders, & Westel, 1975) demonstrated that procedures aimed at altering highly specific self-verbalizations may be effective in reducing phobic behavior and other patterns of maladaptive responding.

Evaluation

This perspective is difficult to evaluate for the same reason that it was difficult to present: it is not one perspective but a collection of perspectives (not even an amalgamation) with a more or less unifying theme (learning theory). But it is difficult to evaluate for another reason, too. Many of the criteria used in the evaluation of other perspectives either do not apply or do not apply in the same ways here as there. For example, the meaning of "cure" is not the same as in other perspectives; the mode of, and rationale for treatment are different. How do you compare an approach whose aim is to rid this client of a specific phobia or that one of a bad habit, with an approach whose aim is to lead its clients to self-actualization, responsibility, or social interest? Apples and potatoes are both nutritious food, but how do you compare their unique contributions to the human body? I suppose the most honest answer is "cautiously."

As Carkhuff and Berenson (1977) pointed out, the major contributions of the various behavioral approaches seem to lie in their systematic and scientific approach to treatment, their well-defined criteria for outcome (in behavioral terms), and their capacity for offering some viable hope to a segment of the client population offered little or no hope by the other perspectives: the many wretched individuals on the back wards of mental hospitals.

More than the other perspectives, the behavioral approach provides clients with an understanding of the treatment process by supplying them with concrete information about their role in that process and their level of progress through it. It also provides them with useful information about the reinforcements in their environment that maintain both adaptive and maladaptive behaviors.

The major limitations seem to be the "flip side" of some of its advantages. The very specificity that focuses treatment on a specific behavior or set of behaviors introduces the risk that the treatment is limited to facilitating a minimal coping with the world. The power of the techniques opens the way to abuse of that power by an unethical practitioner. Finally, in my opinion, the major objection to the behavioral approaches is that they take the major responsibility for effecting a "cure" away from the client and give it to the counselor.

REFERENCES

ALBERTI, R. E., & EMMONS, M. L. *Your perfect right* (2nd ed.). San Luis Obispo, CA: Impact Press, 1970.
AYLLON, T., & AZRIN, N. H. *The token economy: A motivational system for therapy and rehabilitation.* New York: Appleton-Century-Crofts, 1968.

BANDURA, A. *Principles of behavior modification.* New York: Holt, Rinehart, & Winston, 1969.

BANDURA, A., BLANCHARD, E. B., & RITTER, R. The relative efficacy of desensitization and modeling approaches for inducing behavioral, affective, and attitudinal changes. *Journal of Personality and Social Psychology,* 1969, *9,* 173–199.

BANDURA, A., & PERLOFF, B. Relative efficacy of self-monitored and externally imposed reinforcement systems. *Journal of Personality and Social Psychology,* 1967, *7,* 111–116.

BANDURA, A., & WALTERS, R. H. *Adolescent aggression.* New York: Ronald Press, 1959.

BLAKE, B. G. The application of behavior therapy to the treatment of alcoholism. *Behavior Research and Therapy,* 1965, *3,* 75–85.

BLANCHARD, E. B. Brief flooding treatment for a debilitating revulsion. *Behavior Research and Therapy,* 1975, *13,* 193–195.

CARKHUFF, R. R., & BERENSON, B. G. *Beyond counseling and therapy* (2nd ed.). New York: Holt, Rinehart, & Winston, 1977, Chap. 8.

DAVISON, G. E. Systematic desensitization as a counterconditioning process. *Journal of Abnormal Psychology,* 1968, *73,* 91–99.

DeMOOR, W. Systematic desensitization vs. prolonged high intensity stimulation (flooding). *Journal of Behavior Therapy and Experimental Psychiatry,* 1970, *1,* 45–52.

EMERY, J. R., & KRUMBOLTZ, J. D. Standard vs. individual hierarchies in desensitization to reduce test anxiety. *Journal of Counseling Psychology,* 1967, *14,* 204–209.

EYSENCK, H. J. *Behavior therapy and the neuroses.* New York: Pergamon, 1960.

FELDMAN, M., & MacCULLOCH, M. *Homosexual behavior: Theory and assessment.* Oxford: Pergamon Press, 1971.

FITCHETT, S. M., & SANFORD, D. A. Treatment for habitual gambling. In J. D. Krumboltz & C. E. Thoresen (Eds.), *Counseling methods.* New York: Holt, Rinehart, & Winston, 1976, 138–144.

HALL, S. M. Self-control and therapist control in behavioral treatment of overweight women. *Behavior Research and Therapy,* 1972, *10,* 59–68.

HEDQUIST, F. J., & WEINGOLD, B. K. Behavioral group counseling with socially anxious and unassertive college students. *Journal of Counseling Psychology,* 1970, *17,* 237–242.

HERSEN, M., EISLER, R. M., & MILLER, P. M. An experimental analysis of generalization in assertive training. *Behavior Research and Therapy,* 1974, *12,* 295–310.

HODGSON, R. J., & RACHMAN, S. An experimental investigation of the implosion techniques. *Behavior Research and Therapy,* 1970, *8,* 21–27.

HOLLIS, J. W., & WANTZ, R. A. (EDS.). *Counselor preparation 1980: Programs, personnel, trends* (4th ed.). Muncie, IN: Accelerated Development, Inc., 1980.

HOSFORD, R. E., Behavioral counseling: A contemporary overview. *The Counseling Psychologist,* 1969, *1* (4), 1–32.

JAKUBOWSKI, P., & LANGE, A. J. *The assertive option: Your rights and responsibilities.* Champaign, IL: Research Press, 1978.

KANFER, F. H., & SASLOW, G. Behavioral diagnosis. In C. M. Franks (Ed.), *Behavior therapy: Appraisal and status.* New York: McGraw-Hill, 1969.

KAZDIN, A. E., & WILCOXON, L. A. Systematic desensitization and non-specific treatment effects: A methodological evaluation. *Psychological Bulletin,* 1976, *83,* 729–758.

146   Behavior Therapies

Krasner, L.   The reinforcement machine. In B. G. Berenson & R. R. Carkhuff (Eds.), *Sources of gain in counseling and psychotherapy.* New York: Holt, Rinehart, & Winston, 1967.

Krumboltz, J. D.   Behavioral goals for counseling. *Journal of Counseling Psychology,* 1966, *13,* 153–159.

Krumboltz, J. D.   Changing the behavior of behavior changers. *Counseling Education and Supervision,* 1967 (Special Issue).

Krumboltz, J. D., & Thoresen, C. E. (Eds.).   *Counseling methods.* New York: Holt, Rinehart, & Winston, 1976.

Lafleur, N. K.   Behavioral views of counseling. In H. M. Burks, & B. Stefflre. *Theories of counseling* (3rd ed.). New York: McGraw-Hill, 1979, Chap. 6.

Lange, A. J., & Jakubowski, P.   *Responsible assertive behavior: Cognitive behavioral procedures for trainers.* Champaign, IL: Research Press, 1976.

Lavin, N. I., Thorpe, J. G., Barker, J. C., Blakemore, C. B., & Conway, C. G.   Behavior therapy in a case of transvestism. *Journal of Nervous and Mental Disease,* 1961, *133,* 346–353.

Lindsley, O. R.   Operant conditioning methods applied to research in chronic schizophrenia. *Psychiatric Research Reports,* 1956, *5,* 118–153.

Mahoney, M. J., Moura, N., & Wade, T.   The evaluative efficacy of self-reward, self-punishment, and self-monitoring techniques for weight loss. *Journal of Consulting and Clinical Psychology,* 1973, *40,* 404–407.

McCutcheon, B. A., & Adams, H. E.   The physiological basis of implosive therapy. *Behavior Research and Therapy,* 1975, *13,* 93–100.

McFall, R. M., & Lillesand, D. B.   Behavior rehearsal with modeling and coaching in assertion training. *Journal of Abnormal Psychology,* 1971, *77,* 313–333.

McFall, R. M., & Twentyman, C. T.   Four experiments on the relative contributions of rehearsal, modeling, and coaching to assertion training. *Journal of Abnormal Psychology,* 1973, *81,* 199–218.

Meichenbaum, D. H., & Cameron, R.   Training schizophrenics to talk to themselves: A means of developing attitudinal controls. *Behavior Therapy,* 1973, *4,* 515–534.

Meichenbaum, D. H., & Goodman, J.   Reflection—impulsivity and verbal control of motor behavior. *Child Development,* 1969, *40,* 785–797.

Morse, S. J., & Watson, R. I., Jr.   An introduction to behavior therapy. In S. J. Morse & R. I. Watson, Jr. (Eds.), *Psychotherapies: A comparative casebook.* New York: Holt, Rinehart, and Winston, 1977, Chap. 15.

Paul, G. L.   *Insight vs. desensitization in psychotherapy: An experiment in anxiety reduction.* Stanford, Calif.: Stanford University Press, 1966.

Phillips, E. L., Phillips, E. S., Fixen, D. L., & Wolf, M. M.   Achievement place: Modification of the behaviors of predelinquent boys within a token economy. *Journal of Applied Behavior Analysis,* 1971, *4,* 45–59.

Rachman, S.   Studies in desensitization—II: Flooding. *Behavior Research and Therapy,* 1966, *4,* 1–6.

Rathus, S. A.   An experimental investigation of assertive training in a group setting. *Journal of Behavior Therapy and Experimental Psychiatry,* 1972, *3,* 81–86.

Rimm, D. C.   Behavior therapy. In D. C. Rimm & J. W. Somervill (Eds.), *Abnormal psychology.* New York: Academic Press, 1977.

Rimm, D. C., Hill, G. A., Brown, N. N., & Stuart, J. E.   Group assertive training in the treatment of expression of inappropriate anger. *Psychological Reports,* 1974, *34,* 791–798.

RIMM, D. C., & LITVAK, S. B.   Self-verbalization and emotional arousal. *Journal of Abnormal Psychology*, 1969, *74*, 181–187.

RIMM, D. C., & MAHONEY, M. J.   The application of reinforcement and participant modeling procedures in the treatment of snake-phobic behavior. *Behavior Research and Therapy*, 1969, *7*, 369–376.

RIMM, D. C., SAUNDERS, W., & WESTEL, W.   Thought-stopping and covert assertion in the treatment of snake phobias. *Journal of Consulting and Clinical Psychology*, 1975, *43*, 92–93.

RUSSELL, P. L., & BRANDSMA, J. M.   A theoretical and empirical investigation of rational-emotive and classical conditioning theories. *Journal of Consulting and Clinical Psychology*, 1974, *42*, 389–397.

RYCHLAK, J. F.   *Introduction to personality and psychotherapy* (2nd ed.). Boston: Houghton Mifflin, 1981.

SACHS, L. B., BEAN, H., & MORROW, J. E.   Comparison of smoking treatments. *Behavior Therapy*, 1970, *1*, 465–472.

SKINNER, B. F.   *Science and human behavior.* New York: Macmillan, 1953.

STAMPFL, T. G., & LEVIS, D. J.   Implosive therapy—A behavior therapy? *Behavioral Research and Therapy*, 1968, *6*, 31–36.

THORESEN, C. E., & COATES, T. J.   What does it mean to be a behavior therapist? *The Counseling Psychologist*, 1978, *7* (3), 3–21.

WOLPE, J.   *Psychotherapy by reciprocal inhibition.* Stanford, CA: Stanford University Press, 1958.

WOODY, R. H.   Behavioral counseling: Role definition and professional training. In *The Counseling Psychologist*, 1969, *1* (4), 84–88.

YOUNG, E. R., RIMM, D. C., & KENNEDY, T. D   An experimental investigation of modeling and verbal reinforcement in the modification of assertive behavior. *Behavior Research and Therapy*, 1973, *11*, 317–319.

CHAPTER EIGHT
GESTALT THERAPY

If you thought Albert Ellis was unique, wait until you meet Fritz Perls! He was, by his own acknowledgment, a physician, a psychoanalyst, a scholar, a pilot, and a "dirty old man" (Perls, 1969c). A phrase that keeps recurring in his autobiography is, "Don't push the river; it flows by itself." That phrase seems to epitomize Perls' philosophy of life. The autobiography is written in stream-of-consciousness style without page numbers. That makes it a bit difficult to cite, but it shows Perls' reluctance to be pinned down. The title of the autobiography was taken from the first line of a poem written by Perls (1969c):

> In and out the garbage pail
> Put I my creation,
> Be it lively, be it stale,
> Sadness or elation.
>
> Joy and sorrow as I had
> Will be re-inspected;
> Feeling sane and being mad,
> Taken or rejected.
>
> Junk and chaos, come to halt!
> 'Stead of wild confusion,

Form a meaningful gestalt
Of my life's conclusion.

As you read this chapter, remember: don't push the river.

HISTORICAL DEVELOPMENT

Personal Background

Frederick Solomon "Fritz" Perls (1893-1970) was born in Berlin of lower-middle-class Jewish parents. He has not revealed much about his early years or about his family. He had a younger sister whom he loved and an older sister whom he did not love. He saw his father's selective participation in Judaism as hypocritical. He received his M.D. degree from Frederich Wilhelm University in 1920. He studied at both the Vienna and Berlin Institutes of Psychoanalysis under Wilhelm Reich, Otto Fenichel, and Karen Horney. In Berlin he met and married Lore (Laura) who was a graduate student of Kurt Goldstein, the gestalt psychologist.

When Hitler's pressure on Jews in Germany became intolerable (about 1933) Perls left for Amsterdam. He remained there a year under conditions not unlike those of Anne Frank. In 1934, he fled Holland—barely ahead of the Nazis—and took a position as a psychoanalyst in Johannesburg, South Africa. He founded the South African Institute for Psychoanalysis in 1935. With the rise of apartheid in 1946, Perls left South Africa for New York. In 1952, he, his wife Laura, and Paul Goodman founded the New York Institute for Gestalt Therapy. He became dissatisfied with life in New York in general and life with Laura in particular; and in 1956, he went to Miami with one of his patients. After several other liaisons in several other cities, he joined the staff of the Esalen Institute at Big Sur, California, as resident associate psychiatrist (1964). He remained there until 1969, when he moved to Vancouver Island, British Columbia. He was attempting to establish a gestalt commune there when he died in March 1970 (Patterson, 1980; Perls, 1969c).

Theoretical Background

Perls began his psychiatric career as a Freudian psychoanalyst, and he never fully resolved his quasi-oedipal relationship with Freud. As a result, there are many psychoanalytic influences evident in gestalt therapy. In the 1920s, Perls met Max Wertheimer, Wolfgang Kohler, and Kurt Koffka. These theorists were developing a system of psychology that was diametrically opposed to the analytical stimulus-response behaviorism that was beginning to be popular in Germany at this time. They conceived of behavior as based on the concept that psychological phenomena are organized and synthesized wholes, rather than constellations of specific parts. They called their system gestalt psychology.

Gestalt is a German word with no exact English equivalent. *Configuration, structure, unique pattern,* or *meaningful organized whole* are approximations of its meaning. The word implies that the whole is something more than, or different from, the sum of its parts. The organization of the component parts creates a structure that has its own unique character. In the act of perceiving or experiencing, we add a meaning or importance to the incoming stimuli by virtue of the particular patterns or gestalts that we form.

Gestalt psychology focused principally on perceptual and learning processes, but Perls translated several of the principles of gestalt psychology into gestalt therapy. Passons (1975, pp. 12–13) outlined the major principles.

> 1. A person tends to seek closure. A gestalt that is incomplete or unfinished demands attention until it is completed. A total conversation is disrupted when someone asks, "Who starred in that film?" and no one can remember. Finally someone recalls the name, the gestalt is completed, and the conversation continues.
>
> 2. A person will complete gestalts in accordance with current needs. Flash a circular object in front of playful children and they will report it as a ball; hungry children may perceive an apple or a hamburger.
>
> 3. A person's behavior is a whole that is greater than the sum of its specific components. Listening to a piece of music is a process that involves something more than hearing specific notes, just as a melody is more than a constellation of notes.
>
> 4. A person's behavior can be meaningfully understood only in context. The cowering of a child when approached by a teacher carrying a ruler is understood in the light of beatings by parents with sticks.
>
> 5. A person experiences the world in accordance with the principle of figure and ground. When regarding a painting, he or she attends to colors and shapes as figure. At that moment, the frame and the wall are ground. If attention is shifted to the frame, it becomes figure and the painting is ground.

Gestalt therapy is, philosophically, a form of existentialism. Existentialism is concerned with how people experience their immediate existence, while gestalt psychology is concerned with how that existence is perceived. In gestalt therapy, Perls united the two.

Perls assimilated ideas from other theorists as well. The idea of experiencing feelings by acting them out was borrowed from Moreno's psychodrama. Rogers' idea of feedback as a therapeutic agent was utilized through including body posture, voice tone, eye movements, feelings, and gestures. Throughout gestalt therapy, there are examples of existential and humanistic views of human nature from Eastern religion and thought (Passons, 1975; Stewart, 1974).

THEORY OF PERSONALITY

Definition of Terms

Acknowledgment.   Through acknowledgment, individuals discover themselves. Personal acknowledgment leads children to develop a sense of self and an appreciation of their own existence.

Adaptation.   This is the process by which the individual discovers the boundaries within which he exists and differentiates self from nonself.

Aggression.   Aggression is the organism's means of contacting its environment to satisfy its needs and of meeting resistance to the satisfaction of its needs. Its purpose is not destruction, but simply overcoming resistance.

Approbation.   Approbation is a process through which people develop splits in their personalities and create a self-image: a notion of self based on external standards. Approbation interferes with the development of a sound and healthy notion of self.

Awareness.   Awareness is the process of observing and attending to your thoughts, feelings, and actions, including body sensations, as well as visual and auditory perceptions. It is seen as a flowing panorama that constitutes your "now" experience.

Figure.   Figure is that which occupies the center of a person's attentive awareness—what the person is now paying attention to.

Ground.   That part of the perceptual field that is not "figure" is identified as ground. Taken together, figure and ground constitute a gestalt.

Introjection.   Introjection is the uncritical acceptance of other people's concepts, standards of behavior, and values. The person who habitually introjects does not develop his or her own personality.

Organismic self-regulation.   This is the process by which an individual, confronted by either an external demand or an internal need, strives to reduce tension by maintaining the organismic balance between demands and needs.

Projection.   Projection is the process by which the individual places in the outside world the parts of the personality that the organism refused (or is unable) to identify.

Retroflection.   This is a process by which some function that originally is directed from the individual towards the world changes direction and is bent back towards the originator. The result is a split between the self as doer and the self as receiver.

Self.   The self is the creative process that leads the individual to actualizing behaviors by responding to emergent needs and environmental pressures. The fundamental characteristic of the self is the formation and distinction of gestalts.

Self-image.   The self-image is the part of the personality that hinders creative growth by imposing external standards.

View of Human Nature

Despite his psychoanalytic training (he would probably say "because of it") Perls believed that people can rid themselves of "historical baggage" and live fully in the present. He believed that each person is potentially free to make his own choices and is responsible for his own behavior (Elson, 1979).

Self-actualization. Perls' optimistic view of people is based on his assumption that all living things are inherently ordered toward self-actualization; i.e., to bring their selfs (not "themselves") from potency to act. He saw this, of course, as an unending process: we are constantly becoming; we have never fully "arrived." This innate self-actualizing tendency is the motivation for all human behavior; all other needs are rooted in it (Elson, 1979). For some gestaltists, this becoming is not a striving to become what one is not, but rather being what one is.

Perhaps a brief rather shallow philosophical digression will hone your understanding of "self-actualization." My dictionary is balanced precariously at the edge of my desk—51 percent on, but 49 percent off. It is *actually* on the desk. "Being-on-the-deskness" is present in the book right now. However, also present in the book is the possibility—potential—of falling off the desk. So, while the book is on the desk, there are two conditions present in it: "being-on-the-deskness" is there in act; "falling-off-the-deskness" is there in potency. If my elbow nudges the book off the desk, the same two conditions are in it, but in opposite order. Now "falling-off-the-deskness" is in act, and—until I pick it up and put it back—"being-on-the-deskness" is in potency. When we speak of self-actualization, then, we are talking about bringing to act, to realization, the parts of the self that are there now only in potency. Unlike the book, which, once fallen, must remain until I pick it up, the self is capable of an unlimited series of transformations from potency to act.

Self-regulation. Perls, Hefferline, and Goodman (1951) held that every organism tries to reach homeostasis by gratifying or eliminating needs that arise and upset the balance. They called this homeostatic process 'organismic self-regulation." When it experiences some form of pain—imbalance—the organism can regulate itself either by discharging tension through intense emotional experience or by meeting the need. The implication is that, although we have the capacity to know of our own imbalance and to right it, we actually do so only by living fully in the here-and-now. Thus, the core of organismic self-regulation is awareness (Elson, 1979).

Awareness. Awareness is the key to gestalt theory: the entire approach is based on the quantity and quality of the client's awareness. Avoiding awareness only exacerbates the problem, because, instead of directing energy towards meeting the need, one spends it in suppressing the need or the emotions that announced the need.

Perls was more interested in action and experience than in philosophy. He recognized the importance of philosophy of gestalt therapy, but he was ambivalent about developing a systematic philosophy of gesalt therapy. Yet, whether they are explicit or implicit, there are assumptions about the nature of humanity and experience in gestalt therapy. Several primary assumptions about the nature of man form the base of gestalt therapy (Passon, 1975, p. 14):

1. Man is a whole who is (rather than has) a body, emotions, thoughts, sensations, and perceptions, all of which function interrelatedly.
2. Man is part of his environment and cannot be understood outside of it.
3. Man is proactive rather than reactive. He determines his own responses to external and proprioceptive stimuli.
4. Man is capable of being aware of his sensations, thoughts, emotions, and perceptions.
5. Man, through self-awareness, is capable of choice and is thus responsible for covert and overt behavior.
6. Man possesses the wherewithal and resources to live effectively and to restore himself through his own assets.
7. Man can experience himself only in the present. The past and the future can be experienced only in the now through remembering and anticipating.
8. Man is neither intrinsically good nor bad.

Structure of Personality

According to Perls, personality results from an individual's interaction with his perceived environment. From the moment of birth onward, an individual is interacting with the environment. Growth occurs when material from the environment is assimilated through adaptation, acknowledgment, and approbation. Throughout this process, the individual endeavors to meet current needs by forming gestalts (Hansen, Stevic, & Warner, 1982).

Personality is composed of three separate parts: self, self-image, and being. Being is the essential existence of the organism, analogous to Rogers' "organism"; the self is the creative aspect of personality that promotes actualization; the self-image is the darker side of personality that hinders growth. Self and self-image seem to have some aspects of the right brain/left brain configuration; or, in another metaphor, self and self-image seem to share some properties of ego and superego, respectively. In any case, when the individual contacts the environment, either self or self-image develops. Since each has equal potential for development, an internal conflict arises between what the self wants to do and what the self-image says *ought* to be done (Hansen et al., 1982).

Development of Personality

Perls did not describe personality development in the same organized progression as Freud or Rogers, because he did not conceive of it that way. The development of personality, for Perls, was not a sequence of chronological stages, nor was it a clear path to some specified end point. Rather, it was a continuous unfolding, an ongoing actualizing of potential brought about by "creative adjustments" (Perls et al., 1951). The emphasis is on the process of moving from environmental to self-support; this process is Perl's definition of maturity (Perls, 1969b). One of the major facilitators of growth, according to Perls (1969b), is frustration—more precisely, the opportunity to overcome frustration. When parents protect children from frustration, the children learn to direct their energies to avoiding rather than toward overcoming the frustration. This is tantamount to preventing growth. Learning to overcome frustration is essential to growth. If parents would make appropriate use of both frustration and support, their children would learn how to develop their own resources for independent functioning. This facilitates the development of the self and the curtailing of the self-image. Unfortunately, parents frequently shield their children from frustration, thus facilitating the development of the self-image and curtailing the development of the self. This most often occurs when parental support is given in the form of approval. Because it is parental approval, the children perceive it as a "should" and turn it into an external standard to be measured up to. Thus, instead of profitably using their energies for creative growth, they waste them trying to measure up to someone else's standard. It is this internalized standard that Perls calls the "self-image."

Both self and self-image grow though interaction with the environment. When the self-image "takes charge," people lacking confidence in their innate capacities, attempt to exercise deliberate control over the self-regulating tendency, thus blocking awareness and frustrating self-actualization. On the other hand, when they identify with the self, instead of trying to control the situation—and themselves—they simply adjust creatively to the situation, becoming what they are rather than futilely trying to become what they are not. The healthy personality, then, could be described as a gestalt: a unified, meaningful whole. Wholeness, however, is achieved only through identification with, and emergence of, the self (Elson, 1979).

Development of Maladaptive Behavior

Individuals who exhibit pathological behavior attempt to override their spontaneous self-regulating tendencies by exercising deliberate control over themselves. Rather than trying to be self-actualizing, they try to actualize their self-image—a distorted and unrealistic view of themselves (Ward & Rouzer, 1974). There are several characteristic ways in which people manifest maladaptive behavior, each of which involves identification with the self-image. Gestalt therapy sees all maladaptive behavior, regardless of the form it takes, as a growth disorder, an abandonment of self for self-image (Elson, 1979).

Projection.   Unacceptable thoughts, feelings, attitudes, or actions that are seen as inconsistent with the self-image may be projected onto others. What has been projected is then seen as being directed back toward the projector (Elson, 1979). Perls said it best: "We sit in a house lined with mirrors and think that we are looking out" (Perls, 1969a, p. 158).

Introjection. The "holes" that result from alienating parts of the self by projection are filled up by introjections: faulty identifications based on external demands. Projection deals with the "shalt nots" of the self-image, and introjection handles the "shalts."

Retroflection. In projection, a part of the self is projected onto the environment; in introjection, a part of the environment is directed toward the self; in retroflection, both happen. Retroflection usually occurs when behavior directed toward the environment is unsuccessful and then is redirected back (retro-) toward the self, usually in a disguised form. For example, a person who feels a need for nourishment from the environment may typically stand or sit with his arms wrapped around himself as if hugging himself, since no one else will hug him (Elson, 1979; Ward & Rouzer, 1974).

Passons (1975) has divided the kinds of problems people have into six areas:

1. *Lack of awareness* is usually seen in people with rigid personalities. By investing too much energy in attempting to meet the demands of the self-image, they lose contact with the "what" and "how" of their behavior. They lose the creative ability to deal with the environment: they become people to whom things happen; merely existing, not living.

2. *Lack of responsibility* is manifested by one's attempting to manipulate the environment rather than direct oneself. Perls thought of responsibility as "response-ability"—the ability to respond creatively to the environment. One who refuses to take the responsibility decides that he cannot be held accountable and thus is free to assume the role of blamer.

3. *Loss of contact with the environment* can take either of two forms. In the first instance, the person's boundaries have become so rigid that no input from the environment is accepted. Catatonia or autism are extreme examples of this form of withdrawal. The second form of this problem area is seen in the person who needs so much approbation that she literally loses her self in the environment: her boundaries are so undifferentiated that there is little or no distinction between self and self-image.

4. *Unfinished business* of incompleted gestalts is another type of problem. The unfinished business is an unfulfilled need, an unexpressed feeling, or some other incompleted interpersonal situation of significance to the individual. Resentments are the most usual form of unfinished business: for example, the individual who feels angry at a spouse but is unable to express that anger directly. The feeling is then carried as resentment into the individual's other activities and relationships. When unfinished business becomes strong enough, he is beset with preoccupation, compulsive behavior, wariness, oppressive energy, and much self-defeating activity. The unfinished business causes him to strive to complete the business, even in his current activities. Obviously, an individual who is preoccupied with unfinished business cannot bring his full awareness to bear on the current situation.

5. *Fragmentation* occurs when someone acts to deny one of her needs; for example, the need to be aggressive. Instead of directing energy toward constructive satisfaction of the need, she denies the existence of the need and thereby loses the energy it produces.

6. *Dichotomizing the self*, another form of fragmentation, takes the form of seeing oneself only at one pole of the continuum, such as strong or weak, masculine or feminine, powerful or powerless.

THEORY OF COUNSELING

Rationale for Change

In gestalt therapy, change is allowed. It is not planned, sought, or demanded. Perls did not explicitly delineate a gestalt theory of change, but his own views on the matter can be gleaned from his writing and his practice. Change occurs when one becomes what one is, not when one strives to become what one is not. In other words, therapeutic change occurs in me when I become more me, not when I become less me by becoming more someone else (Beisser, 1970).

Process of Counseling

"In essence, gestalt therapy is an experience between I and thou in the here and now. The client is helped to discover what and how he avoids by means of focusing of awareness, directed experimentation, amplification of behavior and feeling, and skillful frustration and support, which allow fully experienced awareness of avoidances, projections, and other processes by which the client interferes with his living fully and satisfyingly. Gradually developed capacity for awareness leads to responsibility which in turn permits choice" (Rader, 1977, p. 559).

Perls (1969b) said that to understand the process of gestalt therapy one must focus on the "now and how" of the client's behavior. Only the present is available to us: we can recall the past and anticipate the future, but we cannot directly do anything to or in either of them. We can live and act only in the present. Therefore, our awareness must be in the present: now. In the now, the individual must focus on those specific behaviors that manifest an attempt to avoid painful unfinished business. Awareness of these behaviors provides a clue to the individual's emotional modus operandi. Thus, the process of gestalt therapy involves focusing on the "now and how" in order to expand the client's awareness, which, in turn, frees the self for creative adjustment to the environment (p. 44).

Goals of Counseling

According to Perls (1969b p. 26), "we have a specific aim in gestalt therapy . . . the aim is to mature, to grow up." This maturity is achieved by moving from environmental support to self-support. Self-support comes through being responsible. A second major goal of gestalt therapy is integration. People who are more integrated function as a systematic whole, comprised of feelings, perceptions, thoughts, and a physical body whose processes cannot be divorced from the more psychological components. When people's inner states and behavior match, there is little energy wasted within their organisms, and they are more capable of responding appropriately (for them) to meet their needs. Less well-integrated people have voids or splits in their selves that inhibit full mobilization of their resources.

The goals of gestalt therapy, then, are to teach people to assume responsibility and to facilitate the functioning of the self. These goals are achieved only in approximation (Passons, 1975). "There is no such thing as total integration. Integration is never completed; maturation is never completed. It's an ongoing process forever and ever. . . . There's always something to be integrated; something to be learned" (Perls, 1969b, p. 64). It is evident from the foregoing that adjustment to society is *not* a goal of gestalt therapy (Passons, 1975).

Training of the Counselor

Training in gestalt therapy typically begins in a traditional counselor education graduate program in the form of contact with (classes under) one or more professors whose professional identity is "gestaltist." More specific and more intense training is obtained in one of the Gestalt Institutions listed below.

Gestalt institutes provide training for professionals, growth groups, and referral services. The following is not designed to be an exhaustive listing, nor an endorsement of any program. Institutes are proliferating rapidly, and there is, as yet, no procedure for the evaluation of professional staffs and programs. The first four listed institutes provide the most extensive training available in gestalt therapy in the United States.

New York Institute for Gestalt Therapy, 7 West 96 Street, New York, New York 10025. The first Gestalt institute in America, begun by Fritz and Laura Perls, and Paul Goodman, now directed by Laura Perls. The New York Institute does not have a published curriculum.

Gestalt Institute of Cleveland, 12911 Euclid Avenue, Cleveland, Ohio 44112. This institute was established by Fritz Perls and some of his Cleveland students. Next to the New York Institute, Cleveland has the longest training history in the United States. This institute has the most comprehensive training, public service, workshop, and publications program.

Gestalt Therapy Institute of Los Angeles, 337 South Beverly Drive, Suite 206, Beverly Hills, California 90212. Perls and a group of his students started this institute in the early 1960s. Like the Cleveland and San Francisco institutes, this group offers extensive training in gestalt therapy, with emphasis on didactic and experiential learning.

Gestalt Institute of San Francisco, 1719 Union Street, San Francisco, California 94123. Again, Perls and a group of his students were responsible for beginning this institute in 1968. The training program consists of a two-year curriculum that also emphasizes personal therapy.

More recently, additional institutes have been established. These include: Gestalt Training Center—San Diego, 7255 Gerard Avenue, La Jolla, California 92037; Gestalt Therapy Institute of Canada, Lake Cowichan, Box 39, Vancouver, British Columbia, Canada; Gestalt Institute of Chicago, c/o Bob Shapiro, Oasis Midwest Center for Human Potential, Chicago, Illinois; Gestalt Institute of the Southwest, 7700 Alabama Street, El Paso, Texas 79904 (Kogon, 1976, pp. 794–795).

Function of the Counselor

Consistent with the theory of change, the major function of the gestalt therapist is to facilitate the client's awareness. To accomplish this, the therapist first establishes a relationship with the client by entering the client's "now." He does not interpret but focuses on the "what" and "how" of the client's experience in the moment. The therapist will use many different means to enhance the client's awareness. These are usually presented as experiments for the client to try. The client is helped to be aware of the discrepancies between his verbal and nonverbal expressions. All of these functions are aimed at increasing the client's awareness of his "now." Awareness, then, is both method and goal, in somewhat the same sense as Marshall McLuhan (1967) declared the medium (television) to be the message (Passons, 1975).

In some instances, gestalt therapists must serve as effective parents for their clients: providing support while allowing the client to deal with frustration; giving clients permission to be who they are, and, at the same time, encouraging them to take risks; communicating nurturance while avoiding overprotection. At other times, gestalt therapists function as teachers, instructing clients in effective living and coping skills (Levin & Shepherd, 1974).

Levitsky & Perls (1970) indicated six rules to guide the gestalt therapist: (a) stay with the here and now; (b) promote direct experiencing rather than other activities such as talking about, analyzing, speculating, etc.; (c) emphasize self-discovery by the client; (d) focus on the client's awareness; (e) make skillful use of frustration; and (f) emphasize responsibility and choice. Within this framework, techniques are limited only by the creativity of the therapist.

PRACTICE OF COUNSELING

Major Techniques

The following are presented as a brief survey of the kinds of things gestalt therapists do; the list is neither prescriptive nor exhaustive—only representative (Elson, 1979).

1. *Directed awareness.* Simple, direct questions focus the client's awareness on the now and how: "What are you aware of in your hands?" "How are you doing your anger?" "What are your hands doing?"

2. *Games of dialogue.* The therapist may ask the clients to develop a dialogue between two conflicting parts of themselves. For example, a student having trouble writing a paper may be asked to discuss the problem with the paper (the client—student—would play both roles, himself and the paper).

3. *Playing the projection.* When clients are unaware of their projections, they are asked to role-play the behavior or attitude they are projecting. For example, a client who accuses another person of being conceited will be asked to act as conceited as possible.

4. *Reversal techniques.* In this technique, clients are asked to behave in ways that are just the opposite of their typical behavior. An aggressive "loud mouth," for example, may be asked to play the part of a meek, deferential "milquetoast."

5. *Assuming responsibility.* The therapist asks the clients to add the phrase, "and I take responsibility for it," after each statement they make. The purpose of this technique is to help the clients realize that they alone are responsible for their thoughts, feelings, and actions. Thus, a client may say, "I feel angry, and I take responsibility for it."

6. *Staying with a feeling.* Clients often want to avoid their strong feelings. This technique forces the client to keep the feeling in figure so that closure on it can be achieved. The counselor may even ask the client to exaggerate the feeling in order to saturate the need for avoidance.

7. *"May I feed you a sentence?"* Another way to bring the client to awareness of a previously denied feeling or attitude is for the counselor to phrase a statement for the client. The statement makes explicit a feeling or an attitude of which the client was not aware.

8. *Personalizing pronouns.* "It-talk" or "you-talk" is one way that people distance themselves from their experiences. Someone may say, for example, "It sure is hot in here," or "You could tell that he was really angry." A gestalt counselor would have the client rephrase the sentence: "I am very hot"; "I could tell that he was angry." In this way, clients become more aware of their experiences and are better able to integrate them into their total experience.

9. *No questions.* Careful listening often reveals that the questioner was, not seeking information, but avoiding making a statement. The counselor may suggest that the client "make the statement that is behind the question," thus again bringing the client face-to-face with a denied part of self.

10. *Dream work.* Unlike psychoanalysts, gestalt counselors do not interpret dreams. Rather, they want the client to bring the dream back to life and to "participate" in it as if it were happening now. The dreamer becomes an active part of the dream. This is accomplished by having the dreamer "become" each element in the dream: each person, each mood, each object, each event. In this way, the elements of the dream dialogue with each other, thus playing out the client's projections (Patterson, 1980).

Treatment Parameters

Far more gestalt therapy is done on a one-to-one basis than is done in groups. At the end of his life, Perls was conducting gestalt therapy workshops—essentially individual counseling with an audience—but that is not the usual mode of most gestalt therapists.

CASE STUDY   *(Simkin, 1970, pp. 162–166)*

Client: I was aware, when I sat down in the chair and put my hands on the arms right here, of the warmth that was still here for Leo and experiencing the warmth in my cold hands. *(Flat voice.)* And . . . I'm perspiring and . . . my heart's beating fast, and I'm feeling . . . I'm swallowing, I'm holding my breath. *(Pause.)* A feeling, a stiffness in my shoulders and . . .

Therapist: Sounds like you're doing a lot of squeezing.

C: Yes, I'm squeezing, squeezing in.

T: Can you either go with your sqeezing in or the reverse?

C: Squeezing in and pulling. Being very cl-close, closed . . . just kinda all in a knot. *(Sigh, tremulous voice.)* And when I can open *(arms unfolded, legs uncrossed)*, when I'm not like this, I feel like I let people—the room—come in, and can be aware of what is going on in the room or aware of Jim, Leo, Bill, and all the rest, and then when I'm like this *(arms folded, legs crossed)*, then the rest of it—you—begin to disappear. I'm aware of only me.

T: Yeah. What did you just do?

C: I swallowed. And I experienced a cutting off my breath, the jerkiness of it in here and here *(points to chest)*.

T: *(Talking ostensibly to the group)* I'm always impressed with the phenomenon that I see over and over again—somebody will learn something about himself: if he does this, something happens; if he does that, something happens—and then he discards what he's learned immediately. I don't understand.

C: It's a beautiful avoidance.

T: Yes. "I'll work on this tomorrow." "I'll tuck this into my computer and store it until next week."

C: Um-hum. *(Pause.)* And it always leaves me with unfinished business.

T: It?

C: I leave myself with unfinished business.

T: How?

C: By not staying with my feelings.

T: I'd like to reinforce your *this* and *this* *(referring to client's hand gestures of squeezing in)*. And I object to your avoiding the experiment. *(Pause.)* Now I'm stuck. If I don't do anything, Mary will sit there. *(Sighs.)* A perfect trap.

C: You—you are saying to go ahead with the experiment of the squeezing, with the feeling I get from it?

T: I wish I had Fritz's cigarette *(to wait out Mary's helplessness)*.

C: I don't know where to go from here.

T: (*Beginning dialogue with himself.*) Jim, shall Mary squeeze herself? Yes, but if you ask Mary to squeeze herself, then *she* isn't doing anything. She's just doing what *you* want. So how can Mary get out of her bind, Jim? The hell with Mary, how can I get out of my bind? (*General gentle laughter.*) You've got *yourself* stuck. (*Long pause.*) What do you experience now?

C: I experience wanting to . . . giving you the power . . . to get me out of the bind . . . and I'm feeling helpless and . . . "What do I do?"

T: What *are* you doing?

C: I'm sitting here, in the chair, and my left leg is over my right, and I'm looking at you. (T: Umhum.) And I swallowed. And my hand is going in and out of the arm of the chair. (*Pause.*) I want to—to push away, to move about. (*Pause.*) I want you to reach out and pull me back in.

T: I know. This is what I've been experiencing with you from the beginning. And I think this is the key to how I get stuck with you and how you get stuck. What you want from me is for me to pull you. What I want from you is for you to support yourself and do something for yourself, and I sit back and expect, "Ah! Now Mary's going to work on this." But (*laughing*) Mary wants *Jim* to pull her. (*Pause.*) And so your expectation and my expectation just don't get along.

C: They can't. (*Laughs.*) At least I'm aware of this, which I haven't been aware of before. (*Voice stronger.*) And this clearly, I would like to try again and see if I can find out if I can support myself.

T: I'm perfectly willing.

C: (*Pause.*) I'm supporting myself here in the chair. (T: Umhum.) And I'm breathing for myself, and all the body parts of it I'm doing for myself.

T: All the body parts of *it* you're doing for yourself?

C: For me. Breathing, my heart's beating—it's not like what I'm doing now.

T: What are you doing now?

C: (*Pause.*) Queer, when I am responding to *please* you—to get recognition in this way (*thoughful voice*)—

T: OK, do you want my recognition?

C: Er . . . yes.

T: I'm willing to acknowledge you and recognize you when you do the experiment.

C: OK (*Pause.*) Would you tell me again what the experiment is that you want me to do?

T: *Oh, no!* Absolutely not. I've told you once.

C: (*Long pause, then very fast.*) Well, I'm not sure at this point, but I think the experiment is to go back and experience what I am feeling when I am all, well, when I'm tense and all tied up like *this*. (*Wraps arms around her body and pauses.*) And when I'm here pulling in . . . and with my eyes closed . . . it's the feeling that it's dark—

T: *It's* dark?

C: I'm dark. I'm alone. (*Pause.*) And I'm frightened.

T: Right.

C: (*Pause.*) I want to scream and somehow I can't. (*Voice becomes tight.*)

T: Do you have any idea what you want to scream?

C: (*Pause.*) HELP! HELP!!!

T: Did you see what you did with your feet when you screamed, "Help"?

C: I brought them up.

T: Yes.

C: (*Crying.*) I can't get away. Somebody's beating me. I scream (*catches breath*), but even if I scream nobody hears. (*Sob and sharp intake of breath. Cries.*) And I have the feeling—I remember being tied to a post (*sobbing,*) . . . when I was a little girl. (*Pause. Continues crying.*) And they're leaving me here. And I can't get loose.

T: This is when you are a little girl. Yes? (*Voice very gentle.*)

C: Um-hum.

T: Are you still a little girl?

C: (*Voice stronger.*) No, but—

T: Can you untie yourself.

C: (*Blows nose.*) Yes, I can untie myself.

T: I'd like to see you.

C: (*Long pause, voice controlled.*) Now, I'm back here in this room, but I'm still a little girl all tied.

T: Right.

C: I'm closed in—alone.

T: (*Softly.*) Now I want you to talk to your little girl—to tell your little girl that she knows exactly how to untie herself and how to open up, and I care too much for that little girl to do anything that would interfere with her doing it for herself.

C: Um-hum. (*Long pause.*) "Little girl, you don't . . . you've been . . . you no longer need to stay tied. OK now, open your eyes." Seeing where I am—here in this room with Sandy, Abe, Bill, Bob, Jim, Leo, Joan, Elizabeth, Art, Miriam, and Cooper. (*Slowly.*) And the ropes are getting looser, and I can take the hands and . . . (*sigh*). I'm beginning to breathe. (*Voice gets firmer.*) I have some space there to take in. (*Pause.*) My feet are untied. I can move. (*Gets up slowly, stretches.*) Support myself way up to the ceiling and back. I can move around.

T: Now I recognize you.

C: I can see! I can feel!

Applications

Gestalt therapy can be practiced in a variety of ways. Perls preferred the intensive workshop format; some prefer to apply gestalt therapy methods in a more-or-less traditional group therapy setting; others follow the gestalt approach in individual sessions. In deciding whether or not to use gestalt theory and/or practice, the counselor should be aware of Shepherd's (1970) caveats:

"In general, Gestalt therapy is most effective with overly socialized, restrained, constricted individuals—often described as neurotic, phobic, perfectionistic, ineffective, depressed, etc.—whose functioning is limited or inconsistent, primarily due to their internal restrictions, and whose enjoyment of living is minimal" (pp. 234–235).

Some of the gestalt awareness exercises would seem to be useful with children as a developmental teaching device, particularly if these exercises are separated from their usual confrontive mode.

CRITIQUE

Research Support

Perls and his followers have been more concerned with developing the clinical features of their approach than with formal evaluation of therapeutic efficacy or research on the theoretical assumptions. There has been very little research involving gestalt therapy or its principles.

Gannon (1972) made a systematic evaluation of gestalt group counseling. He studied three groups of high school students who were in counseling because of unacceptable behaviors such as absence, chronic tardiness, and conflict with the police. The first group received gestalt therapy for nine hours a week for one semester. The second group participated in special team teaching, group discussions, and field trips. A third group attended classes as usual. As expected, the gestalt group showed greater gains in openness and interpersonal relations than either of the other two groups.

Lieberman, Yalom, and Miles (1973) studied seventeen growth-oriented groups representing nine different theoretical approaches, including two gestalt groups. Expert observers evaluated each group on a number of outcome measures including negative outcome or casualties among individual participants. One of the two gestalt groups was highly successful. It received the highest ranking as being a pleasant experience and was tied for first as being a constructive experience in terms of the participants' learning. At the final follow-up assessment, this group ranked second among the seventeen groups.

The other gestalt group stood at the opposite end of the scale! It had the highest casualty rate and was judged the least beneficial to its members. However, the difference in the two groups was found to be in the personality characteristics of the respective group leaders and the differing atmosphere they engendered in their groups. The leader of the first group was confrontive, yet highly supportive. He was rated high in empathy, warmth, and genuineness. By contrast, the other leader was unpredictable, sarcastic, belittling, and obtrusive. The members did not admire him and, in fact, saw him as ineffective and uncaring.

Evaluation

It is neither fair nor scholarly to make an assessment on the basis of only two studies, even though they are fairly representative of others. Perhaps the most honest judgment would be that the research evidence seems to indicate that in the hands of a competent, effective therapist, gestalt therapy can offer the possibility of significant beneficial change. In the wrong hands, it can have tragically destructive effects. Since both the "good" and the "bad" of gestalt therapy seem more a function of the therapist than the therapy, I am not suggesting that we abandon gestalt therapy. I do suggest, however, that both the buyer and the seller beware.

As with all of the perspectives on counseling, there is some good news and some bad news for gestalt therapy. The good news is that it avoids the abstract intellectualizations of some of the other perspectives, and it encourages clients to be aware of and use the full range of their emotional capacity. It seems to be particularly useful with individuals who are rather inhibited and overly intellectual. Its emphasis on the present frees clients from the tyranny of the past, and its positive view of human nature relieves the pessimism of some other approaches. Probably the greatest contribution comes in the prescriptive use of gestalt techniques by other approaches. I particularly like the use of "I" statements, turning questions into statements, and the idea of owning one's response to the environment.

And now, the bad news. A major limitation of the gestalt perspective is the rather narrow range of client population for which it is applicable. This narrowing is due to several factors including (a) the confrontive role of the counselor, (b) the intensity of the client's emotional experience in therapy, and (c) the highly individualistic philosophy which seems to hold in contempt any social system or life style but its own.

Although Perls' followers have written more extensively on the theory of gestalt therapy than the master, it still seems to be tied very closely to Perls' personality and personal views rather than a clear and consistent philosophy of human nature. Finally, Perls' admonitions to "lose your mind and come to your senses" and "do your own thing" seem not just egocentric, but, in a counseling context, irresponsible hedonism. I don't recommend throwing the baby out with the bath water, but I do recommend knowing the difference. As you study that difference, remember not to push the river.

REFERENCES

BEISSER, A. L.   The paradoxical theory of change. In J. Fagan & I. L. Shepherd, *Gestalt therapy now.* Palo Alto, CA.: Science & Behavior Books, 1970.

ELSON, S. E.   Recent approaches to counseling: Gestalt therapy, transactional analysis, and reality therapy. In H. M. Burks, Jr., & B. Stefflre, *Theories of counseling* (3rd ed.). New York: McGraw-Hill, 1979.

GANNON, W.   *The effects of the gestalt-oriented group approach on the interpersonal contact attitudes of selected high school students.* Unpublished doctoral dissertation, Case Western Reserve University, 1972.

HANSEN, J. C., STEVIC, R. R., & WARNER, R. W., JR.   *Counseling: Theory and process.* (3rd ed.). Boston: Allyn & Bacon, 1982, Chap. 7.

KOGON, J.   The genius of gestalt therapy. In C. Hatcher & P. Himelstein (Eds.), *The handbook of gestalt therapy.* New York: Jason Aronson, 1976.

LEVIN, L. S., & SHEPHERD, I. L.   The role of the therapist in gestalt therapy. *The Counseling Psychologist,* 1974, *4* (4), 27–30.

LEVITSKY, A., & PERLS, F. S.   The rules and games of gestalt therapy. In J. Fagen & L. L. Shepherd (Eds.), *Gestalt therapy now.* Palo Alto, CA.: Science & Behavior Books, 1970.

LIEBERMAN, M., YALOM, I. D., & MILES, M. B.   *Encounter groups: First facts.* New York: Basic Books, 1973.

McLUHAN, M., & FIORE, Q.   *The medium is the message.* New York: Bantam Books, 1967.

PASSONS, W. R.   *Gestalt approaches in counseling.* New York: Holt, Rinehart, & Winston, 1975.

PATTERSON, C. H.   *Theories of counseling and psychotherapy* (3rd ed.). New York: Harper & Row, 1980, Chap. 12.

PERLS, F. S.   *Ego hunger and aggression.* New York: Random House, 1969a.

PERLS, F. S.   *Gestalt therapy verbatim.* Moab, UT.: Real People Press, 1969b.

PERLS, F. S.   *In and out of the garbage pail.* Moab, UT.: Real People Press, 1969c.

PERLS, F. S., HEFFERLINE, R. F., & GOODMAN, P.   *Gestalt therapy: Excitement and growth in the human personality.* New York: Julian Press, 1951.

RADER, G. E.   Gestalt therapy. In D. C. Rimm & J. W. Somervill (Eds.), *Abnormal psychology.* New York: Academic Press, 1977.

SHEPHERD, I. L.   Limitations and cautions in the gestalt approach. In J. Fagen & I. L. Shepherd (Eds.), *Gestalt therapy now.* Palo Alto, CA.: Science & Behavior Books, 1970.

SIMKIN, J.   Mary: A session with a passive patient. In I. J. Fagen & I. L. Shepherd (Eds.), *Gestalt therapy now.* Palo Alto, CA.: Science & Behavior Books, 1970.

STEWART, R. D.   The philosophical background of gestalt therapy. *The Counseling Psychologist,* 1974, *4* (4), 13–14.

WARD, P., & ROUZER, D. L.   The nature of pathological functioning from a gestalt perspective. *The Counseling Psychologist,* 1974, *4* (4), 24–27.

CHAPTER NINE
CLIENT-CENTERED THERAPY

"At ten o'clock on the morning of June 7, 1969," reads a Somona State College publication, "some 1500 friends of the Class of 1969 gathered by the side of a beautiful little lake to share in the Eighth Annual Commencement Exercises." Carl Rogers was to deliver the commencement address. He began by explaining, "As an undergraduate I majored in medieval history. I have enormous respect for the scholars of the Middle Ages and their contributions to learning. But I want to speak to you as Carl Rogers in 1969, not as a medieval symbol. So I hope I will not offend you if I remove these medieval trappings—this nonfunctional cap, this handsome but useless hood, and this robe designed to keep one warm even in the rigors of a European winter." He proceeded to remove the garments and to address the graduating class on "The Person of Tomorrow" (Kirschenbaum, 1979, p. 395).

That's vintage Rogers!

HISTORICAL DEVELOPMENT

Personal Background

Carl Rogers was born in 1902 in Oak Park, Illinois, a suburb of Chicago. His family was well-to-do, Protestant, close-knit, loving, practical, and dedicated to Christian principles and to the virtues of hard work. At the age of twelve, he moved to a large farm thirty miles west of Chicago. His father, a successful contractor, employed a manager to administer the farm on a modern, scientific basis. Through reading about scientific agriculture and through activities on this farm, Carl developed a lasting interest in and respect for science and the experimental method.

While majoring in history at the University of Wisconsin, Rogers became deeply involved with student religious groups. After graduating from the University of Wisconsin, he spent two years at the Union Theological Seminary before transferring to Columbia University's Teachers College to complete a Ph.D. in clinical and educational psychology. At Columbia he became acquainted with the measurement trend in American psychology, the view of John Dewey on the value of experiential learning, and Leta Hollingsworth's warmly human and commonsense approach to clinical work. During a year of internship at the Institute for Child Guidance, Rogers was exposed to the Freudian orientation, and he engaged in his first regular therapy with clients.

Over the next twelve years, Rogers immersed himself in practical clinical work in a child guidance clinic in Rochester, N.Y. This was a time of relative professional seclusion, during which he focused on his own experiences as he worked with children and their parents. Through social workers on the staff, he became acquainted with the work of Otto Rank, Jesse Taft, and Frederick Allen. His first book, *The Clinical Treatment of the Problem Child*, published in 1939, was devoted mostly to general clinical issues and procedures; but two chapters about existing points of view about treatment interviews foretold his future interest in relationship therapy.

Rogers became a professor in clinical psychology at Ohio State University in January 1940; and client-centered therapy was born about a year later. He was given an appointment at the University of Chicago in 1945 and went to the University of Wisconsin in 1957. During those twenty years in Chicago and Madison, the client-centered approach matured.

In 1964, Rogers became a Resident Fellow at the Western Behavioral Sciences Institute and later at The Center for the Studies of the Person, which he helped found in 1968. After he left Wisconsin, his writing and professional practice focused chiefly on encounter groups, interpersonal relationships, and extending the client-centered approach to the philosophy of science, to education, and to issues of alienation and powerlessness. In the early 1980s, he was rethinking parts of client-centered theory; and, at more than 80 years of age, Rogers still participates in professional work and writing (Grummon, 1979).

Theoretical Background

Rogers grew up in a family where hard work and a highly conservative (almost fundamentalist) Protestant Christianity were about equally revered (Rogers, 1959). Although he rejected that view of religion, he did pursue his interest in philosophy and religion at the Union Theological

Seminary. The freedom of philosophical thought and respect for honest attempts at resolving problems that he found there introduced him to unconditional positive regard.

He studied medieval history, philosophy, and religion before he began the study of psychology. John Dewey's emphasis on the project method and on the importance of the phenomenal world of the learner had a definite influence on Rogers' thought. At Teachers College, he encountered not only Dewey's ideas, but psychology as it was developing in the United States, with emphasis on the control and manipulation of operationally defined variables. Rogers also had extensive contact with major personality theory orientations, but only the approach and theory of Otto Rank directly affected the development of client-centered therapy.

Constantly assessing and defining his view of man in relation to the philosophies of other approaches helped Rogers clarify his own conceptions. In the child guidance clinic at Rochester, Rogers' ideas about therapy began to take shape. Here, too, he discovered the value of listening attentively to the client, especially listening for the feelings behind the client's words (Holdstock & Rogers, 1977).

Rogers' theory and practice has moved through four stages.

The nondirective stage (1940–1950).   December 11, 1940, was the day on which the nondirective stage was begun. Reflection of feelings and nondirective techniques characterized this period. His major publication during this time was *Counseling and Psychotherapy* (1942).

The client-centered stage (1950–1957).   The change from nondirective counseling to client-centered counseling was signalled by the publication *Client-Centered Therapy* in 1951. It was during this time that Rogers developed his theory of personality and psychotherapy, stressing that the person seeking help was not to be treated as as dependent patient, but rather as a responsible client. The therapist, on the other hand, was seen as a catalyst, but not as a person in therapy.

The experiential stage (1957–1975).   During this stage the counselor became free: the therapist's organismic experience became as important a referent in guiding the therapist's behavior as was the client's. Full development of the mutuality of the professional relationship between psychotherapist and client paved the way for widespread application of the theory (Holdstock & Rogers, 1977).

The person-centered stage (1975).   Since the former client-centered stage evolved into the person-centered stage gradually, an exact starting date is not possible to discern. However, it was during the middle to late 1970s that Rogers began to shift his interest from individuals (whether encountered individually or in groups) to broader aspects of society—education, industry, and society itself—in terms of the source of power for personal and even international growth through interpersonal relationships.

THEORY OF PERSONALITY

Definition of Terms

Actualizing tendency. The actualizing tendency is an inherent tendency of the organism as a whole to develop all its potential in ways that serve to maintain and enhance the organism.

Anxiety. As experienced phenomenologically, anxiety is a state of uneasiness or tension whose cause is unknown.

Awareness, symbolization, consciousness. These terms all refer to the mental representation of some portion of experience.

Congruence. Congruence is the state in which self-experiences are accurately symbolized in the self-concept.

Empathy. Empathy is the act of perceiving the internal frame of reference of another with accuracy and with the emotional components and meanings that pertain thereto as if one *were* the other person, but without ever losing the "as if" condition.

Experience (noun). This term denotes all that is going on in the organism at a given time—whether in awareness or only potentially available to awareness—of a psychological nature.

Experience (verb). To experience is to receive the impact of exterior and interior events at a given moment in time.

Extensionality. This refers to perception that is differentiated, dominated by facts, with awareness of both the space-time anchorage of facts and the different levels of abstraction.

Ideal self. The ideal self is the self-concept the individual would most like to possess.

Incongruence between self and experience. Incongruence refers to a discrepancy between the perceived self and actual experience.

Intensionality. This describes the characteristics of the behavior of the individual who is in a defensive state: rigidity, overgeneralization, abstraction from reality, absolute and unconditional evaluation of experience.

Internal frame of reference. This refers to all of the realm of experience that is available to the awareness of the individual at a given moment.

Organismic valuing process. This is an ongoing process in which values are never fixed or rigid, but experiences are being accurately symbolized and continually and freshly valued in terms of the satisfactions organismically experienced.

Psychological maladjustment. This condition exists when the organism denies or distorts experiences in awareness in such a way that these experiences cannot be incorporated into the self.

Self, self-concept, self-structure.   The self is an organized conceptual set (gestalt) of perceptions and characteristics of the "I" or the "me," and the perceptions of the relationships of the "I" or the "me" to others and the various aspects of life, together with the values attached to these perceptions.
Threat.   Threat is the state that exists when an experience is perceived or anticipated as incongruent with the structure of the self.
Unconditional positive regard.   This is the perception of the self-experiences of another without discrimination as to greater or lesser worthiness.
Vulnerability.   This is defined as the state of incongruence between self and experience with emphasis on the potential of this state for creating psychological disorganization.

View of Human Nature

Rogers has always been wary of anything that may interfere with personal freedom, and he especially abhors the "therapist as expert." On the other hand, he is very optimistic about the possibilities for a rich and rewarding life for those who are free to live according to their own choices. He deeply believes that humans are innately good, trustworthy, and rational. Therefore, Rogers is convinced that society's needs are best met when individuals are free to "pull their own strings." Since his emphasis is almost exclusively on process, rather than on outcome, he has not spelled out his views of the good life. Clearly, however, he sees it as an ever-changing process rather than a state of being or static goal of life. Those who accept their freedom and live nondefensively according to their own organismic valuing process become creatively involved with the process of living. For Rogers, that is the good life.

Client-centered therapy is based on the following assumptions (Rogers, 1951):

1. Every individual exists in a continually changing world of experience of which he is the center. This private world includes all that is experienced by the organism, whether or not these experiences are consciously perceived . . . An important truth in regard to this private world of the individual is that it can only be known, in any genuine or complete sense, to the individual himself (p. 483).
2. The organism reacts to the field as it is experienced and perceived. This perceptual field is, for the individual, "reality" (p. 484).
3. The organism reacts as an organized whole to this phenomenal field (p. 486).
4. The organism has one basic tendency and striving—to actualize, maintain, and enhance the experiencing organism. . . . We are talking here about the tendency of the organism to maintain itself—to assimilate food, to behave defensively in the face of threat, to achieve the goal of self-maintenance even when the usual pathway to that goal is blocked. . . . Its movement . . . is in the direction of an increasing self-government, self-regulation, and autonomy, and away from heteronymous control, or control by external forces (pp. 487–488).
5. Behavior is basically the goal-directed attempt of the organism to satisfy its needs as experienced, in the field as perceived (p. 491).

6. Emotion accompanies and in general facilitates such goal-directed behavior, the kind of emotion being related to the seeking versus the consummatory aspects of the behavior, and the intensity of the emotion being related to the perceived significance of the behavior for the maintenance and enhancement of the organism (p. 492).

7. The best vantage point for understanding behavior is from the internal frame of reference of the individual himself (p. 494).

8. As a result of interaction with the environment and particularly as a result of evaluational interaction with others, the structure of self is formed—an organized, fluid, but consistent conceptual pattern of perceptions of characteristics and relationships of the "I" of the "me," together with the values attached to these concepts (p. 498).

9. Most of the ways of behaving which are adopted by the organism are those which are consistent with the concept of self (p. 507).

10. Psychological maladjustment exists when the organism denies to awareness significant sensory and visceral experiences, which consequently are not symbolized and organized into the gestalt of the self-structure (p. 510).

11. As the individual perceives and accepts into his self-structure more of his organic experiences, he finds that he is replacing his present value *system*—based so largely upon introjections which have been distortedly symbolized—with a continuing organismic valuing *process* (p. 522).

Structure of Personality

When reviewing Rogers' concept of the structure of personality, you should keep in mind his conviction that personality is not static, but always "becoming." In answer to a question about the Freudian construct of unconscious, Rogers replied, "I think I see the same sort of phenomena that Freud saw, for which he developed this concept [unconscious]. I think that psychologists . . . tend to make things out of these concepts when they are really attempts by someone to understand an observable set of data. I prefer to think of a range of phenomena: first, those in sharp focus in awareness right now—the height of consciousness; secondly, a range of material which could be called into consciousness . . . but [is not] in "figure" right now—it is "ground" or background; finally, some phenomena which are more and more dimly connected with awareness, to material that is really prevented from coming into even vague awareness because [this] would damage the person's self-concept (Evans, 1975, p. 6).

Although not clearly brought together under the rubric of structure of personality, Rogers' views on the matter seem to fall into three clusters: the organism, the phenomenal field, and the self (Hansen et al., 1982). *Organism* refers to all that a person is: physical, emotional, and intellectual aspects. According to Rogers (1951), we react organismically to our experiences; that is, our entire being responds to stimuli, whether internal or external.

The *phenomenal field* refers to all that a person experiences. It is the ever-changing world of experience; and experience includes not only those things external to the individual but also events that are internal. Some of these events are consciously perceived, but some are not. It is also important to note that what is perceived by the individual in the phenomenal field is what is relevant to that individual, not the actual reality (Rogers, 1951).

The most important of Rogers' principles of personality is his concept of the *self*. As he sees it, the self is a differentiated portion of the phenomenal field composed of a series of perceptions and values about the "I" and the "me." In Rogers' conception of the structure of personality, the self is the center of the structure, the focal point around which the personality evolves. The self develops out of the organism's interaction with the environment. As it develops, it tends to integrate as well as distort some of the values of other people. The self strives to maintain consistency of behavior and its own consistency. Experiences that are consistent with the concept of self are integrated; those that are inconsistent with the self are perceived as threats. Central to the concept of the self is the idea that it is always in process; it grows and changes as a result of its continuing interaction with the phenomenal field (Rogers, 1961).

Development of Personality

By Rogers' (1959) own admission, the development of a theory of personality has not been a high-priority issue in client-centered therapy. On the other hand, Rogers' research interests and existential philosophy of life provided the impetus for such a theory. It is more of a field theory than a genetic theory (such as Freud's). The forces that shape an individual's development are inherent in that individual's environment, especially in his or her interpersonal relationships, rather than in some intrapersonal dynamics.

To understand client-centered personality theory, you must begin with the human infant at birth. For the neonatal infant, the only world that exists is the world of his or her experience; this, and this alone, is reality. Innate in all humans is one motivational force: the self-actualizing tendency. This force is operationalized by the infant when he positively values experiences he perceives as enhancing his organism and when he negatively values those experiences he perceives as detrimental to the organism. This intuitive appraisal of experiences Rogers calls the "organismic valuing process."

The self-concept. As the infant develops, she begins to be aware of objects and events "out there" that are "not-me." After a time, she is able to accurately discriminate "me" from "not-me" and to correctly assign ownership to one or the other. Out of the gradually focusing awareness of the difference between "me" and "not-me," grows the child's self-concept: an ever-deepening awareness of "I" and "me" (self as subject and as object). This awareness of self distinct from nonself, together with the values attached to self-experience, is the developing self-concept (Meador & Rogers, 1973).

Need for positive regard.   As the awareness of a self emerges, a need for positive regard also arises. This need is innate and thus is present in all human beings. Unfortunately, this need for positive regard can be satisfied only by others, and so it is frequently thwarted. (I need you to regard me positively; but your perception of me as worthy of positive regard is based on *your* needs, not mine.) Out of the myriad experiences of satisfaction and frustration of the need for positive regard, the infant develops a learned sense of self-regard based on the regard (positive or negative) he has been given by significant others. The need for positive self-regard is so potent it may override the organismic valuing process (Meador & Rogers, 1973).

Conditions of worth.   Sooner or later, the child's need to have the positive regard of significant others comes into conflict with the existential needs of the organism. Her self-developed values may be contrary to parental values. Behavior based on organismic values may be unacceptable to parents or others. When this happens, the child begins to suppress her own organismic valuing process and to assume, as if they were her own, the value discriminations of those significant others whose regard she so desperately needs. In other words, experiences are now labeled satisfying or not, not because they are so experienced by the child, but because the child perceives them as so experienced by the significant other. When a self-experience is sought (or avoided) solely because it is more (or less) worthy of self-regard, the individual is said to have acquired a condition of worth, which becomes incorporated into her self-regard system. When she acts in accordance with conditions of worth, she achieves positive self-regard; when she does not so act, she feels negative self-regard (Meador & Rogers, 1973).

Development of Maladaptive Behavior

Client-centered therapy views human behavior on a continuum, with self-actualizing behavior at one end and disorganized behavior at the other; normal and defensive behavior fall somewhere between, with both somewhat closer to the self-actualizing end. "On a continuum" means that they are regarded as differing in degree, not in kind; i.e., the degree of incongruence between self-concept and self-experience. For example, when an individaul who sees herself as a good student fails a test, her experience doesn't "fit into" her self-concept. Moderate incongruence may be manifested by rationalization: "My average is high enough; I'll still get an A." Extreme incongruence may be manifested by denial ("That's not my exam paper") or bizarre behavior ("I'm going to get that SOB who flunked me!").

The development of incongruence.   As the person develops, his need for self-respect remains; but meanwhile, he has also acquired conditions of worth. As a result, he begins to perceive his experiences selectively. He will either deny awareness of, or selectively perceive, those experiences that are not in accord with his conditions of worth. As a result of this distortion or selective perception, an incongruence develops between the person's experience and his self-concept. He is now vulnerable to anxiety and, to some degree, is psychologically maladjusted (Price, 1972).

Rogers makes a general distinction between defensive behaviors and disorganized behaviors. Among the defensive behaviors are included behaviors conventionally thought of as "neurotic"—for example, rationalization, projection, phobias—as well as some behaviors often regarded as psychotic—for example, paranoid behaviors such as suspicion or projection. Disorganized behaviors, on the other hand, include much of what is usually associated with "acute psychotic" reactions.

The development of defensive behaviors.   When an individual perceives his or her experience distortedly or selectively, the resulting incongruence between the perceived experience and the self-concept (burdened with conditions of worth) makes that individual vulnerable to threat. Although the precise parameters vary with the individual and his or her experiences, the core of all threat is the fear that the constancy of the self is endangered. If the incongruity is great enough, the person will be unable to fulfill his or her conditions of worth and will experience anxiety—the organism's signal that all is not well. Defensive behavior occurs when the person tries to turn off the alarm and to prevent the anxiety from arising. Thus, defensive behavior results from the distortion or selective perception of experience in order to artificially make that experience "fit" the self-concept as amended by conditions of worth (Price, 1972).

The development of disorganized behavior.   The degree of incongruence between self and experience may be great for a particular individual who is confronted with the incongruity suddenly and without warning. If this should occur, the process of defense may not work adequately, if at all. When defenses are ineffective, the threatening experience is not distorted but symbolized accurately in awareness. When this happens, disorganization, not defensiveness, results.

Once the disorganization has begun, it may follow one of two paths. The individual may attempt to build a defense against her awareness of herself (become catatonic) or she may take on a different identity (paranoid delusion). Another possibility is that the self-concept may change in order to include the previously unacceptable experience: "Of course I acted crazy; I *am* crazy" (Price, 1972).

THEORY OF COUNSELING

Rationale for Change

The only way to break the cycle of threat and defensiveness is to remove the need for defense by removing the perceived threat. This process is begun by first stripping away the conditions of worth (somewhat like removing an old coat of paint), so that the real, unfettered self-concept is available to experience. Next, the individual must be led to awareness of his or her own experience and to his or her own unique evaluation of that experience. (My image is that of Margaret Sullivan introducing Helen Keller to water, tree, earth.) According to client-centered therapy, this occurs in the context of a corrective relationship with another individual who makes no demands but offers "unconditional positive regard."

In 1957, Rogers presented a formal theory of the conditions that are both *necessary* and *sufficient* to get the process of therapeutic personality change moving: that is, the process will begin only if the stated conditions are present and no other conditions are necessary. Since then, Rogers has agreed that it is difficult, if not impossible, to establish the necessary and sufficient conditions of therapy; but he still believes that the therapist's attitudes can account for much of the constructive change that occurs in counseling and psychotherapy (Grummon, 1979; Rogers, Gendlin, Kiesler, & Truax, 1967).

The newer formulation states that the amount of process movement and the amount of constructive personality change are dependent upon the degree to which (a) the therapist is congruent and genuine in the relationship; (b) the therapist experiences unconditional positive regard for the client; and (c) the therapist exhibits accurate empathic understanding of the client's internal frame of reference. These are termed the "facilitative conditions." Three other variables are added for the sake of completeness and clarity: (d) the client and therapist are in contact with each other; (e) the client is in a state of incongruence and is vulnerable (preferably anxious); and (f) the client perceives, at least to a minimal degree, the therapist's genuineness, unconditional positive regard, and accurate empathy (Grummon, 1979).

Process of Counseling

Rogers developed his (1961) "process conception of psychotherapy" by distilling and abstracting many hours of recorded therapy interviews. There appears to be a regular progression through the stages, and at any given time, a client could be rather accurately described by a narrow band on the continuum. As in any process, there are occasional retreats, along with the advances.

First stage.   This is the stage of rigidity and distance from experience. Clients are unwilling to reveal themselves; they communicate—if at all— only about externals. They are unaware of even the possibility of personal meanings or feelings, and their personal constructs are extremely rigid. Since they fail to recognize any problems and have no desire to change, it is very unlikely that a client at this stage would come voluntarily to therapy. Such people have little recognition of or interest in the world around them. Discrimination of personal experience is minimal and crude—in terms of "always" or "never." These clients are extremely difficult to reach; the therapist's best shot is to try some form of group therapy or play therapy where the client can experience being accepted without having to give.

Second stage.   Clients at this stage are only slightly more open than at the first stage. They begin to discuss non-self topics but all self-references are omitted: They have no sense of personal responsibility in their own situations. Feelings may be manifested (they may show anger, for example) but they do not recognize or own the feeling. Any discussion of feeling is in the past tense. Personal constructs are still rigid and seen as facts rather than constructs. Contradictions may be expressed without being recognized as such.

Third stage.   At this stage clients seem able to talk about themselves and their current experiences, but only as objects. They see themselves as people to whom things happen. Their awareness of self is limited to an image reflected in others. They talk freely about past feelings but either deny or disparage current feelings. They begin to recognize constructs as constructs, not established facts; and those constructs are slightly less rigid, less global. They are frequently frustrated and discouraged by their inability to make or effectively carry out personal choices. Most people entering therapy are at stage three.

Fourth stage.   Clients in this stage are able to recognize and own intense feelings from the past, but present feelings are usually depersonalized or externalized. Strangely, these clients often recognize and own their present fear of recognizing and owning their feelings! Both experience and the way it is interpreted are a bit less rigidly structured: there is a slight lessening of the "always" or "never" framework. The validity of personal constructs begins to be questioned, and contradictions and incongruities are no longer accepted. There is even some acceptance of personal responsibility for problems. Clients at this stage are like swimmers testing the water before going into a pool: they are still afraid of a close therapeutic relationship, but they are intrigued by it and cautiously test it to see if it will hurt. This stage characterizes the bulk of therapy.

Fifth stage.   In this stage, feelings are freely expressed in the present and, for the most part, are experienced in the present. However, when these feelings emerge, they are usually accompanied by fright and fear rather than pleasure. These clients are increasingly able to own feelings about themselves; their experiencing is much less structured, less remote. There is a growing tendency toward accurate representation of feelings, experience, and constructs together with a greater acceptance of personal responsibility for personal problems. These clients are close to their organismic valuing process, close to being in the stream of their feelings rather than watching them from the bank. Experiencing is no longer rigid, and internal communication—awareness and ownership of feelings—is more accurate.

Sixth stage.   This stage is characterized by the "unsticking" of previously "stuck" feelings: previously inhibited feelings now flow freely and are experienced with immediacy and usually delight. These clients no longer merely perceive their experience as object: now they subjectively live it in the moment. The psychological loosening is accompanied by a physiological loosening: tears, sighs, laughter, relaxation are frequent. Incongruence is swallowed up by congruence, and its disappearance is experienced with great joy. Clients at this stage have no more "problems," whether internal or external. Rather, they subjectively live a phase of their lives that previously had been objectified as "problem." From this point on, the client has little need of a therapist.

Seventh stage.   This stage rarely occurs within therapy, because, by this time, the client no longer needs therapy. At this level, new feelings are experienced with immediacy and richness. People (no longer clients) accept and own, not only their feelings, but also the changes in their feelings: they trust and enjoy the process of their experiencing. Experiencing now is a process because it has lost most, if not all, of its former rigidity. The rigidly structured self has evolved into a freely flowing subjective awareness of experiencing. Personal constructs are tentatively formulated pending validation against experience, and even then, they are loosely held.

Goals of Counseling

The goal of client-centered counseling is a reorganization of the self. According to Rogers (1961), successful counseling dissolves conditions of worth, increases openness to experience, and, thus, broadens the degree of congruence between self-concept and experience. Through this process, the client becomes a more fully functioning person (Grummon, 1979). The fully functioning person is one who has attained optimum psychological adjustment and maturity, complete congruence, complete openness to experience, and complete extensionality.

There are three salient characteristics of the fully functioning person, which are manifested organismically; i.e., holistically (Patterson, 1980, p. 488).

1. Fully functioning people are open to all their experiences. This doesn't mean that they experience everything that can be experienced, but rather that they are free to consider accepting or rejecting any given experience and that there are no barriers to fully experiencing whatever is accepted.
2. Openness to experience means that fully functioning people live existentially; i.e., participate in the experience without the need to control it. Living is characterized by flexibility and adaptability, rather than rigidity.
3. Fully functioning people are able to do what "feels right" because they trust the organismic valuing process as a guide to satisfying behavior.
4. Fully functioning people may be "non-conformist," may not be "adjusted to society," but do live constructively and creatively.
5. Since fully functioning people are free of defensiveness, they are able to be realistically socialized: neither aggressive nor timid, but assertive, trustworthy, and strong.
6. Since fully functioning people live existentially, their behavior is dependable, but not predictable.
7. Fully functioning people are free: they think their own thoughts, feel their own feelings, do their own thing—not anarchistically, but creatively; not anti- or even asocially, but existentially.

The value directions that develop in people as they become fully functioning are not idiosyncratic or unique, but have a commonality that extends through different cultures, suggesting that they are indigenous to the human species. These directions include being real rather than presenting a façade, valuing one's self and self-direction, valuing being in process, rather than having fixed goals, valuing sensitivity to, and acceptance of, others valuing deep relationships with others, and finally, valuing an openness to all one's experiences, including the feelings and reactions of others. This ideal, fully functioning person does not exist.

Training of the Counselor

Rogers and his colleagues were the first to develop brief workshops for the training of psychotherapists and to attempt to measure their effectiveness. They specified graded procedures for facilitating experiential learning of the counseling process and specified the characteristics of the effective counselor. Rogers' graded experiences included (a) listening to tape-recorded interviews of experienced therapists, (b) role-playing therapist with fellow students, (c) observing a series of live demonstrations by a supervisor, (d) participating in group or multiple therapy, (e) supervision of the student's counseling interviews, and (f) personal therapy (Matarazzo, 1978).

In addition to the La Jolla Program of summer workshops, most client-centered training is done in traditional counselor education settings: a 36 to 45 semester-hour master's degree program. According to Hollis and Wantz (1980); of the graduate counselor training programs surveyed in August of 1979, 24 percent claimed an eclectic orientation and 21 percent identified themselves as Rogerian. It is likely that the eclectic group included many who were "more or less" Rogerians.

Function of the Counselor

The attitudes that are most important for releasing the potential for growth appear on the basis of research findings to be (a) a sensitive and accurately empathic understanding of the client; (b) the therapist's complete acceptance of, or unconditional positive regard for, the client; and (c) the therapist's genuineness or congruence. These attitudes seem to be differentially important depending on the life situation a person is in. Congruence seems to be most important in ordinary, everyday situations. In certain other special situations, such as between parent and child or between therapist and "out-of-touch" psychotic, caring or prizing may turn out to be the most significant. However, therapy appears to be most effective when all three are present to a high degree.

Accurate empathy.   One of the most important functions of the therapist is understanding what the client thinks, feels, and experiences and how the client perceives his or her own behavior. This involves a genuine and accurate sensing of the meanings and feelings of the client as they flow, ever-changing through his or her experience. It means that the therapist must be secure enough in his or her own world to live—temporarily but comfortably—in the client's world. What is more, it means not only living in that world, but also accepting the client's judgments about that world. The therapist accepts, not that the judgments are true, but that they are truly the client's. Finally, the therapist must not only understand the client's world as the client perceives it, but also must accurately communicate that understanding to the client (Holdstock & Rogers, 1977).

Unconditional positive regard.   Another function of the therapist is to offer a kind of caring for the client that Rogers calls "unconditional positive regard" (Rogers, 1951). This means accepting the client "as is," valuing the client as a person, regardless of the client's appearance or behavior. Unconditional positive regard depends on accurate empathy as its vehicle: the effort to understand the client without exercising control or judgment is the primary mode for communicating unconditional positive regard (Holdstock & Rogers, 1977).

Congruence. To fulfill Rogers' third function, the therapist must have some of the characteristics of the fully-functioning person, so that he or she is able to respond to and interact with the client as a person, not just through the role of therapist. This involves being relatively transparent to the client, being open to the feelings, thoughts, and attitudes of the moment, not in a way that burdens the client, but in a way that reveals the therapist.

PRACTICE OF COUNSELING

Major Techniques

Some of the early formulations of nondirective therapy saw the therapist as a nonentity in the process and thus stressed techniques (Rogers, 1942). More recently, however, the therapist is seen as an active partner in the therapeutic relationship, and attitudes and philosophy are therefore given more weight than techniques per se (Patterson, 1980). Evidently, since techniques are the means of implementing attitudes and philosophy, they must be consistent with them. Questioning, probing, interpreting, and analyzing are all but absent from the client-centered therapist's repertoire.

The best known client-centered technique is reflection of feeling. Actually, that is not a very accurate description of the process. It is more paraphrase than mere reflection and more feeling and content or general state than just feeling. Whatever the words, it is an attempt to let clients know that they (not just their words) have been heard, understood, and accepted as is. Accurate empathy is the vehicle for both positive regard and congruence. Part of the package, though not formally a technique, is the therapist's hovering attentiveness (eye contact, tones of voice, rate of speaking, and choice of words).

Treatment Parameters

Because the client-centered approach is used in a wide variety of situations, there is no one typical physical setting that would be generally acceptable. The setting for a one-to-one client-therapist relationship might be a traditional office, while a group of Peace Corps volunteers might meet in a trailer on an Indian reservation (Meador & Rogers, 1973). Generally, individual sessions are 50 to 60 minutes once a week, while group sessions are one-and-a-half to two hours twice a week. However, both the duration of each session and the frequency of the sessions will depend on the age of the clients and the purpose of the interaction. The number of sessions also depends on the severity and type of problem brought to therapy. However, by nature, **client-centered** therapy tends to be at least six months or more in length.

CASE STUDY *(Meador & Rogers, 1973, pp. 140–141).*

Therapist: I see there are some cigarettes here in the drawer. Hm? Yeah, it is hot out. *(Silence of 25 seconds)*

T: Do you look kind of angry this morning, or is that my imagination? *(Client shakes head slightly)* Not angry, huh? *(Silence of 1 minute, 26 seconds)*

T: Feel like letting me in on whatever is going on? *(Silence of 12 minutes, 52 seconds)*

T: *(Softly)* I kind of feel like saying that "If it would be of any help at all, I would like to come in." On the other hand, if it's just something you'd rather . . . if you just feel more like being within yourself, feeling whatever you're feeling within yourself, why that's OK too. I guess another thing I'm saying, really, in saying that is, "I do care. I'm not just sitting here like a stick." *(Silence of 1 minute, 11 seconds)*

T: And I guess your silence is saying to me that either you don't want to or can't come out right now and that's OK. So I won't pester you but I just want you to know I'm here. *(Silence of 17 minutes, 41 seconds)*

T: I see I'm going to have to stop in a few minutes. *(Silence of 20 seconds)*

T: It's hard for me to know how you've been feeling, but it looks as though part of the time maybe you'd rather I didn't know how you were feeling. Anyway it looks as though part of the time it just feels good to let down and relax the tension. But as I say, I don't really know how you feel. It's just the way it looks to me. Have things been pretty bad lately? *(Silence of 45 seconds)*

T: Maybe this morning you just wish I'd shut up—and maybe I should, but I just keep feeling I'd like to—I don't know, be in touch with you in some way. *(Silence of 2 minutes, 21 seconds)* *(Jim yawns)*

T: Sounds discouraged or tired. *(Silence of 41 seconds)*

Client: No, just lousy.

T: Everything's lousy, huh? You feel lousy? *(Silence of 39 seconds)*

T: Want to come in Friday at 12:00 at the usual time?

C: *(Yawns and mutters something unintelligible. Silence of 48 seconds)*

T: Just kind of feel sunk way down deep in these lousy, lousy feelings, hm?—Is it something like it?

C: No.

T: No? *(Silence of 20 seconds)*

C: No. I just ain't no good to nobody, never was, and never will be.

T: Feeling that now, hm? That you're just no good to yourself, no good to anybody. Never will be any good to anybody. Just that you're completely worthless, huh?—Those really are lousy feelings. Just feel that you're no good at all, hm?

C: Yeah. (*Muttering in low, discouraged voice*) That's what this guy I went to town with just the other day told me.
T: This guy that you went to town with really told you that you were no good? Is that what you're saying? Did I get that right?
C: M-hm.
T: I guess the meaning of that—if I get it right—is that here's somebody that meant something to you and what does he think of you? Why, he's told you that he thinks you're no good at all. And that just really knocks the props out from under you. (*Jim weeps silently*) It just brings the tears. (*Silence of 20 seconds*)
C: (*Rather defiantly*) I don't care though.
T: You tell yourself that you don't care at all, but somehow I guess some part of you cares because some part of you weeps over it. (*Silence of 19 seconds*)
T: I guess some part of you just feels, "Here I am hit with another blow, as if I hadn't had enough blows like this during my life when I feel that people don't like me. Here's someone I've begun to feel attached to and now *he* doesn't like me. And I'll say I don't care. I won't let it make any difference to me. But just the same, the tears run down my cheeks."
C: (*Muttering*) I guess I always knew it.
T: Hm?
C: I guess I always knew it.
T: If I'm getting that right, it is that what makes it hurt worst of all is that when he tells you you're no good, well, shucks, that's what you've always felt about yourself. Is that the meaning of what you're saying? (*Client nods slightly, indicating agreement*) Um-hm. So you feel as though he's just confirming what you've already known. He's confirming what you've already felt in some way. (*Silence of 23 seconds*)
T: So that between his saying so and your perhaps feeling it underneath, you feel about as no good as anybody could feel. (*Silence of 2 minutes, 1 second*) End of interview.

This was a young man who had caused trouble in the institution. He frequently felt mistreated, easily took offense, and often fought with the staff. He revealed that he had no tender feelings and was bitter against others. However, in this interview (and the following, not reported here) he began to experience the depth of his own feelings of worthlessness, of having no excuse for living.

Applications

The client-centered approach can be used any time someone feels misunderstood, wants understanding, and is willing to be open about thoughts and feelings. There are four categories of helping situations in which client-centered principles are most effectively applied (Meador & Rogers, 1973).

Counseling and psychotherapy.   The client-centered approach has been effective in individual counseling with all types of clients. Pastoral counseling, school counseling, play therapy, and marriage and family counseling have utilized this approach (Meador & Rogers, 1973).

Human relations training.   Client-centered principles have been widely used in the training of both professional and para-professional helpers. This includes all levels of school personnel, social workers, nurses, physicians, and Peace Corps and Vista volunteers (Meador & Rogers, 1973).

Encounter groups.   Rogers was largely—though not solely— responsible for the growth of the growth group movement. In fact, from the late 1960s to the middle 1970s, he all but abandoned individual counseling in favor of encounter groups. These groups dealt with labor-management disputes, Black-White relations, student-faculty concerns, and other polarized relationships, as well as the more basic interpersonal relations of individuals and groups.

Institutional change.   This has included faculties of individual schools as well as entire school systems, industrial plants, businesses, churches, and organizations such as YWCA/YMCA. It has even been used with several government agencies.

CRITIQUE

Research Support

A distinctive feature of the client-centered approach has been a strong research orientation. Probably it is more extensively researched than any other method of therapy, except perhaps behavior therapy.

The therapist-offered variables of empathy, respect, and genuineness have been researched extensively; and the findings provide strong support for this part of Rogerian theory. At least in client-centered counseling, empathy, genuineness, and nonpossessive caring do seem causally related to many process variables, such as depth of self-exploration and to successful outcomes (Barrett-Lennard, 1962; Rogers et al., 1967; Truax & Mitchell, 1971). Some evidence suggests that low levels of these core conditions may be associated with a worsening of the client's situation (Bergin, 1963, 1966; Truax & Carkhuff, 1967).

Rogers hypothesized that genuineness, empathy, and nonpossessive caring are important growth-facilitating conditions in all psychotherapeutic approaches and in interpersonal relationships generally. This hypothesis was confirmed by Truax and the Johns Hopkins Group (Truax, Wargo, Frank, Imber, Battle, Hoen-Saric, Nash, & Stone,

1966) and by Kurtz and Grummon (1972). However, Garfield and Bergin (1971) were unable to replicate these findings and suggested that the Rogerian constructs may be valid only for client-centered counseling and psychotherapy.

Rogers and Gendlin both theorized that process movement should be greater in successful than in unsuccessful cases, and some preliminary research confirmed this (Rogers, 1961). Higher levels on the experiencing scale and on other closely related process scales do, in fact, differentiate successful from unsuccessful cases; however, the successful ones are high on the experiencing variables even at the start of therapy. Clients who enter therapy with the ability to engage in experiential focusing became the success cases, while those low in the ability became the failures. Thus, process level on the experiencing scale rather than process movement is associated with success; and the client-centered counselor was doing little in most cases to improve the client's experiential focusing ability. Nor is openness to one's ongoing experiential process equivalent to psychological health, because many clients scored high on this ability when they entered therapy, even though they were quite maladjusted (Rogers, 1967). Instead of defining psychological health, experiencing variables and other process scale variables seem to measure behaviors that enable a person to profit from counseling (Grummon, 1979).

Some early research by Rogers and Dymond (1954), Hogan (1948), and Raskin (1949) indicated that as a counseling relationship progresses, there is a decrease in the amount of the client's defensiveness, an increase in congruence between self and experience, and a tendency for the client to see the self as the locus of evaluation. Studies by Truax and Carkhuff (1967) and Carkhuff and Berenson (1967) showed that, given the necessary and sufficient conditions described by Rogers, clients will move into self-exploration, which will lead to positive changes. Not only are these conditions factors in clients' growth, but levels of these conditions have been found to be significant, according to the research of Truax (1963) and Truax and Carkhuff (1965).

Halkides (1958) related the presence of the core conditions to success in therapy. On the basis of several criteria, ten cases were identified as successful and ten as unsuccessful. Blind judges rated the degree to which the core conditions were present in the interview tape recordings of these cases. Halkides found that all three of the conditions were significantly associated with the successful cases. Barrett-Lennard (1959) studied the core conditions from the vantage point of the client rather than judges' interview ratings. After the fifth interview and at the end of therapy, clients completed the Barrett-Lennard Relationship Inventory. He found that clients' improvement in adjustment was significantly related to their perception of their therapist's (after five interviews) having respect, genuinesness, and empathic understanding for them.

Among the most definitive studies of the client-centered approach were those conducted by Rogers et al. (1967) at the Wisconsin Psychiatric Institute. This large-scale project showed that (a) patients whose therapists offered high levels of non-possessive warmth, genuineness, and empathy showed significant positive personality and behavior change; (b) patients whose therapists offered low levels of those core conditions exhibited deterioration in personality and behavioral functioning. A nine year follow-up of these results (Truax & Mitchell, 1971) indicated that the effects found at the end of treatment tend to persist. Patients whose therapists had offered high levels of the core conditions had a significantly better post-hospitalization history than those patients whose therapists had offered low levels of the conditions. They were also significantly better off than a matched control group of patients who had not received therapy.

Finally, the Wisconsin studies indicated that the client's level of involvement in the therapy process at the beginning of therapy is an important predictor of improvement. Contrary to expectations, increases over the course of therapy in the client's level of self-exploration were not related to outcome, whereas the client's initial level was related to outcome.

One of the best studies comparing different therapeutic orientations was conducted by Raskin (1974). He selected eight-minute audiotape segments from the therapy sessions of six expert therapists, each of whom had agreed that the segment selected was representative of the way he worked. The therapists represented the following orientations: RET, experiential, psychoanalytic, Jungian, client-centered, and direct analytic. Eighty-three therapists then rated the tapes on a four-point scale as to the degree to which the following therapist variables were present in the tape segment: cognitive, experiential, empathic, therapist-directed, egalitarian, warm and giving, unconditional positive regard, congruent, emphasizes the unconscious, systematically reinforces, self-confident, and inspires confidence (in the judge). In addition to rating the audiotape segments, the judges also rated themselves on the degree to which the therapist variables were present in their own work, and again, on the degree to which the therapist variable should be present in the ideal therapist's work.

Raskin found that the expert therapists were rated as practicing differently from one another, that the orientation and experience level of the judges made little difference in their rating, and that there was a high degree of agreement in their rating of the ideal therapist. Most important, the judges viewed both their own practice and the ideal as being most like the client-centered expert. Regardless of orientation, the judges tended to agree that the experiential aspect of therapy is more important than the cognitive and that empathy and congruence are to be given greater weight than therapist directions, emphasizing the unconscious, and systematic reinforcement. Finally, it was found that the correlations between the client-centered therapist and the ideal was .94; the next highest correlation with the ideal was .57 for the experiential therapist; the remaining four experts all correlated negatively with the ideal, the extreme being -.66 for the Jungian therapist. Thus this study not only supports the importance of the core conditions, but also indicates that the client-centered approach is regarded as quite close to the ideal therapeutic approach by 83 judges, of whom only 23 classified themselves as client-centered (Harren, 1977).

Evaluation

Winston Churchill once said of American democracy, "It is the worst form of government in the world—but the only one that works!" Judging by the number of counselors who claim or appear to be client-centered in their approach, that seems to be a fair assessment of the prevailing attitude of counselors toward the Rogerian approach. Carkhuff and Berenson (1967) found some good news and some bad news for client-centered therapy. The client-centered approach does provide the client with immediate and concrete feedback about what he has just said, an opportunity to express previously denied experiences, and the opportunity to find his own mode of expression. In addition, this approach defines the therapist's responsibilities within ranges safe for both client and therapist and enables the therapist to remain unique and personal in the relationship. On the other hand, the client-centered approach denies to the client an opportunity for real-life conditions for functioning and it fails the therapist by denying him the opportunity to translate commitment into action through directive techniques.

Grummon (1979) pointed out the fact that the client-centered perspective fails to account for the effects of conditions existing prior to treatment and concurrent external events on a client's behavior. Client-centered practice is based on the client's subjective perception of reality rather than on the objective reality itself. However, both theory and practice fail to take into account the effect of reality on perception. Another weakness, also mentioned by Grummon, is that many of the constructs used by Rogers are superficially appealing but are difficult, if not impossible, to operationalize (e.g., self-actualizing tendency, organismic valuing process).

This impreciseness lends itself to misinterpretation by a naïve or careless counselor. Client-centered counseling involves more than just active listening and reflecting feelings. If the counselor has not assimilated the underlying attitudes that are the core of the Rogerian approach, then he or she cannot truly practice client-centered counseling.

I agree generally with these criticisms; but my major objection is that, while it does well what it does, first, it takes forever to do it, and second, the precondition of nondirectiveness eliminates from the counselor's repertoire some very effective techniques or modalities. I am also not convinced that unending unconditional positive regard is always in the client's best interest. I have found that often—not always, but often—I can help a client to move more effectively and more efficiently through therapy by introducing—at later stages—a conditional regard. Always the condition, in essence, is "I won't accept your behavior at a level lower than you have already demonstrated you can achieve and maintain."

In summary, then, in my opinion, the client-centered perspective on human nature, the development of personality, and the development of maladaptive behavior is clear and true. I believe that the nondirective approach, with some modification, is effective in early stages of therapy. However, I have some trouble with the fuzzy language; but most of all I feel trapped by the imperative of unconditional positive regard and nondirectiveness throughout therapy.

Current Status

Rogers' recent thinking is best characterized by the shift from *client-centered therapy* to a *person-centered approach* to far more than therapy. The change in emphasis is an attempt to emphasize a more explicitly existential outlook: the individual is the basic unit of all interactions, not just in terms of some role (client, student, counselor), but rather as *person,* as *being,* as *I am.* It also draws attention to the fact that society is not an amorphous mass of humanity, but an aggregate of unique individuals. In other words, there is no society apart from the individuals who make it up. Although this reflects a broader view of the target population, it does not seem to me to be a real departure from the principles of client-centered therapy delineated four decades ago.

REFERENCES

BARRETT-LENNARD, G. T.,   *Dimensions of the client's experience of his therapist associated with personality change.* Unpublished doctoral dissertation. University of Chicago, 1959.

BARRETT-LENNARD, G. T.,   Dimensions of therapist response as causal factors in therapeutic change. *Psychological Monographs,* 1962, *76,* (43, Whole No. 562).

BERGIN, A. E.   The effects of psychotherapy: Negative results revisited. *Journal of Counseling Psychology,* 1963, *10,* 244–255.

BERGIN, A. E.   Some implications of psychotherapy research for therapeutic practice. *Journal of Abnormal Psychology,* 1966, *71,* 235–246.

CARKHUFF, R. R., & BERENSON, B. G.   *Beyond counseling and therapy.* New York: Holt, Rinehart, & Winston, 1967, Chap. 7.

EVANS, R. I.   *Carl Rogers: The man and his ideas.* New York: E. P. Dutton and Company, 1975.

GARFIELD, S., & BERGIN, A. E.   Personal therapy, therapy outcome, and some therapist variables. *Psychotherapy Theory and Practice,* 1971, *8,* 251–253.

GRUMMON, D. L.   Client-centered theory. In H. M. Burks & B. Stefflre, *Theories of counseling* (3rd ed.). New York: McGraw-Hill, 1979.

HALKIDES, G.   *An experimental study of four conditions necessary for therapeutic change.* Unpublished doctoral dissertation. University of Chicago, 1958.

HANSEN, J. C., STEVIC, R. R., & WARNER, R. W., JR.   *Counseling: Theory and process* (3rd ed.). Boston: Allyn & Bacon, 1982, Chap. 6.

HARREN, V. A.   The client-centered theory of personality and therapy. In D. C. Rimm & J. W. Somervill, *Abnormal psychology.* New York: Academic Press, 1977, Chap. 17.

HOGAN, R.   *The development of a measure of client defensiveness in the counseling relationship.* Unpublished doctoral dissertation. University of Chicago, 1948.

HOLDSTOCK, T. L., & ROGERS, C. R.   Person-centered theory. In R. Corsini (Ed.), *Current personality theories.*   Itasca,   IL: F. E. Peacock,   Publishers,   1977, Chap. 4.

HOLLIS, J. W., & WANTZ, R. A.   *Counselor preparation. 1980: Programs, personnel, trends* (4th ed.). Muncie, Ind.: Accelerated Development Press, 1980.

KIRSCHENBAUM, H.   *On becoming Carl Rogers.* New York: Dell, 1979.

KURTZ, R. R., & GRUMMON, D. L.   Different approaches to the measurement of therapist empathy and their relationship to therapy outcomes. *Journal of Consulting and Clinical Psychology,* 1972, *39,* 106–115.

MATARAZZO, R. G.   Research on the teaching and learning of psychotherapeutic skills. In S. L. Garfield & A. E. Bergin, *Handbook of Psychotherapy and Behavior Change* (2nd ed.). New York: John Wiley & Sons, 1978.

MEADOR, B., & ROGERS, C. R.   Client-centered therapy. In R. Corsini (Ed.). *Current psychotherapies.* Itasca, IL: F. E. Peacock, Publishers, 1973, Chap. 4.

PATTERSON, C. H.   *Theories of counseling and psychotherapy* (3rd ed.). New York: Harper & Row, 1980, Chap. 13.

PRICE, R. H.   *Abnormal behavior: Perspectives in conflict.* New York: Holt, Rinehart, & Winston, 1972.

RASKIN, N. J.   An analysis of six parallel studies of the therapeutic process. *Journal of Consulting Psychology,* 1949, *13,* 206–220.

RASKIN, N. J.   *Studies of therapeutic orientation: Ideology and practice.* Orlando, Fla.: American Academy of Psychotherapists, 1974.

ROGERS, C. R.   *Counseling and psychotherapy.* Boston: Houghton Mifflin Co., 1942.

ROGERS, C. R.,   *Client-centered therapy: Its current practice, implications, and theory.* Boston: Houghton Mifflin, 1951.

ROGERS, C. R.   A theory of therapy, personality, and interpersonal relationships as developed in the client-centered framework. In S. Koch (Ed.), *Psychology: A study of a science* (Vol. 3). New York: McGraw-Hill, 1959.

ROGERS, C. R.   *On becoming a person: A therapist's view of psychotherapy.* Boston: Houghton Mifflin, 1961.

ROGERS, C. R.   Client-centered psychotherapy. In A. M. Freedman & H. I. Kaplan (Eds.), *Comprehensive textbook of psychiatry.* Baltimore: The Williams and Wilkins Company, 1967.

ROGERS, C. R.   *Freedom to learn.* Columbus, OH: Charles E. Merrill, 1969.

ROGERS, C. R., & DYMOND, R. F. EDS.   *Psychotherapy and personality change: Coordinated studies in the client-centered approach.* Chicago: The University of Chicago Press, 1954.

ROGERS, C. R., GENDLIN, E. T., KIESLER, D. V., & TRUAX, C. B.   *The psychotherapeutic relationship and its impact: A study of psychotherapy of schizophrenics.* Madison, WI: The University of Wisconsin Press, 1967.

TRUAX, C. B.,   Effective ingredients of psychotherapy: An approach to unravelling the patient-therapist interaction. *Journal of Counseling Psychology*, 1963, *16*, 256–263.

TRUAX, C. B., & CARKHUFF, R. R.   Personality change in hospitalized mental patients during group psychotherapy as a function of the use of alternate sessions and vicarious therapy pretraining. *Journal of Clinical Psychology*, 1965, *21*, 327–329.

TRUAX, C. B., & CARKHUFF, R. R.   *Toward effective counseling and psychotherapy: Training and practice.* Chicago: Aldine, 1967.

TRUAX, C. B., & MITCHELL, K. M.   Research on certain therapist interpersonal skills in relation to process and outcome. In A. E. Bergin & S. Garfield, (Eds.), *Handbook of psychotherapy and behavior change.* New York: John Wiley & Sons, 1971.

TRUAX, C. B., WARGO, D., FRANK, J. D., IMBER, S. D., BATTLE, C. C., HOEN-SARIC, R., NASH, E. H., & STONE, A. R.   Therapist empathy, genuineness, and warmth and patient therapeutic outcome. *Journal of Consulting Psychology*, 1966, *30*, 395–401.

CHAPTER TEN
HUMAN RESOURCE DEVELOPMENT

Ever since this text was originally conceived as class notes, I have been concerned about my objectivity in this chapter for two reasons. Bob Carkhuff is not just a name, and he is more than a professional acquaintance; he is a friend. More than that, I believe in the Human Resource Development (HRD) model. On the other hand, I never intended this text to be a totally dispassionate, clinically sterile view of anything so flesh-and-blood as perspectives on human behavior. I think you have a right to know my biases. You don't have to abide by them.

Carkhuff has stated his "Credo of a Militant Humanist" in several places (Berenson, 1975; Carkhuff & Berenson, 1976), but nowhere more succinctly than in this paragraph:

> Human nourishment is made up of commitment, discipline, skills, and strategies. Mostly, human nourishment is dependent upon hard work and the acquisition of skills. The commitment is to grow: to be one's best physically, emotionally, and intellectually. The discipline enables one to do what needs to be done without self-indulgence. Skills provide the response repertoire that enables one to live, learn, and work effectively. Systematic strategies provide the means to achieve physical, emotional, and intellectual goals (Carkhuff & Berenson, 1977, pp. 4–5).

HISTORICAL DEVELOPMENT

Personal Background

Robert Carkhuff was born in 1934 of middle-class parents in Linden, New Jersey. He obtained a B.A. in political science from Rutgers in 1956, served three years in the army, and then received his Ph.D. in psychology from the State University of New York at Buffalo in 1963. Following graduation he took a position at the University of Kentucky as co-director of a psychotherapy research unit and at the same time participated in Carl Rogers' (1967) extensive research on schizophrenics. Over the next eight years, he moved first to the University of Massachusetts, then to the State University of New York at Buffalo, and finally to American International College in Springfield, Massachusetts. In 1970, he established Carkhuff Associates, a private consulting firm, and the Human Resource Development Press. Shortly thereafter, he founded the Carkhuff Institute for Human Technology and ended his direct participation in academe. More recently, he developed Human Technology, Inc., an organization dedicated to serving governments and private industry in the development and implementation of organizational training and productivity systems. According to the Social Science Citation Index, he is the author of three of the 100 most-cited books by social scientists: *Toward Effective Counseling* (1967, with C. B. Truax) and *Helping and Human Relations,* vols. I & II, published in 1969 (Carkhuff, 1982).

Theoretical Background

In the early 1960s, the helping professions were confronted with the challenge that counseling and psychotherapy did not effect a measureable change in the lives of patients (Levitt, 1963; Lewis, 1965). Eysenck discovered that about two-thirds of his patients remained out of the hospital for a year whether or not they had been seen by professional psychotherapists while in the hospital. His conclusion was that psychotherapy is ineffective since spontaneous remission accounts for 67 percent of the success rate.

There are at least two methodological errors with this line of thinking. First, the fact that these patients got no professional help does not mean that they received no help at all (ward attendants, nurses, visitors, and even other patients could have provided some therapeutic experiences). Second, Eysenck failed to look at the variability of change in those treated versus those not treated. This latter approach was taken by several groups of researchers in the late 1960s (Rogers, Gendlin, Kiesler, & Truax, 1967; Truax & Carkhuff, 1967). They discovered that there was considerably more variability of outcome among patients receiving professional treatment than among those not receiving treatment. This suggested two conclusions: psychotherapy does make a difference and that difference may be for better or for worse. In other words, some professionally treated patients improved considerably while others deteriorated significantly.

More recent research has shed new light on the effectiveness of counseling and psychotherapy. Anthony and his associates found that within three to five years of treatment, 65 to 75 percent of the ex-patients return for further treatment and that the gainful employment of ex-patients is below 25 percent (Anthony, Buell, Sharrett, & Althoff, 1972; Anthony, Cohen, & Vitalo, 1978). The bottom line, then, is that traditional counseling and psychotherapy have a stable success rate of about 20 percent. Of the two-thirds of the patients who initially get better, only one-third to one-quarter stay better.

In addition to the alarmingly low success rate, two other implications of the outcome research discussed above were that helping may be for better or for worse and that these effects can be accounted for—at least in part—by the therapist's level of functioning on certain emotional and interpersonal dimensions (Carkhuff & Berenson, 1977; Rogers et al., 1967; Truax & Carkhuff, 1967). That is, clients whose therapists functioned at relatively high levels of these dimensions demonstrated positive change, while clients whose therapists functioned at low levels of the same dimensions showed either no change or deteriorated change.

The therapist dimensions that were investigated were empathy, unconditional regard, and congruence (Rogers et al., 1967). Later, these were modified to emphasize nonpossessive warmth (rather than unconditional regard) and genuineness (rather than congruence), but they remained essentially the same. About the same time, the number of helper (therapist) skills was increased to include self-disclosure, concreteness, confrontation, and immediacy of expression. These new dimensions were the first real departure from Rogers' (1957) formulation and the beginning of a systematic model of helper skills. (Carkhuff prefers the term "helper" to "therapist," or even "counselor," because it emphasizes the fact that the skills of helping are relevant in all walks of life, not just the professional.)

Next, the process of operationally defining each of the helper skills was begun. Through this process, it was found that accurate empathy was the principal modality for communicating respect; and self-disclosure was subsumed under genuineness. When the remaining helper skills were analyzed, two factors emerged: responsiveness (incorporating accurate empathy and respect) and initiative (including confrontation and immediacy). Genuineness and concreteness each loaded uniquely on both factors (e.g., under responsiveness, concreteness takes the form of accurate discrimination of the helpee's [this term replaces "client" or "patient"] frame of reference; under initiative, it involves specificity of direction). Finally, practice revealed the need for an introduction to the process designed to involve the helpee in the process—attending skills—and a bridge from the responding mode to the initiative mode—personalizing skills. The final phase in the development of helper skills involved the refinement of the initiative skills, particularly those involving decision-making and program development.

A number of outcome studies were conducted to determine the effects of helper skills on various measures of helpee outcome (Aspy, 1969; Pierce & Drasgow, 1969; Shilling, 1970; 1976). One of the results of these studies was that Rogers' (1957) "therapeutic personality change" was replaced by "human resource development (HRD)" as the desired outcome. Later, human resource development was operationalized in terms of the quantity and quality of skills in the helpee's response repertoire. Since human behavior involves doing, feeling, and thinking, human resource development must, of necessity, include physical, emotional (interpersonal), and intellectual functioning.

Study of helper skills and helpee outcomes helped define the cause and effect of helping. The next step was to study the process. The work of all the great theorists, from Freud to Rogers, as well as clinical experience in counseling and psychotherapy, dictated that the first phase of the helping process be characterized by an exploration of material of personal relevance to the helpee. Through a series of studies (Pierce, Carkhuff, & Berenson, 1967) in which the helper's level of functioning was experimentally manipulated, it was found that the helpee's level of self-exploration is, in part, a function of the helper's responsive skills. In other words, the helping process is begun by the helper's attentiveness; and the helpee's self-exploration is facilitated by the helper's responsiveness.

The end point of helping is some demonstrable change in behavior. In HRD terms, this involves a demonstrated change or gain in physical, emotional, and/or intellectual functioning; i.e., the helpee must, through some observable action, demonstrate the change. However, research and clinical practice have shown that exploration alone, even thorough and extensive exploration, does not always lead to helpee action. Two additional elements are needed: helpee understanding and helper skill delivery. The helpee must know not only where he is in his world, but also where he is in relation to where he wants or needs to be. Many helpees, even after they thoroughly understand their personal deficits and assets, are unable to eliminate the one and augment the other because they lack the skills to do so. The helper's final function in the helping process is to deliver those skills (Carkhuff & Berenson, 1977).

Summary

Outcome is defined in terms of human resource development: increasing the helpee's level of functioning in the physical, emotional/interpersonal, and intellectual areas. Those outcomes are principally a function of the helper's skills in attending, responding, personalizing, and initiating. The process by which the helpee grows is through exploration and understanding to action.

THEORY OF PERSONALITY

Definition of Terms

Accurate empathy. The helper's ability to communicate at high levels of empathic understanding appears to depend on the helper's ability to allow himself or herself to experience or merge with the experience of the helpee, reflect upon this experience while suspending his or her own judgments and tolerating anxiety, and communicate this understanding to the helpee.

Actualizer. Actualizers are people characterized by a high level of physical energy, emotional commitments to a mission outside themselves, interpersonal relations that lead to incorporating the missions of others, substantive specialty skills leading to skilled expertise, learning skills leading to the effective processing of data, and teaching skills leading to the communication of the processed data.

Attending. Attending involves some physical act on the part of the helper that enables the helpee to become involved in the helping process.

Concreteness. Concreteness, or specificity of expression, involves the fluent, direct, and complete expression of specific feelings and experiences, regardless of their emotional content, by both helper and helpee.

Confrontation. Confrontation is an active, evaluative, subjective response that offers the helpee much-needed feedback about his impact upon the helper. It involves the helper's pointing out a discrepancy between (a) the helpee's expression of what he wishes to be and how he actually expresses himself, (b) the helpee's verbal expression of his awareness of himself and his observable or reported behavior, or (c) how the helper experiences the helpee's expression of his own experience of himself.

Effectiveness. In any operation, effectiveness involves effective people operating effective programs through an effective organization.

Effective organization. Effective organizations are simply ways of relating effective people to effective programs. The function of an effective organization, then, is to appoint the most effective people to the leadership roles and equip them with programs that will not only serve the functions of the operation, but will also develop additional effective leadership within the operation.

Effective people. Effective people are a function of the quantity and quality of responses they have in their interpersonal skills repertoire.

Effective programs. Effective programs offer systematic methodologies for operationalizing goals and for developing step-by-step programs for attaining these goals.

Encouraging. Encouraging is the second step in involving a helpee in the helping process. It means giving the helpee a personal reason to become involved.

Exploration. Self-exploration in interpersonal processes is defined by the voluntary introduction by the helpee of personally relevant material concerning where he or she is in relation to his or her world and the people in it.

Favorability scale. The favorability scale is used in the decision-making process and is "simply a systematic design for determining in advance the sorts of things that will have a positive effect upon any given value" affecting the decision to be made.

Genuineness. Facilitative genuineness in interpersonal processes is defined as the helper's providing no discrepancies between what he or she verbalizes and what other cues indicate he or she is feeling.

Helping. Helping is the act of promoting constructive behavioral changes in an individual, which enhance the affective dimension of the individual's life and permit a greater degree of personal control over subsequent activities.

Human resource development. This refers to the development or actualizing of human potential—the physical, emotional/interpersonal, and intellectual functioning of yourself and your helpees.

Immediacy. Immediacy means understanding and interpreting in the moment what is going on between you (the helper) and the helpee. Immediacy involves the highest levels of responsive and initiative behavior. It means living fully in the moment through responding fully to the helpee's experience and initiating fully from your own (helper's) experience.

Informing. Informing is the first step in involving the helpee in the helping process. It involves letting the helpee know *whom* to see, *when* and *where* the appointment will take place, *how* to get there, and *what* the general purpose of the interview will be.

Initiative. The initiative factor involves the helper's taking the helpee's experience into consideration in developing his or her own experience of the helpee, and, in conjunction with the helpee, in developing goals and action steps to help the helpee get from where he or she is to where he or she wants or needs to be.

Interchangeable response. An interchangeable response is a helper's response to the helpee that communicates the same feeling and reason for the feelings as expressed by the helpee. It frequently takes the form "You feel _____ because _____."

Interpersonal skills. Interpersonal skills are substantive communication skills that facilitate a relationship between two people, enabling one (the helper) to contribute to the actualization of the human potential of the other (the helpee). The interpersonal skills include attending, responding, personalizing, and initiating skills.

Listening skills. The skill of listening involves, first, suspending your own judgment in order to hear the helpee's frame of reference. Next, the helper must listen for cues to the helpee's feelings, level of energy, and degree of congruence. Finally, the helper must listen for the *who, what, when, where, why*, and *how* (5WH) of the helpee's situation.

Observing skills. Observing skills involve the helper's ability to see and understand the nonverbal behavior of the helpee. The helper must observe the aspects of the helpee's appearance and behavior that tell about the helpee's energy level, feeling, and degree of congruence.

Personalizing. Personalizing is a helper skill that tries to enable the helpee to understand where he or she is in relation to where he or she wants or needs to be. It involves building a base of interchangeable responses before personalizing the meaning, the problem, the feelings, and the goal.

Physical fitness. Physical fitness involves having physical energy and resources to function at your best, physically, emotionally, and intellectually. It is measured principally by cardiovascular endurance and secondarily by flexibility and dynamic strength. It does not involve athletic ability.

Positioning. Positioning is a cluster of physical attending skills, including level, angle, inclination, and eye-contact.

Primary steps.   The major steps of a program are called the primary steps. Developing primary steps is the first phase of program development. It involves identifying the goal as the most complex step in the program, then the starting point as the simplest, and finally, intermediate steps at appropriate intervals of time or difficulty.

Program development.   In a broad sense, program development involves (a) assessing (exploring) where you are, (b) operationally defining where you want to be, and (c) operationally defining the steps you need to take to get where you want to be. More specifically, program development is step (c): developing and implementing the steps to achieve an operationally defined goal.

Respect.   Respect or positive regard in interpersonal processes is defined by the helper's communication of positive respect and concern for the helpee's feelings, experiences, and potential.

Responding.   Responding is a helper skill that involves the helper's verbal and nonverbal response to the content, feeling, and meaning of the helpee's expression of his or her experience.

Response repertoire.   An individual's response repertoire is a collection of verbal and nonverbal responses to his or her current experience. It may involve a verbal response to a person or an action response to a situation.

Responsiveness.   Responsiveness emphasizes responding to the helpee's experience at the level at which the helpee expresses that experience. It is based totally on the helpee's experience and the helper's skills to discriminate that experience and to communicate accurately his or her understanding of that experience.

Secondary steps.   Secondary steps are the fillers between the primary steps of a program. Developing secondary steps is the second step of program development. It is characterized by turning already developed primary steps into minigoals and then developing new steps to these goals. The final phase of the process involves attaching time units to each step.

Self-disclosure.   Self-disclosure is the helper's revelation of personal details in a way that facilitates the helpee's self-exploration and/or self-understanding.

Skills.   Skills are observable, measurable, replicable, and teachable (behaviors). Skills are the operational representations of the dimensions of human potential.

Specialty-area skills.   Specialty-area skills are those required for the effective execution of one's learning or working functions (such as study skills for the student; teaching skills for the teacher).

Think steps.   Think steps support the do steps of a program. There are three categories of think steps: (a) before-think steps prepare the helpee for a given do step, (b) during-think steps allow the helpee to keep track of progress while actually involved in the do-step activity, and (c) after-think steps make it possible for the helpee to consolidate learning and to make sure that the do steps have been completed satisfactorily.

Understanding.   Self-understanding in interpersonal processes is defined by the helpee's ability to add to his exploration of where he is and understanding of where he wants or needs to be in relation to his world and the people in it.

Value hierarchy.   An individual's value hierarchy is a ranking of the personal values having a direct bearing on the choice of a given course of action.

Whole person.   The whole person is a fully functioning, self-actualized individual whose life is made up of actions that integrate physical, emotional, and intellectual resources in such a way that these actions lead to a stronger, more adequate self: self-actualization (Carkhuff & Berenson, 1977). Wholeness, like self-actualization, is an ideal, not an actually attainable goal.

View of Human Nature

Carkhuff views human nature as a vast reservoir of almost unlimited—and mostly untapped—potential: All humans have vast reservoirs of energy, which many fail to tap. Most of us have in reserve far more physical energy than we use; but we allow our bodies to atrophy without exercise, adequate rest, or proper diet. All of us have the emotional potential not only to enjoy our own lives but also to embrace our brothers and sisters, too; but we crawl into our shells and pull our feelings in after us. All of us have the intellectual potential to understand far more than we do; but we are so afraid of new learnings that we tell all our teachers, "don't teach me anything I don't already know!" We are enormously wealthy with potential, but too many of us are buried with our riches—even before we are dead.

This view is both optimistic and pessimistic: optimistic in regard to human potential, pessimistic in regard to the actualization of that potential. It is pessimistic, not because the potential cannot be actualized, but because, in the main, this potential is not being actualized. Many professional helpers are not teaching people how to actualize their potential.

Carkhuff's view of human nature has an Adlerian flavor, a sense of social interest: "Developing human resources means developing our own as well as others. We cannot develop our resources fully if we are not also involved in developing those of others. Developing human resources is a simultaneous and reciprocal process between the helper and the person being helped" (Carkhuff, 1981, p. 149).

Carkhuff views human nature as a dynamic process rather than as a static entity. Although he is not particularly enamored of the methods of existential psychology, he is quite comfortable with this view: life is growth; the only reason to live is to grow; growth is expanding to become one with the world.

Structure of Personality

The HRD model does not espouse a theory of personality structure. Such a theory and the constructs (ego, id, etc.) through which it is articulated are far too static. When Carkhuff has written about such psychoanalytic constructs, his tone has been somewhat less than cordial: "The unconscious is the major psychological component for those who cheat and abuse their resources and ask others to do the same" (Carkhuff & Berenson, 1977, p. 105). He acknowledges a certain structure to human potential: since we are operationally defined by doing, feeling, and thinking, we are both limited and set free by this structure—we cannot move outside it, but within it our horizons are unlimited.

Development of Personality

Consistent with his view of personality as an individual's potential for effective functioning in the physical, emotional, and intellectual areas, Carkhuff discusses personality development in terms of developing physical, emotional, and intellectual resources. Again, consistently, he looks at the dynamic process of development, not the static result of the process. Thus, he eschews traditional theories that trace development through a series of identifiable stages, because such an approach cannot be translated to human benefits. Rather, he looks at research efforts to discover and explain the causes and effects of development in the physical, emotional, and intellectual areas.

Physical development. There are three lines of recent research relevant to physical development: (a) the modification of autonomic functions through conditioning techniques (e.g., biofeedback), (b) the effect of sensory stimuli on physical development (e.g., sensory deprivation experiments), and (c) the effects of environmental stress on physical functioning (e.g., zero gravity). Studies such as these increase our understanding of physiological development. As a result of these new learnings, future physical development programs will begin to add to fitness attempts to modify bodily functions in order to bring about cognitive control of well being (Carkhuff, 1981).

Emotional development. In his original formulations (Carkhuff, 1969; Carkhuff & Berenson, 1976; 1977), Carkhuff used the term "emotional" to refer principally to interpersonal interactions and/or interpersonal interaction skills. More recently he has modified this slightly to include intrapersonal factors—he coined the term "emotivation," as opposed to motivation. The intrapersonal factor involves developing a mission outside oneself—"a cause for justice for specific subpopulations such as women, minorities, or children" (Carkhuff, 1981). The interpersonal factor involves committing yourself to someone else's mission. This somewhat circular language means that one who has the intrapersonal factor "feeds a man a fish," while those who possess the interpersonal factor "teach the skill of fishing." A fully actualized person cooks on both burners.

But how does one light both burners? How are these emotional—emotivational—factors developed? It can occur only through extended contact with people functioning at high levels of these factors. When Carkhuff writes of training in interpersonal skills (Carkhuff & Anthony,

1979; Carkhuff & Berenson, 1976), he is almost exclusively concerned with training professional or paraprofessional helpers to function in professional settings. However, by extension, it seems obvious that charity begins at home: parents functioning at high levels are apt to have children who begin to function at higher levels than children whose parents function at low levels of these factors. If these "high-level" children then meet other actualized adults outside the home, their chances of also becoming actualized are greatly increased.

Intellectual development. According to Carkhuff, "there is as yet no commonly accepted developmental sequence of cognition" (1981, p. 24); but he then summarizes the theories of Piaget, Dewey, Gagne, Bloom, and Guilford as contributing to the operationalizing of cognitive development. Later, in the same work (pp. 83–91), when he writes of the intellectual factors of the actualizers, he identifies three major dimensions. The first is the individual's substantive specialty; the degree to which that person has acquired the skills and knowledge needed to function effectively in his or her world. The second concerns the person's learning skills and processes: the ability to bring to any learning situation an effective means for gathering, analyzing, and interpreting information. The third intellectual factor involves the person's teaching or communication skills: assisting others in developing courses of action based on understanding. It would seem that intellectual development, too, can take place only in the context of contact with an actualized person.

Development of Maladaptive Behavior

All behavior is learned: both adaptive and maladaptive. Whether the behavior learned is adaptive or maladaptive, for better or for worse, is a function of the quantity and quality of skills learned, which, in turn, is a function of the quality of the learning experience.

All learning begins with the learner's frame of reference. If the helper (parent, teacher, counselor, spouse) does not have the skills to facilitate this initial exploration, there can be no learning. All learning must culminate in a skill objective that is directly useful in the learner's world. If the helper does not have the skills to identify the helpee's assets and deficits, to identify needed skills, and to develop programs to attain them, whatever insight may have been gained in the exploration will be lost in a sea of futility: it just won't work.

Even if the helper is functioning at high levels of interpersonal skills, if he or she is unable to deliver substantive skills, the helpee is left holding an empty bag. A large number of people grow up starved for even minimal levels of understanding, love, respect, genuineness, and direction. Others have been victimized by helpers who are, themselves, victims: parents, teachers, counselors, employers, or spouses without substantive skills. The effect of a limited repertoire of responses is perhaps most clearly seen in the typical juvenile delinquent, whose intellectual, interpersonal, and even physical responses are severely limited and whose likelihood of receiving effective help is even more limited. It is the limited repertoire of responses that dictates an individual's low probability of functioning effectively in a given situation. The typical human relationship peaks with the first contact and declines thereafter and is characterized by the parties to the relationship essentially ignoring one another (Carkhuff & Berenson, 1976; 1977). "Our children are lost because we are lost. Our children are undernourished because we don't know how to nourish them. We cannot provide human nourishment because we don't have the skills to do so" (Carkhuff & Berenson, 1977, p. 4).

In the HRD perspective, then, dysfunction or maladaptive behavior is due, not to some mysterious intrapsychic battle, but rather, to a lack of skills or the inability to function effectively in one's own world. This is why Carkhuff is able to make the statement that "psychopathy . . . is the preoccupation with irrelevancies" (Carkhuff & Berenson, 1977, p. 45). In a sense (vastly oversimplified, but basically true) he is saying that people aren't crazy or bad: they are unskilled. They are unskilled because no one has taken the trouble to see their lack of skills or to teach them the skills they need.

THEORY OF COUNSELING

Rationale for Change

If the problem is defined as a lack of skills—interpersonal and specialty skills—then, obviously, the solution is to acquire those skills. The goal (skills to be acquired) has already been defined by the deficit (lack of skills). It remains, then, to operationalize the process of acquisition. In order to set up his position, Carkhuff takes the traditional therapies to task: "If therapy fails, it does so because it fails to enter fully the helpee's frame of reference . . . , it fails to deliver to the helpee the skills which the helpee needs to make it effectively in his or her world . . . , [and] it fails to prepare the helpee for the everyday world" (Carkhuff & Berenson, 1976, p. 61).

If therapy has failed, and Carkhuff is convinced that it has, then a new system is needed: a system in which teaching is treatment; a system that recognizes that all learning begins with the learner's frame of reference; a system that emphasizes the delivery of skills because all learning culminates in a skill objective; a system that delivers substantive skills because all learning is transferable to real life. Carkhuff defines his human resource development as a human (humane) technology: a construct technology as opposed to the destruct technology of a weapons system (or a failed therapeutic system). Such a human system functions on the three principles of learning identified above, and, in addition, (a) is directed toward specific achievable goals identified by the individual, (b) evaluates the goals on the basis of the individual's current behavioral assets and deficits, and (c) develops action steps that are determined by the individual's explicit value judgments. In order to be effective, it must be a fully human technology; technology alone is reduced to mere logic and humanism alone is impotent to achieve the goals it has identified (Carkhuff, Note 2).

Process of Counseling

Useful learning, whether in humans or in one-celled paramecia, must be demonstrated in observable, measureable behaviors. In other words, the learner must act in some way to demonstrate that learning has taken place, that a skill has been acquired. Human learning follows an orderly sequence of exploration, understanding, and action.

In order to demonstrate constructive change in behavior, a person must begin by exploring his or her world: the people, events, and things that make up the world as that person sees it. This means exploring that world from the person's (client's) frame of reference. But it also means exploring the world as others see it: reality testing. Not a static, sterile, clinical diagnosis of the way someone else thinks the world should be, but a fluid, dynamic, personal investigation—diagnosis—of the world as it is for this person. The purpose of exploration is understanding: the individual explores where he or she is in the world to be able to understand—identify and own—his or her own personal behavioral assets and deficits; assets that facilitate growth, deficits that retard it. But simply knowing where you are or where you want to be doesn't move you from one to the other. Understanding and owning both assets and deficits enables the individual to develop effective courses of action to maximize the assets and minimize the deficits.

Goals of Counseling

Counseling goals can be described in a variety of ways (see Chapter 1). As a dynamic system, the HRD perspective emphasizes process rather than state, becoming rather than being. However, Carkhuff does write about "the whole person" and "actualizers" as end products of the process. The HRD perspective encompasses three levels of goals: (a) ultimate goals: self-actualization; (b) intermediate goals: skills; and (c) immediate or process goals: exploration, understanding, and action. These goals will be considered in reverse order.

Process goals. The goal of all helping is change or gain in behavior. In order that the change be real and not merely apparent, the helpee must demonstrate the new behavior. The first goal of helping, then, is exploration. The exploration centers first on the helpee and where he is in relation to his world and the people in it. Later stages of exploration include reality testing and diagnosis in the real world. The second goal of helping is for the helpee to understand where he is in relation to where he wants or needs to be. This includes defining and operationalizing personal behavioral deficits, then defining and operationalizing the goals to eradicate those deficits. Part of the process of goal definition includes developing the values that dictate the goals. Finally, the helpee uses the fruits of his exploration and understanding to take appropriate and effective action to get from where he is to where he wants to be; i.e., to acquire the skills which he now lacks (Carkhuff & Berenson, 1977).

Intermediate goals. Skills are the result of achieving process goals. Physical skills include not only fitness exercises, but also functional nutrition habits and adequate rest. Interpersonal skills, such as attending, listening, responding, and initiating, serve the emotional dimension. Cognitive skills, such as analyzing, synthesizing, and interpreting, lead to intellectual development.

Ultimate goals. People actualizing their physical potential function at high levels of fitness in terms of cardiovascular endurance, dynamic strength, and flexibility. This fitness gives them the physical energy to function effectively in any task they undertake. People actualizing their emotional potential function at high levels of responsiveness and initiative. They are able to respond to the human experience—their own and others'—and to initiate courses of action based on a deep understanding of that experience. People actualizing their intellectual potential function at high levels of cognitive skills. They are able to organize the facts and concepts of daily life into principles and then to translate those principles into skills and skill steps (Carkhuff, 1981).

Training of the Counselor

Training philosophy. It is important to remember that training in helping skills is another instance of interpersonal learning processes in general. Just as helping looks for a change or gain on the part of the helpee, so training asks for a constructive change or gain in trainee functioning. Helping seeks to aid the helpee to become a whole person; training seeks to make the trainee a whole helper—a fully functioning actualizer in process.

The purpose of training is to build the helping skills repertoire of the trainee so that he or she is able to lead a helpee to constructive change. A second purpose of training is to provide the trainee with the skills to develop new helping and training programs for new crises and situations. While Carkhuff's research-development approach to effective helping is very clear and specific about what works and what doesn't, it also takes into account that a creative helper can't be boxed in. "An effective helper does not allow him- or herself to be institutionalized in any system—including mine" (Carkhuff, 1978).

The training experience.   Both training and counseling work toward constructive change and increased levels of interpersonal skills. Both training and counseling draw on the same basic sources of learning in an integrated approach. Both training and counseling are experientially based; that is (as is true of all learning processes), what is critical is the learner's experience of the process. Finally, both trainer and counselor serve as effective role models for training and/or counseling. Thus, for effective training to take place, the trainee must be open to his or her experience and committed to constructive change. In addition, the trainer must be whole, or at least in the process of becoming whole, since his or her limitations place severe limitations on the growth of the trainee (Carkhuff & Berenson, 1977).

The content of training.   The content of training is the content of helping. This means that the trainee learns the details of attending, responding, personalizing, and initiating. The training takes place in the effective helping and learning skills: (a) the trainee begins as a helpee and progresses, on the basis of demonstrated skills, to helper, then to trainer, and finally, to master trainer (trainer of trainers). Some trainees elect to stop at an intermediate level, and some are unable to demonstrate the higher level skills. Some special individuals progress beyond master trainer to human resource development consultant and some to the highest level of community resource consultant (Carkhuff & Berenson, 1976).

This training is carried out either in extended workshops of 100-250 hours duration or in the context of a graduate program in counseling or psychology. In the former, the major emphasis is on learning the behavioral skills; in the latter, skill building still takes the major role, but more emphasis is given to theoretical rationale than in the workshop format. The most complete and longest running program is directed by Dr. Bernard Berenson at The American International College in Springfield, Massachusetts. Other institutions offer counselor training with emphasis on the HRD model (e.g., Georgia State University, the University of Georgia, and Texas Woman's University).

Function of the Counselor

To be effective, a counselor must be more than a dispenser of information and advice, do more than hold hands. Effective counseling involves both helping and teaching. Helping includes attending to the helpee, entering the helpee's frame of reference, facilitating the helpee's ownership of his or her experience, and working with the helpee to achieve his or her goals. Teaching involves developing the helpee's functional knowledge of his or her world, diagnosing the helpee's level of functioning in terms of that knowledge, setting goals in terms of the diagnosis, and finally, delivering to the helpee the skills he or she needs to achieve the goals. Both helping and teaching facilitate movement toward the goal (Carkhuff & Berenson, 1976.).

In other words, an effective helper must:

1. Enter the helpee's frame of reference. In every helping situation, whether it be five minutes or five sessions, part of the time must be devoted to facilitating the helpee's exploration of his or her world.
2. Enter the environment of the helpee. This means physically entering the home, school, or work environment of the helpee as a "reality check" of the helpee's experience.
3. Relate the helpee's frame of reference to goals in his or her environment. The helpee's goals must lie in his or her own—not some other—environment.
4. Relate the environment's goals to the helpee's functioning within the environment. The home, school, work, and community environments have expectations about the helpee's living, learning, and working performance within those environments.
5. Bring helping to a course of action related to achieving the helpee's goals. It is not enough to identify the goal or even to choose a course of action; the course must be implemented.
6. Use teaching and training procedures to implement the course of action. The helper, either personally or through another, trains the helpee in any of the specialty skills needed to reach the goal.
7. Teach transferable skills. Skills must be directly applicable in the life of the helpee.
8. Teach the environment how to support the helpee. This means teaching the significant others in the helpee's environment the skills they need to support the helpee's gain.
9. Follow up the helping-teaching activities. This involves helping the helpee to make living, learning, or working applications in his or her real world.
10. Assess the outcomes of the helping-teaching efforts. Obtaining and using feedback to revise a process is the only way to prevent a system from stagnating.

PRACTICE OF COUNSELING

Major Techniques

Techniques generally follow and are operationally defined by the appropriate phase of the helping process. The four major categories of techniques are attending, responding, personalizing, and initiating. While these are techniques, they are so heavily embedded in personal qualities such as empathy, respect, genuineness, and so on, it is not possible to just "technique it," or attempt to use the techniques without benefit of the personal quality the technique is rooted in.

Attending. There are four steps in the attending phase. The first of these is *preparing* the helpee to become involved in the helping process. This is accomplished in three substeps. First, the helper must *inform* the helpee of the helper's availability through a personal invitation (who the helpee is, when and where the meeting will take place, and how to get there). Next, the helper *encourages* the helpee to participate by stressing the specific personal benefits to be gained by the helpee (what will happen and why the helpee wants it to happen). Finally, the helper can assure that the helpee will continue to come for help by *arranging the setting* in such a way that the helpee perceives his or her involvement. For example, in a one-to-one setting, there should be two similar chairs facing each other at a distance of three to four feet. In a small group, chairs should be arranged in a circle so that each one can see every other person's eyes (not around a table). In a large group, chairs should be placed theater style, and the helper should stand facing the group.

Positioning. The second attending skill involves *positioning*, which encompasses five subskills: (a) The optimum *distance* in a one-to-one situation is about three to four feet, although the helpee's reaction may necessitate adjustment. (b) Whenever possible, the helper should try to take a position at the same level as the helpee in order to communicate an attitude of "helpful equality" rather than "remote superiority." (c) The best *angle* for the helper is the one in which he or she is fully squared, shoulder to shoulder, with the helpee. This communicates attentiveness and eliminates distractions. (d) The helper should sit, or stand, slightly *inclined* towards the helpee in order to communicate interest and involvement. (e) Finally, the helper should maintain appropriate *eye-contact* with the helpee. The duration of the eye-contact will depend upon the helpee's reaction to it; but it should be real eye-contact, not just glancing over the helpee's head or shoulder.

It is good to remember that helping is for the helpee. Therefore, distance, level, angle, inclination, and eye-contact, while important and useful, are means to the end of helping, not ends in themselves. If, with a given helpee, inclining does not facilitate helping, it should be abandoned; if, with a given helpee, direct eye-contact is interpreted negatively, it should be modified or abandoned.

Observing. The third attending skill involves the helper's ability to *observe* the helpee's appearance and behavior in order to draw inferences about the helpee's level of energy, feelings, and degree of congruence. It is important to distinguish between observation and inference. What is observed is appearance and/or behavior ("he is neatly dressed and well groomed" or "she is frowning and won't look at me"). What is inferred is related to level of energy ("his bright eyes and alert attentiveness tell me his energy level is high"), feelings ("she is frowning and won't look at me while disagreeing with me . . . perhaps she is angry with me"), or degree of congruence ("he says he feels good, but he looks like he's been through a wringer").

Listening. The final attending skill involves *listening,* not just hearing, but attentive, active listening. It is imperative that the helper listen for the content and tone of expression personally relevant to the helpee. In listening for content, the helper is alert to pick up on the "5WH": who, what, when, where, why, and how. Furthermore, the helper must listen for tone of voice: volume, pitch, rapidity, and any changes in these indicators. Even this is not enough! The helper must be alert for the personal meaning of what the helpee says ("she's talking about her mother, but what is she telling me about herself?"). While listening, the helper must suspend his or her own judgment, or more accurately, his or her own frame of reference. It is only by temporarily abandoning his or her own frame of reference and moving freely within the helpee's that the helper can make an accurately empathic response.

Finally, all of the attending skills are directed toward enabling the helper to ascertain the helpee's personally relevant feeling and meaning contained in each expression. Attending involves the helpee in the helping process and sets the stage for the next phase (Carkhuff, 1980a; Carkhuff & Anthony, 1979).

Responding. By attending, observing, and listening, helpers can define and individualize their understanding of each helpee's unique frame of reference during initial interactions. At this second stage, the helper's primary job is to enter, understand, and respond to each helpee's unique set or frame of reference so that the helpees can explore their immediate situation, the immediate meaning this situation has, the immediate feelings prompted by the situation, and the immediate reason for these feelings.

(Immediate means now, current, not something dredged up from the past.)

During the initial exploratory phase of any counseling session, the goal for the helpee is to discuss information relative to specific, concrete *situations* (i.e., the 5WH of content). In order to facilitate this exploration, the helper responds with expressions like "what you are saying is . . . " when the helpee expresses material that has clear situational specificity. In instances when the helpee has difficulty volunteering specific details, the helper can combine specific questions (5WH) with a response to each answer.

The next step is to facilitate the helpee's exploration of the immediate *meaning* that each experience has. While always implicit in the content, the meaning is not always coextensive with content. For example, "my husband slammed the door in my face" (content): "he doesn't respect me" (meaning). The helper can facilitate exploration of the immediate meaning with the response format, "You mean. . . . " For example:

> He.: Whenever they get mad at each other, they wind up yelling at me.
> Hr.: You mean they take out their anger on you.

At the next level of exploration, the helpee's goal is to express the immediate and specific *feelings* about the situation. The helper can facilitate this exploration by responding, "you feel. . . . " Responding to the helpee's feeling says, not only that the helper understands, but also that he or she cares. Since there are many categories and levels of feelings, the helper must work to build a feeling-word vocabulary so that his or her responses will be accurately empathic in terms of the helpee's frame of reference. The helper may be able to determine the most accurate feeling word by asking "if I were this person with the same past and present, and I looked and acted the same and said the same words, how would I feel?"

Once the helpee's feelings have been determined and responded to, the helper's next step is to respond to the immediate reason for the feelings. The helper must respond to the helpee's feelings in order to communicate understanding and acceptance of the helpee, not just as a human being, but as a unique individual of worth. While necessary, responding to feelings alone is not sufficient. The helper must also respond to the helpee's immediate reasons for his or her feelings in order that the helpee begin to associate that inner reality with the personally relevant exterior world. A further reason is that responding to both feeling and reason puts the helper in direct contact with the helpee's world, thus establishing the bond that is a prerequisite to helping.

The typical response at this level is "you feel . . . because he/she/they/it. . . . " This is not the helper's guess at what he or she thinks the helpee is feeling, but it is a true response to or paraphrase of what the helpee has already communicated. Helpee self-exploration is a function of the helper's accurately empathic response to the helpee's immediate situation, feelings, and reasons for the feelings. While this exploration is taking place, the bond between helper and helpee is being built—a bond which is the base of all effective helping (Carkhuff, 1980a; Carkhuff & Anthony, 1979).

Personalizing. This phase of helping involves helpee understanding: the helpee's recognition and acceptance of personalized meanings, personalized problems, personalized feelings, and personalized goals. After the empathic base has been laid by the helper's responses to the helpee's exploration, the helper directs the relationship to a new level by responding to the personal meaning(s) implicit in the helpee's statements. In other words, the helper translates the helpee's comments on external reasons underlying his or her feelings into a statement that reflects the personal—interior—meaning that the situation has for the helpee. The format here is "you feel . . . because you. . . . " The effect of personalizing the meaning is to begin to focus the helpee's attention on his or her contribution to the situation: "I get frustrated because the kids keep coming between us in our marriage" becomes "I get frustrated because I don't have enough time to spend with my wife."

Once the helpee is able to see that he or she is making some contribution to the problem situation, the next step is to get him or her to "own" the problem by seeing it in terms of limited capability, if not personal deficit. At this level, the helper must first identify the deficit theme and then respond to this theme in terms of a personalized problem. To identify the deficit theme, the helper asks him- or herself "what is the helpee doing or failing to do that contributes most directly to the problem?" The response format at this level is "you feel . . . because you can't. . . . " The goal for the helpee is to identify and own the personal behavioral deficit that represents his or her contribution to the problem: "You feel frustrated because you can't organize your time better."

At this point, the helpee's increased understanding and awareness of his or her personal deficits may result in a different level and/or category of feelings. The helper personalizes these new feelings by relating them to the behavioral deficit, using the same format but introducing the new feeling word.

In the final step of the personalizing phase, the helper identifies the personal goal that is implicit in the helpee's own expressions. The latter point is often overlooked: the goal is the helpee's, not the helper's; it is the "flipside" of the helpee's problem, not a "shot in the dark" by the helper. The response format here is "you feel . . . because you can't . . . and you want to. . . . ": "You are angry with yourself because you can't seem to arrange your schedule so that you can spend more time alone with your wife." The helpee's acceptance of the helper's statement of the goal indicates his or her readiness for the next phase of the helping process (Carkhuff, 1980a; Carkhuff & Anthony, 1979).

Initiating: Decision making. The helping process began with exploration of the helpee's world, because all learning begins with the learner's frame of reference. It continued with deepening understanding of the helpee's personal deficits and unique assets. Unfortunately, many helpers, assuming that insight will generate action, stop here. However, experience as well as research has demonstrated that, while both insight and action are necessary to promote lasting change, neither necessarily leads to the other: both must be present to assure effective action. Another principle of learning is that all learning must transfer to real life. Unless the helpee acts on the understanding gained in helping, no behavioral change can occur.

The first step in the initiating phase is defining the helpee's goal in terms that are meaningful, measureable, and realistic; meaningful in that it is directly and fully related to the original problem; measureable because an imprecise goal is impossible to attain except by accident; realistic in that the attainment of the goal is within the helpee's power. The 5WH format is a good way to define a goal in meaningful, measureable, and realistic terms.

The second step in initiating is exploring alternative ways to reach the goal in order to select the most effective course of action. The helper can facilitate this exploration by continuing to attend and respond and, when appropriate, to make concrete suggestions. In this way, the helpee is encouraged to "brainstorm," and explore all viable alternatives.

The next step is to help the helpee develop his or her value hierarchy as a means of choosing among alternatives. This process has four steps: (a) exploring existing values, (b) defining those values related to one of the alternative courses of action, (c) developing a favorability scale for each value, and (d) weighting all values numerically.

The helper can facilitate the helpee's exploration of existing values by continued use of attending and responding skills and also by a new application of the 5WH technique: Who really counts in your life? What things are really important to you? Where do you want to spend your time? When do you want to have reached your goal? Why does this alternative look good to you? How do you feel about this value? After the helpee's values have been identified, they must be defined in concrete terms—usually relating to amount and/or time. The question to be answered is, "What does this value mean to the helpee in terms of the number of things done in a given period of time?"

The next step is the development of a personalized favorability scale. This is simply a systematic design or paradigm for determining the relative importance of different values. Symbolically, the scale looks like this:

++   very favorable
+   favorable
+−   acceptable
−   unfavorable
−−   very unfavorable

This general scale must be individualized in terms of the helpee's unique values. For instance, one helpee may decide that two of his or her values stack up like this:

VALUE	DEFINITION	SCALE	
Finances	# of $ in debt	+	$0
		+	$50-100
		+−	$101-200
		−	$201-300
		−−	$301-400
Family	# waking hours together per week	++	20-30
		+	15-19
		+−	10-14
		−	5- 9
		−−	0- 4

Once the favorability scale for each value is established, the helpee must then rank the values from least important to most important. After ranking, numerical weights should be assigned to each value in order to more accurately discriminate the relative importance of the values. The least important value is assigned a weight of 1, and each other value is assigned a weight in increasing magnitude up to 10. This allows the helpee to indicate that two values are of equal importance (same weight) or that, for example, one value (weight 6) is twice as important as another (weight 3).

The final step in decision making is making the decision based on the systematic approach described above. This is a simple, mechanical (mathematical) process. The first step is the construction of a matrix that includes both the alternate courses of action and the weighted values. For example,

		ALTERNATIVES		
Values	wt.	Keep job	Change jobs	Go to school
Family	(10)			
Friendship	(7)			
Finances	(1)			

The helpee now considers each alternate course of action in terms of the favorability scale and weight of each value. For example, keeping the same job will not increase time with the family, but it will allow the helpee to continue the same twelve hours a week he now spends with his family. He has indicated that this is favorable (+). When that favorability score is multiplied by the weight of the first value, the result (+10) is assigned to the first cell of the matrix. Keeping the job has the same effect on the second value; but, since the weight is different, the result is different (+4). This is assigned to the second cell. Keeping the job doesn't change the money picture, so the net result (+1) + (−1) is 0. When this process is continued for each cell, the completed matrix may look like this:

		Keep job		Change jobs		Go to school	
Family	(10)	+	+10	−	−10	++	+20
Friendship	(4)	+	+ 4	− −	− 8	++	+ 8
Finances	(1)	+ −	0	++	+ 2	− −	− 2

The next step is to get the algebraic sum of each column:
+14   −16   +26

The preferred course of action is the one with the highest positive total. In this example, the helpee would opt to go to school, despite the financial disadvantage, because his other values are prepotent (Carkhuff & Anthony, 1979).

Initiating: Program development.   Deciding which course of action to follow is one thing, but implementing that decision is quite another. The first phase of program development involves identifying and operationally defining the primary steps of the program: (a) the last step—that which leads directly to the goal, (b) the first step of the program, and (c) intermediate steps to bridge the gap from the first to the last. It is the helper's job to be sure that each step is defined in behavioral terms, that the helpee is (or will be) able to master each step, that the final step leads directly to the goal, and that a sufficient number of steps are developed so that the helpee doesn't "bite off more than he can chew."

Next, the helpee must develop check steps to assure that he or she is on target. These are think steps, as opposed to the do steps by which the program is executed. There are "before-think steps," "during-think steps," and "after-think steps." The before-think steps prepare the helpee for each do step: Do I have what I need to do this? Have I set aside the time to do it? Am I physically, emotionally, and intellectually prepared to do it? The during-think steps enable the helpee to monitor his or her progress while actually involved in the do steps: Am I ready for the next step?

These are not idle *pro forma* questions, but vitally important checks designed to ensure the successful attainment of the goal. The helper must provide the helpee with encouragement as well as tactical support in this phase of the program; this attention to the details of success is one big way to do it (Carkhuff, 1980a; Carkhuff & Anthony, 1979).

Communicating with immediacy and confrontation. Two final techniques that may be appropriate at various stages of the helping process are communicating with immediacy, and confrontation. Communicating with immediacy refers to the helper's response to the immediate relationship between him- or herself and the helpee. The helper can assess the situation by asking "how does what the helpee is saying about the problem relate to what is going on between us right now?" or "is the helpee acting out his or her part in the problem?" or "does the helpee perceive me (helper) as doing things that he or she has described others as doing?" Once the helper has determined the helpee's immediate feelings in the situation, he or she can respond with immediacy by saying something like, "Right now, with me, you feel . . . because you can't . . . . " For example, to a helpee who has expressed a pervasive mistrust of others and manifested undue caution in regard to the helper, the latter might say, "Right now you feel miserable because you can't trust me even when I seem to understand you." Responding with immediacy assists the helper to personalize the helper-helpee relationship, and it provides the helpee with a role model of someone who is able to communicate fully and accurately. Responding with immediacy can be used by a skilled helper at almost any point with little threat to the helpee or the relationship (Carkhuff & Anthony, 1979).

Confrontations are a different matter. Confrontation is neither necessary nor sufficient for helping and should be used cautiously, if at all, and never until after a strong empathic base has been built. Confrontations may take many forms, but they can generally be reduced to two major categories: mild, and strong or direct confrontations. In confronting, the helper attempts to increase the helpee's personalized understanding by pointing out a discrepancy in the helpee's communication. A mild confrontation might take the form of "on the one hand, you say/do . . . , while on the other hand, you say/do. . . . " A mild confrontation is limited to the helpee's frame of reference.

A direct or strong confrontation stresses external, observable data. A typical format is "You say/do/feel . . . , but it looks to me like you say/do/feel . . . . " A confrontation is not an interpretation ("You say you feel confident, but you are not"), but the manifestation of a discrepancy in the helpee's communication (verbal or nonverbal). Because of the potential severity of the threat to the helpee, there are two important caveats to be observed: (a) never confront if an effective alternative is available and (b) never use a direct confrontation if a mild one will suffice (Berenson & Mitchell, 1974; Carkhuff & Anthony, 1979).

Summary

The HRD perspective is a systematic learning/problem-solving approach to counseling. The techniques employed serve this end in that they are based on three principles of learning. (a) All learning begins with the learner's frame of reference. The HRD helper begins by involving the helpee in the helping process (attending skills) and then facilitating self-exploration (responding skills). (b) All learning must culminate in a skills objective. The goal of exploration is the development of understanding of the helpee's personal behavioral assets and deficits so that he or she can acquire the skills to resolve the problem and reach the goal. The helper facilitates this process by his or her personalizing skills. (c) All learning must transfer to real life. In the final phase of helping, understanding must lead to action; otherwise, the goal will be known, but not attained. The helper facilitates action by his or her decision-making and program-development skills.

Treatment Parameters

HRD trainers work with groups of varying size but usually use one trainer for every 15 to 20 trainees. Ideally, the group would meet twice a week for 75 to 90 minutes per session and, depending upon the goals of the group, may involve from 15 to 250 hours of training. If the group is small, it is arranged in a circle, including the trainer; if it is large, the group is seated theater style, with the trainer at the point of the triangle. The size of the meeting room would, of course, depend on the size of the group.

In one-to-one counseling, the HRD helper would meet the helpee once a week for 50 to 60 minutes. The sessions would continue as long as the helpee's need demanded but rarely would go beyond ten or fifteen sessions. The helper's office should be neat and attractive and should include some elements reflecting the helper's frame of reference as well as that of the helpee—something to make the helpee feel at ease (Carkhuff & Pierce, 1977).

CASE STUDY   *(Carkhuff & Berenson, 1977, pp 155–159)*

The process of learning begins and ends with exploration, understanding, and action. The efficacy of any act depends upon its efficacy in achieving a goal or facilitating progress toward a goal. Full understanding depends upon the degree to which goals can be operationalized so that they reflect personal needs and experience. The detailed definition of a goal and actions to achieve the goal rest on exploring fully where the helpee starts.

Helpee: I don't think I can handle my daughter. She is only eight and rules the house.

Helper: You feel anxious because things are getting out of control.

He.: They are out of control; and I don't know what to do.

Hr.: It's a desperate feeling when you are not in control of your children or yourself.

He.: I know it's me. Nothing is right: home, the children—I feel stupid.

Hr.: You feel scared because you cannot handle things you were able to handle before.

He.: It's like I used to be smart; now I am dumb. Even the kids are smarter than I am.

Hr.: You're afraid for yourself and the children because you can't do what a mother should do.

The helper is communicating that she listened and understood at the level the helpee presented herself. The helpee began to examine the implications of her feelings—lack of control of self, home, children—and began to explore feeings of failure in her function as parent. The introduction of mild helper initiative in the last helper response began to personalize the problem.

He.: That's it. I don't think or feel like a mother because my daughter runs me.

Hr.: You feel helpless because you can't help your daughter or yourself.

He.: I should be able to. I've tried everything. I hold the children: I spank them. Sometimes I just give up; and they know it. And it gets worse.

Hr.: You get to feel overwhelmed because you cannot find a way to get back on top.

He.: I'm not sure what else there is. Maybe there's no answer: but there has to be.

Hr.: You're terrified because you can't be the mother you desperately want to be.

He.: I do. I do want to be a good mother. It's up to me—but how?

The helper initiated to the level of personalizing the problem by focusing on the helpee and her role as mother. The helper, in addition, looks at the "flip side" of the problem and takes steps toward defining a personally relevant goal for the helpee: wanting to be a good mother. The helpee began to entertain the goal and look for more direction.

Hr.: You feel angry with yourself because you cannot be the mother you need to be, but you want to be an effective mother.

He.: Oh, yes! It has been the most important thing in my life. That's why I work so hard in the house—even in my school work. I try to learn things that will help at home. I need to start somewhere and soon—perhaps with me.

Hr.: You're impatient to get something going because time is running out. Your goal is to get back on top of being a good mother to your children. Perhaps the first steps involve getting yourself together.

He.: I think so. I'm exhausted most of the time; I don't have any energy.

Hr.: The first goal is to increase your energy and the first step here is to look at how much rest you get and then plan a rest program related to other factors that influence your energy level.

The helper not only initiated to define a first goal that has relevance for the helpee's problem but also begins to focus on the development of steps to do something about achieving the goal.

Applications

Because it emphasizes basic interpersonal skills in a training format, the application of the HRD perspective is practically unlimited. It is, of course, limited by the helper's communication skills and the helpee's ability to receive and understand the helper's communication. It works best with those willing and able to learn. The skills encompassed by the HRD perspective can be used to great advantage to all concerned by counselors, teachers, parents, librarians, salespeople—in short, anyone who interacts with another human being. Its use is not limited to the formal therapeutic arena, but it is also an effective instrument there.

CRITIQUE

Research Support

Attending skills. Genther and Moughan (1977) investigated the effect of counselor's posture (incline) in helpee's ratings of the counselor's attentiveness. In every case, the counselor in the forward-leaning position was rated more attentive. Other research on verbal and nonverbal communication support the contention that there is a relationship between positioning, observing, and listening (Baker, 1971; Mehrabian, 1972).

Responding skills. The early research identified the relationship between specific helper skills and helpee self-exploration (Carkhuff, 1969; Rogers et al., 1967; Truax & Carkhuff, 1967). In addition, a series of experiments corroborated this conclusion. The helpee's level of self-exploration could be increased or decreased by systematically varying the helper's level of responding (Cannon & Pierce, 1968; Holder, Carkhuff, &

Berenson, 1967; Piaget, Berenson, & Carkhuff, 1967). The results of these experiments showed that when the helpers were more responsive, the helpee's explorations were more personally relevant; when the same helpers became less responsive, their helpees' explorations became less personal.

Personalizing.   In another series of experimental manipulations, a trained client was instructed to explore herself deeply during the first third of an interview, talk only about irrelevant and impersonal details during the middle third, and return to the original mode in the final third of the interview. Her counselors were unaware of these instructions. Analysis of the results revealed that in the middle third of the interview, when the client began to withdraw from the therapeutic encounter, the higher functioning therapists became more initiative—i.e., they became more interpretative, more immediate, more confrontive, more personalized in their understanding of the helpee's immediate problems (Alexik & Carkhuff, 1967; Carkhuff & Alexik, 1967).

Initiating.   Smith (1976) trained one group of counselors to define observable goals for helpees and then compared the outcome of their counseling against another group of counselors not so trained. At the end of eight weeks of counseling, helpees whose helpers had been trained to define goals showed significantly greater gains on a variety of outcome indices. Willer and Miller (1978) found that client satisfaction as well as prediction of recidivism are both related to goal attainment. Other experimental studies have suggested that outcome is positively affected by feedback about goal attainment (Walker, 1972) and training in goal-setting techniques (Latham & Rinne, 1974). Goal-setting manipulations have been demonstrated to have a positive effect on performance in the world of work (Bucker, 1978), administrative decision making (Alden, 1978), and assertiveness training (Flowers, 1978; Flowers & Goldman, 1976).

In 1971, Carkhuff suggested that training clients directly in the skills that they need to function in society could be a potent treatment method. Five years later, he developed the technology to implement that idea (Carkhuff & Berenson, 1976). Others have followed suit (Authier, Gustafson, Guerney, & Kasdorf, 1975; Ivey, 1976; Sprinthall & Mosher, 1971). Many of the skills-training programs have been directed to interpersonal skills: psychiatric inpatients (Pierce & Drasgow, 1969; Vitalo, 1971), parents (Carkhuff & Bierman, 1970; Reed, Roberts, & Forehand, 1977), mixed race groups (Carkhuff & Banks, 1970), marriage counseling (Valle & Marinelli, 1975), college counseling center clients (Cabush & Edwards, 1976), delinquent youth (Collingwood, Douds, Williams, &

Wilson, 1978), minority-group dropouts (Berenson, Berenson, Berenson, Carkhuff, Griffith, & Ranson, 1978), and interracial community relations (Shilling, 1970).

Evaluation

Lambert and DeJulio (1977) took Carkhuff to task for poor research methodology. Some of their complaints are that (a) he failed to specify the nature of the treatment (training), which seemed to vary from one study to another, (b) control groups were either nonequivalent or nonexistent, (c) there was excessive testing-treatment interaction, and (d) minimal—though occasionally statisically significant—gains. Carkhuff's more recent works (Carkhuff, 1980a; Carkhuff & Anthony, 1979; Carkhuff & Berenson, 1976; 1977) seem to answer the first objection adequately. The last (minimal gains) is really not a fair assessment. There were many studies resulting in minimal gains; but there were many more (not cited by Lambert & DeJulio) resulting in large gains (Friel, 1972; Megathlin & Porter, 1969; Shilling, 1970; 1976). The other objections, insofar as they relate to the studies reviewed by Lambert and DeJulio, are less easily dismissed. Until there is another review of the nature and scope of the Lambert and DeJulio paper, one can only hope that the more recent research by Carkhuff and his associates does not suffer from the same methodological problems. Meanwhile, the growing body of literature about the HRD perspective, the enormous quantity of material coming from the HRD Press, and, especially, the quantity and quality of testimonials from satisifed users—both helpers and helpees—suggest that, research methodology aside, perhaps the HRD perspective has something good to offer.

My own assessment of the HRD model is that, despite the methodological problems, the obscure language, the overkill, and the seemingly haughty approach, it is one of the more promising of the perspectives considered in this text. In my opinion, the HRD perspective—more than any other, except, possibly, reality therapy—deals with real people in a real world. It is truly scientific in that it seeks to discover all the facts about a given situation (the client and his or her problem) without filtering them through preconceived ideas. It is truly pragmatic in the sense that it looks for what works in *this* situation, not for some panacea that might work in *all* situations. It is truly eclectic in the sense that, within the framework of the stated principles of learning, it pulls from other perspectives those aspects that are most effective and uses them when and where they are most applicable. It is truly universal in the sense that it is not inextricably bound to the personality of the "founder." It is a construct technology that works when the "worker" makes it work.

REFERENCES

ALDEN, J.   Evaluation in focus. *Training and Development Journal,* Oct., 1978, 46–50.

ALEXIK, M., & CARKHUFF, R. R.   The effects of manipulation of client self-exploration upon high- and low-functioning counselors. *Journal of Clinical Psychology,* 1967, *23,* 210–212.

ANTHONY, W. A., BUELL, G. J., SHARRAT, S., & ALTHOFF, M. E.   Efficacy of psychiatric rehabilitation. *Psychological Bulletin,* 1972, *78,* 447–456.

ANTHONY, W. A., COHEN, M. R., & VITALO, R.   The measurement of rehabilitation outcome. *Schizophrenia Bulletin,* 1978, *4,* 365–383.

ASPY, D. N.   The effect of teacher-offered conditions of empathy, positive regard, and congruence upon student achievement. *Florida Journal of Educational Research,* 1969, *11,* 39–48.

AUTHIER, J., GUSTAFSON, K., GUERNEY, B., & KRASDORF, J. A.   The psychological practitioner as teacher. *Counseling Psychologist,* 1975, *5* (2), 31–50.

BAKER, L. I.   *Listening behavior.* Englewood Cliffs, N.J.: Prentice-Hall, 1971.

BERENSON, B. G. (ED.).   *Belly to belly, back to back: The militant humanism of Robert R. Carkhuff.* Amherst, MA: Human Resource Development Press, 1975.

BERENSON, B. G., & MITCHELL, K. M.   *Confrontation: For better or worse.* Amherst, MA: Human Resource Development Press, 1974.

BERENSON, D. H., BERENSON, S. R., BERENSON, B. G., CARKHUFF, R. R. GRIFFITH, A. H., & RANSOM, B. M.   The physical, emotional, and intellectual effects of teaching learning skills to minority group drop-out learners. Research Reports, Carkhuff Institute of Human Technology, 1978, *1* (3).

BUCKER, L.   Joint effect of feedback and goal setting on performance: A field study of residential energy conservation. *Journal of Applied Psychology,* 1978, *63,* 428–433.

CABUSH, D. W., & EDWARDS, J. J.   Training clients to help themselves: Outcome effects of training college students in facilitative self-responding. *Journal of Counseling Psychology,* 1976, *23,* 34–39.

CANNON, J. R., & PIERCE, R. M.   Order effects in the experimental manipulation of therapeutic conditions. *Journal of Clinical Psychology,* 1968, *24,* 242–244.

CARKHUFF, R. R.   *Helping and human relations: A primer for lay and professional helpers* (2 vols.). New York: Holt, Rinehart, & Winston, 1969.

CARKHUFF, R. R.   Personal communication, November, 1978.

CARKHUFF, R. R.   *The art of helping IV.* Amherst, MA: Human Resource Development Press, 1980.

CARKHUFF, R. R.   *A human technology for human systems in education.* Keynote address to Phi Delta Kappa convention, University of Minnesota, July 11, 1980.

CARKHUFF, R. R.   *Toward actualizing human potential.* Amherst, MA: Human Resource Development Press, 1981.

CARKHUFF, R. R.   Personal communication, April 28, 1982.

CARKHUFF, R. R., & ALEXIK, M.   The differential effects of the manipulation of client self-exploration upon high- and low-functioning counselors. *Journal of Counseling Psychology,* 1967, *14,* 350–355.

CARKHUFF, R. R., & ANTHONY, W. A.   *The skills of helping: An introduction to counseling skills.* Amherst, MA: Human Resource Development Press, 1979.

CARKHUFF, R. R., & BANKS, G.   Training as a preferred mode of facilitating relations between races and generations. *Journal of Counseling Psychology,* 1970, *17,* 413–418.

CARKHUFF, R. R., & BERENSON, B. G.   *Teaching as treatment: An introduction to counseling and psychotherapy.* Amherst, MA: Human Resource Development Press, 1976.

CARKHUFF, R. R., & BERENSON, B. G.   *Beyond counseling and therapy* (2nd ed.). New York: Holt, Rinehart & Winston, 1977.

CARKHUFF, R. R., & BIERMAN, R.   Training as a preferred mode of treatment of parents of emotionally disturbed children. *Journal of Counseling Psychology,* 1970, *17,* 157–161.

CARKHUFF, R. R., & PIERCE, R. M.   *The art of helping III: Trainer's guide.* Amherst, MA: Human Resource Development Press, 1977.

COLLINGWOOD, T. R., DOUDS, A., WILLIAMS, H., & WILSON, R. D.   *Developing youth resources.* Amherst, MA: Carkhuff Institute of Human Technology, 1978.

FLOWERS, J.   Goal clarity as a component of assertive behavior and a result of assertion training. *Journal of Clinical Psychology,* 1978, *34,* 744–747.

FLOWERS, J., & GOLDMAN, R.   Assertion training for mental health paraprofessionals. *Journal of Counseling Psychology,* 1976, *23,* 147–150.

FRIEL, T.   *Education and career exploration system: The development of a systematic computer-based, career guidance program.* New York: International Business Machines Corporation, 1972.

GENTHER, R. W., & MOUGHAN, J.   Introverts' and extroverts' responses to nonverbal attending behavior. *Journal of Counseling Psychology,* 1977, *24,* 144–146.

HOLDER, B. T., CARKHUFF, R. R., & BERENSON, B. G.   The differential effects of the manipulation of therapeutic conditions upon high- and low-functioning clients. *Journal of Counseling Psychology,* 1967, *14,* 63–66.

IVEY, A.   The counselor as teacher. *Personnel and Guidance Journal,* 1976, *54,* 431–434.

LAMBERT, M. J., & DeJULIO, S. S.   Outcome research in Carkhuff's Human Resource Development training programs: Where is the donut? *The Counseling Psychologist,* 1977, *6* (4), 79–86.

LATHAM, G., & RINNE, S.   Improving job performance through training in goal setting. *Journal of Applied Psychology,* 1974, *59,* 187–191.

LEVITT, E. E.   Psychotherapy with children: A further evaluation. *Behavior Research and Therapy,* 1963, *1,* 45–51.

LEWIS, W. W.   Continuity and intervention in emotional disturbance: A review. *Exceptional Children,* 1965, *31,* 465–475.

MEGATHLIN, W., & PORTER, T.   *The effects of facilitative training provided correctional officers stationed at the Atlanta Federal Penitentiary.* Washington, DC: U.S. Department of Justice, 1969.

MEHRABIAN, A.   *Nonverbal communication.* New York: Aldine-Atherton, 1972.

PIAGET, G., BERENSON, B. G., & CARKHUFF, R. R.   The differential effects of the manipulation of therapeutic conditions by high and low-functioning counselors upon high-and low-functioning clients. *Journal of Consulting Psychology,* 1967, *31,* 481–486.

PIERCE, R. R., CARKHUFF, R. R., & BERENSON, B. G.   The differential effects of high- and low-functioning counselors. *Journal of Clinical Psychology,* 1967, *23,* 212–215.

PIERCE, R. M., & DRASGOW, J.   Teaching facilitative interpersonal functioning to psychiatric inpatients. *Journal of Counseling Psychology,* 1969, *16,* 295–298.

REED, S., ROBERTS, M., & FOREHAND, R.   Evaluation of effectiveness of standardized parent training programs in altering the interaction of mothers and noncompliant children. *Behavior Modification,* 1977, *1,* 323–350.

ROGERS, C. R.   The necessary and sufficient conditions of therapeutic personality change. *Journal of Consulting Psychology*, 1957, *22*, 95–103.

ROGERS, C. R., GENDLIN, E. T., KIESLER, D., & TRUAX, C. B.   *The therapeutic relationship and its impact.* Madison, WI: The University of Wisconsin Press, 1967.

SHILLING, L. E.   *The differential effects of two small-group training procedures on the acquisition of interpersonal communication skills and the extinction of interpersonal anxiety.* Unpublished doctoral dissertation. The University of Georgia, Athens, Georgia, 1970.

SHILLING, L. E.   Implementing humane technology: Short-term training for teachers. *Journal of Educational Research*, 1976, *69*, 193–198.

SMITH, D. L.   Goal attainment scaling as an adjunct of counseling. *Journal of Counseling Psychology*, 1976, *23*, 22–27.

SPRINTHALL, N., & MOSHER, R. L.   Psychological education: A means to promote personal development during adolescence. *The Counseling Psychologist*, 1971, *2* (4), 3–84.

TRUAX, C. B., & CARKHUFF, R. R.   *Toward effective counseling and psychotherapy*, Chicago: Aldine, 1967.

VALLE, S. K., & MARIENALLI, R. P.   Training in human relations skills as a preferred mode of treatment for married couples. *Journal of Marriage and Family Counseling*, 1975, *1*, 359–365.

VITALO, R.   Teaching improved interpersonal functioning as a preferred treatment. *Journal of Clinical Psychology*, 1971, *27*, 166–170.

WALKER, R. A.   The ninth panacea: Program evaluation. *Evaluation*, 1972, *1* (1), 45–53.

WILLER, B., & MILLER, G.   On the relationship of client satisfaction to client characteristics and outcome of treatment. *Journal of Clinical Psychology*, 1978, *34*, 157–160.

CHAPTER ELEVEN
EPILOGUE
MY PERSPECTIVE
ON PERSPECTIVES

There you have it. But what is it you have? Nine perspectives or a pot-pourri of disjointed ideas from, perhaps, disgruntled old men? Or . . . . Many of the authors who write this kind of text (Burks & Stefflre, 1979; Hansen, et al., 1982; Patterson, 1980) generally agree that what you do not have is a set of formal theories. Neither are they totally disjointed ideas; and not all of their proponents are both disgruntled and old. I believe that "perspectives on counseling" based on perspectives on human nature is a fair way to collectively describe them. But, having said that, what do you have? One thing that I get out of that designation is that I don't have to take anything that any of them said as "gospel." Theory is a bit intimidating. If any one of these perspectives were, in fact, a *theory*, I might feel compelled to click my heels and march alongside it. If more than one were true theories, I'd be in big trouble. Since they are only perspectives, I can settle back, watch them viewing human nature and behavior, and make up my own mind.

I am not very comfortable with the Freudian perspective, partly be-cause I am not comfortable with the medical model in general. "Patient" (sufferer) is not a way that I like to be characterized; and I am least patient of all while waiting for a doctor's appointment! I stand in utter awe of Freud's genius. Even those who totally disagree with him share my rever-

221

ence for his creative genius in bridging the gap from the physical to the psychological aspects of human nature and behavior. That quantum leap was not very different from Columbus' testing the flat earth theory. While Freud's perspective may have minimal relevance for the modern counselor, we would do well to remember that none of us would be counselors if it were not for Freud and his imaginative perspective.

Carl Rogers, too, is a genius. (It is a bit more difficult but a lot more satisfying to write about a living genius!) Rogers came along at a time when counselors were to therapy as orderlies were to medicine. Before and shortly after World War II, counselors were not allowed to "do therapy"; and counseling was limited to academic or vocational advisement. Psychoanalysis was the only game in town, and counseling and counselors were no problem because no one had ever heard of them. Rogers changed all that. He moved, not just counseling, not even just psychotherapy, but all of psychology (as a human science) out of the dark ages and into the light. He has been called—and, indeed, has referred to himself—as a "quiet revolutionary." Rogers' revolution was no less creative than Freud's and far more substantial. This quiet revolution has changed the map of counseling and therapy, education, and every form of interpersonal relationship, including international relations. The heart of the revolution—focusing on the client's frame of reference—is, now at least, amazingly simple. Rogers' genius was that he saw it when no one else did. Another of Rogers' major contributions was his insistence on the primacy of the self or self-concept: that alarmingly fragile inner perspective that determines who and how we are. He saw that all behavior is directed toward enhancing or protecting the self. Thus, he decreed all counseling should be directed toward freeing the self to become "more self."

In my opinion, another genius of the same stature as the other two is Robert Carkhuff. His genius is not in designing the plan (as was Freud's and Rogers') but in showing us how to execute it. If Freud moved the study of human nature and behavior out of the Stone Age and into the Dark Ages and Rogers moved us from a medieval perspective to a modern one, Carkhuff propels us into the future. His genius was to take the belief of all his predecessors that humans can be more than they are and to devise a way to teach them how to do it. Freud taught us that what we don't know can hurt us. Rogers taught us that we can become more than we are. Carkhuff taught us how to avoid the former and achieve the latter. As a therapy, the human resource development model makes the most sense to me because it is systematic and truly eclectic: it uses proven procedures at those times when they are most effective for the client. There is no such thing as a panacea, a cure-all, a tool for all situations. I have found that the HRD model works better for me with more clients and with more kinds of problems than other approaches because it is more flexible, more pragmatic.

What about the others? What about Adler, Berne, Ellis, Glasser, Perls, and the behaviorists? Were they not geniuses, too? In the sense that each devised his own hammer or screwdriver, yes; but not in the sense that each created a new system of carpentry as well as a whole tool kit—as Freud, Rogers, and Carkhuff did. A counselor rejects tools essential for his task if he rejects the contributions of these perspectives; but, viewed as contributions, they are not of the same order as those of Freud, Rogers, and Carkhuff.

A final point, which I believe is more important than all the rest: when you are face to face with a client, which perspective was developed by a genius is absolutely irrelevant. All that is relevant is that you be the most effective counselor you can be at that moment. You *cannot*—repeat, *cannot*—be an effective counselor if you try to be Freud or Rogers or Carkhuff or anyone other than yourself. You must learn from these teachers, and anyone else who has something to teach you, but you must not allow yourself to be institutionalized in, immobilized by anybody's system.

That's what I think. What do you think? I would very much like to know what you think. Please write to me at

P.O. Box 23029
TWU Station
Denton, Texas 76204

Lou

NAME INDEX

Abeles, N., 18, 24, 26–27, 30, 32–33, 36, 39, 43
Adams, H. E., 143, 146
Adler, A., 7, 40, 45–47, 49–53, 55, 72, 94, 107, 110, 223
Alberti, R. E., 139, 144
Alden, J., 216, 218
Alexander, F. M., 33, 43
Alexik, M., 216, 218
Allen, G. J., 21, 43
Allen, T. W., 6, 14, 66–67
Althoff, M. E., 192, 218
American Mental Health Counselor's Association, 2, 14
American Personnel and Guidance Association, 2, 14, 83
American Psychoanalytic Association, 33, 43
American Psychological Association, 2
Ansbacher, H. L., 7, 14, 47, 49–50, 56, 66–67
Ansbacher, R. R., 49–50, 67
Anthony, W. A., 192, 198, 206, 208–209, 211–213, 217–218
Arnkoff, D. B., 107–108
Aspy, D. N., 193, 218
Authier, J., 216, 218
Ayllon, T., 137, 142, 144
Azrin, N. H., 137, 142, 144

Baker, L. I., 215, 218
Bandura, A., 126, 128–129, 136, 139, 142–143, 145
Banks, G., 216, 218
Bard, A. T., 96, 107
Barker, J. C., 143, 146
Barrett-Lennard, G. T., 183–184, 187
Battle, C., 183, 189
Bean, H., 142, 146
Beck, A. T., 107–108
Beisser, A. L., 156, 165
Belkin, G. S., 94, 108
Berenson, B. G., 4, 6–7, 11, 15, 42–43, 144–145, 184, 186–187, 190, 192–193, 197–200, 202–204, 213, 216–220
Berenson, D. H., 217–218
Berenson, S. R., 217–218
Bergin, A. E., 183–184, 187
Berne, E., 71–72, 75, 86–87, 91–92, 223
Bierman, R., 216, 219
Blake, B. G., 143, 145
Blakemore, C. B., 143, 146
Blanchard, E. B., 143, 145
Bloom, B., 199
Bostrom, J. A., 57, 68
Brammer, L. M., 2, 14
Brandsma, J. M., 143, 146
Brannon, J. M., 123–124
Brown, M., 72, 75–87, 91–92
Brown, N. M., 143, 147
Browning, B. D., 123–124
Bucker, L., 216, 218
Buell, G. J., 192, 218
Burks, H. M., 72, 74, 221
Burton, A., 8, 15

Cabush, D. W., 216, 218
Cameron, R., 143, 146
Cannon, J. R., 215, 218
Carkhuff, R. R., 4–7, 9, 11, 16, 42–43, 60, 67, 144–145, 183–184, 186–187, 189–193, 197–204, 206, 208–209, 211–213, 215–219, 222–223

Cassel, P., 50, 68
Coates, T. J., 126, 146
Cohen, M. R., 192, 218
Collingwood, T. R., 216, 219
Combs, A. W., 5, 15
Conway, C. G., 143, 146
Corsini, R., 8, 15, 72, 92

Davison, G. E., 142, 145
Dejulio, S. S., 217, 219
Demoor, W., 143, 145
Dewald, P. A., 36, 43
Dewey, J., 167–168, 199
Digiuseppi, R. A., 107–108
Diloretto, A., 66–67, 106, 108
Dinkmeyer, D., Jr., 47, 68
Dinkmeyer, D., Sr., 6, 15, 47, 49–54, 56, 58, 60–64, 68
Douds, A., 216, 218
Drasgow, J., 193, 216, 219
Dreikurs, R., 6–7, 15, 50–52, 54, 56–58, 60, 62, 64, 68, 113, 124
Dymond, R. F., 184, 188

Edwards, J. J., 216, 218
Eisler, R. W., 142, 145
Ellis, A., 66, 68, 93–103, 106, 108, 148, 223
Elson, S. E., 72, 75–76, 80, 82, 86, 88, 92, 110, 112, 114–115, 117, 119, 122–124, 151–152, 154–155, 158, 165
Emery, J. R., 142, 145
Emmons, M. L., 139, 144
English, J., 122, 124
Evans, D. B., 115, 124
Evans, R. I., 171, 187
Eysenck, H. J., 1, 15, 126, 145, 191

Feldman, M., 143, 145
Fine, R., 31, 34, 43
Fiore, Q., 158, 165
Fitchett, S. M., 140, 145
Fitzgerald, P. W., 2, 15
Fixen, D. L., 142, 145
Flowers, J., 216, 219
Ford, D. H., 9, 15
Forehand, R., 216, 220
Frank, J. D., 6–8, 15, 60, 68, 183, 189
Freud, A., 30, 32, 43
Freud, S., 8, 17–19, 22–26, 29, 33, 35, 40, 42–43, 45–47, 50, 76, 153, 171–172, 221–223
Friel, T., 217, 219
Furtmuller, C., 46, 48

Gagne, J., 199
Gang, M. J., 123–124
Gannon, W., 163, 165
Garfield, S., 184, 187
Garfinkel, M. I., 64, 68
Gendlin, E. T., 60, 68, 175, 183–185, 188, 191–192, 215, 220
Genther, R. W., 215, 219
Glasser, W., 109–119, 122–124, 223
Goldman, R., 143, 146, 216, 219
Goodman, J., 143, 146
Goodman, P., 152–153
Greiger, R., 97, 102, 106, 108
Grey, L., 113, 124
Griffith, A. H., 217–218
Grummon, D. L., 167, 175, 177, 184, 186, 188
Guerney, B., 216, 218
Guilford, J. P., 199

Rush, A. J., 106, 108
Russell, P. L., 143, 146
Rychlak, J. F., 46, 51, 68, 132, 146

Sachs, L. B., 142, 146
Sanford, D. A., 140, 145
Saslow, G., 133, 145
Saunders, W., 143, 146
Schoben, C., 6, 16
Semrad, E. V., 18, 23–25, 28, 35, 43
Sharrat, S., 192, 218
Shearn, D. F., 123–124
Shepherd, I. L., 158, 163, 165
Shilling, L. E., 193, 217, 220
Shostrom, E. L., 2, 14
Shulman, B. H., 55, 62, 68
Simkin, J., 160, 165
Skinner, B. F., 125–126, 128, 146
Smith, D. L., 216, 220
Soper, D. L., 5, 15
Spence, D. P., 41, 43
Sprinthall, N., 216, 220
Stampfl, T. G., 140, 146
Stefflre, B., 11–12, 14, 16, 221
Steiner, C. M., 71–72, 75, 79, 90, 92
Stevic, R. R., 153, 165 188, 221
Stewart, R. D., 150, 165
Stewart, R. L., 32, 34–36, 43
Stone, A. R., 6–8, 15, 60, 68, 183, 189
Stripling, R. O., 2, 15
Strupp, H. H., 34, 43
Stuart, J. E., 143, 147
Sue, D. W., 13, 16
Szaz, T., 110
Thoresen, C. E., 126, 134–135, 146
Thorndike, E. L., 126–128
Thorpe, J. G., 143, 146
Tiegerman, S., 107–108
Tolman, E., 126

Truax, C. B., 6–7, 16, 60, 68, 175, 183–185,
    188–189, 191–192, 215, 220
Twentyman, C. T., 142, 146
Tyler, L., 2, 16

Urban, H. B., 9, 15

Valle, S. K., 216, 220
Verger, D., 62, 68
Vitalo, R., 192, 216, 218, 220

Wade, T., 142, 146
Walker, R. A., 216, 220
Walters, R. H., 126, 145
Wantz, R. A., 135, 145, 179, 188
Ward, P., 154–155, 165
Wargo, D., 183, 189
Warner, R. W., 153, 165, 188, 221
Watson, J. B., 126
Watson, R. I., 126–128, 146
Watts, G. E., 122, 124
Weingold, B. K., 143, 145
Wertheimer, M., 149
Westel, W., 143, 146
Wilcoxon, L. A., 142, 146
Willer, B., 216, 220
Williams, H., 216, 219
Wilson, R. D., 217, 219
Wolberg, L. R., 1, 16
Wolf, M. M., 142, 146
Wolfe, J. L., 107–108
Wollams, S., 72, 75–87, 91–92
Wolpe, J., 126, 135, 137, 146
Woody, R. H., 135, 146

Yalom, I. D., 7–8, 15–16, 163, 165
Young, E. R., 142, 146

Zunin, L. M., 110–112, 114–116, 118–119, 124

SUBJECT INDEX

A-B-C Theory, 98
Abreaction, definition, 20
Acknowledgement, definition, 151
Activities:
    definition, 73
    time structuring, 76
Actualizer, definition, 194
Actualizing, tendency, see Self-actualizing
    tendency
Adaptation, definition, 151
Adler, Alfred, personal background, 45–47
Aggression:
    drive, 22
    gestalt definition, 151
Alternative courses of action, 209
Alternatives phase, individual psychology, 57–58
Anal stage, 26
Anxiety, 29, 114, 174
    definition, 20, 169
Anxiety hierarchy, 138
    definition, 129
Applications:
    behavior therapy, 141
    client centered therapy, 182–183
    gestalt therapy, 162–163
    human resource development, 215
    individual psychology, 66
    psychoanalysis, 39–40
    rational emotive therapy, 106
    reality therapy, 122
    transactional analysis, 90

Approbation, definition, 151
Assertiveness training, 138–139, 142–143
    definition, 129
Assessment phase, behavior therapy, 133
Attending, 60, 192, 205, 215
    definition, 194
Autonomy, 86–87
    definition, 86, 111
Awareness, 23, 79, 86, 152–153, 155
    definition, 151, 169
    directed, 159

Basic mistakes, 55–56, 62
    definition, 48
Behavior:
    defensive, 174
    disorganized, 174
Behavior modification, definition, 129
Behavior rehearsal, 138
    definition, 129
Behavior therapy, definition, 129
Behavioral techniques, rational emotive therapy,
    103
Being, 153
Berne, Eric, personal background, 71–72
Biofeedback, 137
Birth order, 53
    definition, 48

Carkhuff, Robert R., personal background, 191

Ego State (continued)
  Parent, 72, 76, 78–79, 81
  Parent, definition, 73
Ellis, Albert, personal background, 93–94
Emotional development, human resource
  development, 198–199
Emotivation, human resource development, 198
Emotive techniques, rational-emotive therapy, 103
Empathy, 5, 61, 175, 179–180, 192
  definition, 169, 194
Encouragement:
  definition, 48
  individual psychology, 57
Encouraging:
  definition, 194
  human resource development, 205
Escape, *see* reinforcement, negative
Evaluation:
  behavior therapy, 144
  client-centered therapy, 186–187
  gestalt therapy, 164–165
  human resource development, 217
  individual psychology, 67
  psychoanalysis, 41–42
  rational-emotive therapy, 107
  reality therapy, 123
  transactional analysis, 91–92
Evaluation/termination phase, behavior therapy,
  134
Exclusion:
  definition, 73
  transactional analysis, 81
Experience:
  (noun) definition, 169
  (verb) definition, 169
Explanation, transactional analysis, 87
Extensionality, definition, 169
Extinction, 127
  definition, 130

Family atmosphere:
definition, 48
individual psychology, 53
Family constellation:
  definition, 48
  individual psychology, 53, 62
Favorability scale:
  definition, 194
  human resource development, 209–210
Feelings:
  reflection, 61, 180
  responding to, 207
  staying with, 159
Fictional goal, definition, 48
Figure, definition, 151
Figure, Gestalt, 150
Fixation, definition, 20
Flooding, definition, 130
Flooding procedures, 139–140, 143
Formula G, transactional analysis, 86
Fragmentation, gestalt, 156
Frame of reference, 171, 199, 204
  definition, 169
Free Association:
  definition, 20
  psychoanalysis, 28, 32, 34–35
Freedom of choice, 9, 51
Freud, Sigmund, personal background, 17–18
Frustration, gestalt therapy, 154
Function of the counselor:
  behavior therapy, 135–136
  client-centered therapy, 179–180
  gestalt therapy, 158
  human resource development, 204

individual psychology, 59–60
rational-emotive therapy, 101–102
reality therapy, 117–118
transactional analysis, 87
Function of the therapist, psychoanalysis, 33–34
Futility position, transactional analysis, 81

Game:
  definition, 73
  transactional analysis, 76, 81
Game analysis, transactional analysis, 84–87
Games of dialog, gestalt therapy, 159
Generalization, definition, 130
Genial stage, psychoanalysis, 27
Genuineness, 5, 175, 192
  definition, 195
Gestalt, definition, 150
Gestalt psychology, 150
Gestalt therapy, 150
Glasser, William, personal background, 109–110
Goal alignment, individual psychology, 60–61
Goal definition, human resource development,
  209
Goal directed behavior, 50, 170–171
Goal-setting phase, behavior therapy, 133
Goals:
  immediate, 202
  process, 202
  ultimate, 202
Goals of counseling, *see* Counseling goals
Graduate training, behavior therapy, 135
  human resource development, 203–204
  individual psychology, 70
  rational-emotive therapy, 101
Ground:
  definition, 151
  gestalt therapy, 150
Group counseling, 163

Hedonism, rational-emotive therapy, 95
Helping, definition, 195
Historical development:
  behavior therapy, 125–129
  client-centered therapy, 166–169
  gestalt therapy, 148–150
  human resource development, 191–194
  individual psychology, 45–48
  psychoanalysis, 17–19
  rational-emotive therapy, 93–94
  reality therapy, 109–111
  transactional analysis, 71–72
Homeostasis, definition, 20
Human Nature:
  behavior therapy view, 131
  client-centered therapy view, 170–171
  gestalt therapy view, 151–153
  human resource development view, 197
  individual psychology view, 49–52
  psychoanalytic view, 21–22
  rational-emotive therapy view, 95–96
  reality therapy view, 111–112
  transactional analysis view, 75–76
Human resource development, definition, 195
Hypnosis, 19

ID, 23–24, 72
  definition, 20
Identification, 30
Identity:
  definition, 111
  failure, definition, 111
  reality therapy, 111–114
  success, definition, 111
Illustration, transactional analysis, 87

definition, 151
Self-involvement, 114
Self-regulation, 152
Self-structure, definition, 170
Self-understanding, 57, 99, 176–177, 193–194, 201–202
    definition, 196
Self-worth, 112–114
    definition, 111
Sex, 19, 22, 25–27
Significance, individual psychology, 50, 63
Silence, individual psychology, 61
Skills, 4, 49, 87, 190, 192–194, 199–201, 203–204, 206–209, 213, 215–217
    definition, 196
Social interest:
    definition, 49
    individual psychology, 49–50, 64, 67, 197
Social learning procedures, behavior therapy, 139, 143
Social learning theory, behavior therapy, 128–129
Somatic child, transactional analysis, 77
Specialty-area skills, definition, 196
Specification, transactional analysis, 87
Spitting in the client's soup, individual psychology, 63
Spontaneity, transactional analysis, 79, 86
Stamps, definition, 74
Stimulus generalization, 127
Stimulus hunger:
    definition, 74
    transactional analysis, 75
Stroke:
    conditional, 75, 79–80
    conditional, definition, 74
    negative, 75, 79–80
    negative, definition, 74
    positive, 75
    positive, definition, 74
    unconditional, 75
    unconditional, definition, 74
Stroking, transactional analysis, 75
Structural analysis, transactional analysis, 82, 87
Structure Hunger:
    definition, 74
    transactional analysis, 75–76
Style of life:
    definition, 49
    individual psychology, 51–55, 61, 72
Superego, 23, 25, 72
    definition, 21
Superiority, definition, 49
    individual psychology, 50, 55
Symbiosis, definition, 74
Symbolization, client-centered therapy, 169

Task setting, individual psychology, 64
Technique implementation phase, behavior therapy, 134
Techniques:
    behavior therapy, 136–140
    client-centered therapy, 180
    gestalt therapy, 158–159
    human resource development, 205–213
    individual psychology, 60–64
    psychoanalysis, 34–36
    rational-emotive therapy, 102–103
    individual psychology, 60–64
    psychoanalysis, 34–36
    rational-emotive therapy, 102–103
    reality therapy, 118–119
    transactional analysis, 87–88

Teleological:
    definition, 49
    individual psychology, 50
Termination, 32, 134
Theoretical background, behavioral therapy, 126–129
    client-centered therapy, 167–169
    gestalt therapy, 149–150
    human resource development, 191–194
    individual psychology, 47–48
    psychoanalysis, 18–19
    rational-emotive therapy, 94
    reality therapy, 110–111
    transactional analysis, 72
Theory, 10–13, 221
Therapist function, psychoanalysis, 33–34
Therapy goals, see Counseling goals
Therapy process, psychoanalysis, 31–32
Think steps:
    definition, 196
    human resource development, 211
Threat:
    client-centered therapy, 172
    definition, 170
Token economies, behavior therapy, 137, 142
Tolerance of others, rational-emotive therapy, 100
Training analysis, definition, 21
Training of the counselor:
    behavior therapy, 135
    client-centered therapy, 178–179
    gestalt therapy, 157–158
    human resource development, 202–203
    individual psychology, 58–59
    rational-emotive therapy, 101
    reality therapy, 116–117
    transactional analysis, 86
Training of the therapist, psychoanalysis, 33
Transaction:
    angular, 83–84
    complementary, 82–83
    complementary, definition, 74
    crossed, 83
    crossed, definition, 74
    definition, 74
    duplex, 83–84
    ulterior, 83–84
    ulterior, definition, 74
Transactional analysis, 82–84, 87
Transactional game diagram, 84
Transference, 19, 31–32, 34–35, 40
    analysis of, 35
    definition, 21
Transference neurosis, 32
    definition, 21
Treatment parameters:
    behavior therapy, 140
    client-centered therapy, 180
    gestalt therapy, 159–160
    human resource development, 213
    individual psychology, 64
    psychoanalysis, 36
    rational-emotive therapy, 103
    reality therapy, 119
    transactional analysis, 88

Unconditional positive regard, see Regard, positive
Unconditional positive regard, definition, 170
Unconscious, 23, 31–32, 35, 52, 96, 171, 197
    definition, 21
Understanding phase, individual psychology, 57